SLAVES FOR HIRE

RENTING ENSLAVED LABORERS IN ANTEBELLUM VIRGINIA

JOHN J. ZABORNEY

LOUISIANA STATE UNIVERSITY PRESS ❧ BATON ROUGE

Published by Louisiana State University Press
Copyright © 2012 by Louisiana State University Press
All rights reserved
Manufactured in the United States of America
First printing

Designer: Barbara Neely Bourgoyne
Typeface: Whitman
Printer: McNaughton & Gunn, Inc.
Binder: Acme Bookbinding, Inc.

Library of Congress Cataloging-in-Publication Data

Zaborney, John J., 1967–
 Slaves for hire : renting enslaved laborers in antebellum Virginia / John J. Zaborney.
  p. cm.
 Includes bibliographical references and index.
 ISBN 978-0-8071-4512-8 (cloth : alk. paper) — ISBN 978-0-8071-4513-5 (pdf) — ISBN 978-0-8071-4514-2 (epub) — ISBN 978-0-8071-4515-9 (mobi)
  1. Slavery—Virginia—History—19th century. 2. Slaves—Virginia—Social conditions—19th century. 3. Slavery—Economic aspects—Virginia—History—19th century. 4. Slaves—Employment—Virginia—History—19th century. I. Title.
 E445.V8Z33 2012
 306.3'620975509034—dc23

                                                                2012000531

The paper in this book meets the guidelines for permanence and durability of the Committee on Production Guidelines for Book Longevity of the Council on Library Resources. ∞

IN LOVING MEMORY OF
Stuart Bruchey
John Hopewell
Marli Weiner
and
John and Eva Zaborney

DEDICATED TO
Kim Sebold
and
John and Delia Zaborney

CONTENTS

ACKNOWLEDGMENTS   ix

Introduction   1

CHAPTER 1
The Origins and Proliferation of Slave Hiring in Virginia   9

CHAPTER 2
Hired Slave Women   28

CHAPTER 3
Slave Hiring and Hired Slaves' Family and Friendship Ties in Rural Areas   46

CHAPTER 4
Hired Slaves, Whites, and Slavery   65

CHAPTER 5
White Ladies, White Men, Masters All: Slave Hiring and White Society   87

CHAPTER 6
Slave Hiring, Hired Slaves, and Urban and Industrial Slavery   120

CHAPTER 7
Slave Hiring and Slavery   149

Conclusion   163

NOTES   167

BIBLIOGRAPHY   193

INDEX   201

ACKNOWLEDGMENTS

Many institutions and persons facilitated my completion of this book. I wish to thank Rand Dotson, my editor at the Louisiana State University Press, for his encouragement and guidance of my manuscript to publication. Thanks are also due Lee Sioles and others at LSU Press who spent their time and effort working with my manuscript and copy editor Lois Crum, whose sharp eyes and expertise enhanced the quality of this book immeasurably. I am also grateful to Charles Dew, who read earlier versions of the manuscript. Professor Dew's expert evaluation and suggestions made the final product immensely better than it was. Any remaining errors or shortcomings are, of course, my own responsibility. Additionally, I wish to thank John Saillant, and also the Afro-American Historical and Genealogical Society, for permission to use previously published material.

In North Carolina and Virginia, the staff at the following archives were cheerful and helpful: the Southern Historical Collection, Wilson Library, at the University of North Carolina at Chapel Hill; the Rare Book, Manuscript, and Special Collections Library, William Perkins Library, at Duke University; the Earl Gregg Swem Library at the College of William and Mary in Virginia; the Albert and Shirley Small Special Collections Library at the University of Virginia; the Library of Virginia; the Virginia Historical Society; the Fairfax Circuit Court Archives at the Fairfax County (Virginia) Judicial Center; and the Sussex (Virginia) courthouse. My work was aided greatly by Andrew W. Mellon Research Fellowships at the Virginia Historical Society and by faculty development funds and a sabbatical leave awarded by the University of Maine at Presque Isle.

Numerous people made my research easier. Sara Bearss, Julie Campbell, Carl Childs, Bob Clay, Conley Edwards, the late John Hopewell, Ervin Jordan, Gregg Kimball, John Kneebone, Chris Kolbe, Nelson Lankford, Jennifer McDaid, Frances Pollard, Connie Ring, Lee Shepard, Brent Tarter, Gwynne Tayloe, Jim Watkinson, Patricia Watkinson, and Minor Weisiger helped me enormously. In Sussex, Virginia, Gary Williams facilitated my research beyond belief. Others who assisted me include Tom Buckley, Julie Curry, Jim Jones, John Saillant, Werner Steger, and Al Tillson. I was lodged by Hood and Deb Frazier, Donna Grubb and Robin Sebold, Susan Hendrickson, Marilyn Hinkley, Rick and Gayle Pougher, Brian and Theresa Quinn, Gregg Riddiford, and Lucille Sebold. I also received much time and feedback from Leah Arroyo, Derek Catsam, Mel Ely, Janette Greenwood, Dick Judd, Maureen Lee, and Angelita Reyes. Marli Weiner gave me much academic buoying, and I miss her very much.

Many in Presque Isle (some of them unknowingly) facilitated my work on this book in various ways, including Meghan, Lauren, Ingrid, Ethelyn, Shara, Denise, Erica, Liza, Tricia, Nancy, Bev, Tyler, Nola, Erin, Debbie, Robin, Bill and Claire, John and Gwen, Ginni, Helen, Guy and Patty, Susan, Kurt and Linda, Charles, Jan, Gene, Lynnelle, Jeanie, Deb, Amanda, KimAnne, Larry, Megan, Todd, Ken, and Rich and Tammy. Linda helped me to produce various versions of the manuscript, and Ed, Marteen, JoAnne, and the computer services and physical plant staffs made my corner of campus function smoothly. Ray, Mike, and Don cheered me on, and thanks to Chris for the 5K. People of the hallway banter, poker games, and choir practices, you know who you are. Elsewhere, Hannah, Jack, Katie, Lily, Oliver, and (thanks to Barbara Farren) the late Sunny made a house a home.

Without Bob, Holmes, Mike, and Lynn, much would have been far different. Bob gave me boundless time and encouragement, and Holmes allowed me to bend his ear at any time. Mike is a real piece of work, and I am one of those fortunate enough to be his friend. Lynn's enthusiasm made my progress easier, and I am glad she is still in the area.

Shannon was first a student, then an advisee, and always a friend. Shannon shared more than just boring, useless information with me because she thought highly of me and trusted me. Ultimately, Shannon found classes offered at times when she could take them and finished her degree under difficult circumstances, and I am proud of her. Shannon's progress paralleled my own work, and she encouraged me from the day she saw me with my box. When I was hopeful about publication, Shannon said, "Oh, I'm certain of it," and that she couldn't wait. When I had theories about what to do next, Shannon said, "What are you waiting for?" My interactions with Shannon mean the world to me. I miss having Shannon in my classes, but I hope to see her have what she deserves: the very best of everything. By now, I know she will not think that sounds corny.

My parents, John and Delia Zaborney, gave me love as I pursued my academic goals. My uncles, John Marchioni and Ron Zaborney, gave great support, and my grandparents, the late John and Eva Zaborney, were models of hard work, decency, thoughtfulness, happiness, and love. I have known Kim just a bit longer than I have been thinking about hired slaves, but she heard a lot about them. Kim and I never had much down time away from work, but we did many little things together, and so established the kind of companionship that has sustained us. Kim always was supportive and proud of all I've done (this book being the most recent thing) because she still sees something in me. All of this is what I thank Kim for, that is, for her love.

SLAVES FOR HIRE

INTRODUCTION

In 1842 Joseph Potts observed a slave at work plowing a wheat field in Fairfax County, Virginia. The man Potts saw that day was George, a hired slave, whom Potts judged "better than the generality of negroes at plowing, & a good Cradler." Had he traveled a greater distance, Potts might have seen other hired slaves, some working in wheat fields, others tending livestock and working on railroads, and still others engaged in a wide variety of other chores. George was one of countless slaves hired out almost everywhere slavery existed in what became the United States, from the institution's beginnings in the British North American mainland colonies through its final destruction by the Civil War.[1]

Slave hiring, or renting, was a practice whereby slaves were transferred temporarily between persons, firms, or institutions for a variety of reasons. Scholarly assessments of slave hiring have varied considerably. Historians of urban slave hiring have shown that many urban hired slaves were male, and they have accented the manner in which slave hiring conferred upon those male slaves advantages such as overwork payments, mobility, and living out; they have proclaimed that slave hiring weakened urban slavery generally. On this basis, in 1960 Clement Eaton characterized slave hiring in the Upper South as "a step toward freedom," and in 1964 Richard Wade maintained that particular characteristics of urban slave hiring were symptomatic of a fundamental incompatibility between slavery and an urban environment. Other scholars have asserted that hired slaves were worked harder and punished more frequently and that they received care inferior to that of non-hired-out slaves. In short, historians' debate about slave hiring has been polarized: hired slaves either enjoyed nearly full autonomy, which weakened slavery generally, or they endured ruthless exploitation.[2]

Several decades after Eaton and Wade published their findings, many historians advanced erroneous assumptions about slave hiring based on earlier findings for urban areas and for male slaves alone. Some historians, for instance, rendered slave hiring synonymous with greater freedom generally and with urban slavery in particular. In 1992, for example, one historian contended that hired slaves somehow "moved between slavery and their temporary employments" and that they acted as liaisons for slaves "who remained on the plantations" while they themselves labored "for hirers in distant and urban places." For this historian, slaves were no longer quite slaves once they were hired out, and they normally were hired out from a plantation to a city. The view that most hired slaves were men also continued to appear in the literature. Believing that slave owners hired out especially skilled male slaves and few females, for example, one historian concluded that "more male than female slaves were artisans and craftsmen, and this made it more difficult to hire out a female slave than a male slave." Another scholar asserted that slave owners normally did not hire out slave women because their "domestic responsibilities were deemed too important to permit protracted absences from the quarters."[3]

Recent investigations of slave hiring have arrived at various conclusions. Midori Takagi's study of slavery in Richmond, Virginia, emphasizes hired-out slaves' opportunities for autonomous activities, but it asserts that slavery, facilitated by slave hiring, sustained the city's economic development. Still others argue that hired slaves, and slave hiring generally, were detrimental to slavery's institutional stability. William Link, for example, writes that hired-out slaves in Virginia evaded their owners' supervision and control, which enabled those hired-out slaves to engage in acts of rebellion. Jonathan Martin, too, concludes that slave hiring undermined slavery because hired-out slaves brought owners and hirers into conflict with each other, which conflict fractured the white racial solidarity upon which slavery rested. The debate remains polarized: some of the most recent studies find that slave hiring fortified slavery and regional economies, while others argue that slave hiring, if not hired slaves themselves, weakened slavery.[4]

In addition to historiographical polarization, historians' debate about slave hiring also has been characterized for several decades by the assumption that slave hiring was an institutional irregularity. Yet findings for Virginia show that slave hiring was an extremely complex practice that eludes many historians' characterizations of it and of individual hired slaves' experiences, which were unique in particular locales and circumstances. This study finds that slave hiring was *integral* to Virginia slavery because slave hiring touched *all* types of slaves, *all* locations and occupations, and *all* types of whites. Virginia slave owners routinely hired out not just men in urban and industrial contexts, but also slave women (including pregnant women) and children and elderly slaves, and the practice was pervasive in rural areas, agriculture, and households. Additionally, the actual operation of slave hiring in Virginia, that is, the various logistical activities whereby slaves were transferred from one person, firm, or point to another, was a multifaceted process that bestowed power over hired slaves upon numerous white men whose tasks moved slaves from owners' to hirers' possession. As a result, white involvement with slave hiring was not confined to owners and hirers alone but was society-wide. This is in addition to the facts that all white economic and occupational groups hired slaves and that, quite frequently, other whites in addition to hirers supervised, or worked alongside, hired slaves as they themselves labored for slave hirers. Consequently, in Virginia, slave hiring meant far more to white society as a whole than relatively rare instances of conflict between white owners and hirers, because so many more whites in addition to owners and hirers were involved with it. Consideration of all slaves, all locations, and all whites in a comprehensive manner reveals that most Virginia hired slaves' experiences differed little from those of nonhired slaves and that slave hiring made Virginia slavery stronger, not weaker, during the years before the Civil War. In telling the full story of slave hiring in one southern state, Virginia, this book also illuminates much about slavery and about the history of African Americans, Virginia, and the South.[5]

In this book I trace the origins and proliferation of slave hiring back to the eighteenth century. During the period from then up through the Civil War, domestic and international developments led to agricultural diversification, urban and industrial growth, and the emergence of a transportation infrastructure in Virginia. These agricultural and economic changes intersected with a rapidly increasing slave population to alter white Virginians' labor requirements, which produced slave surpluses in many areas. Many white

Virginians hired out slaves to solve their superfluous-slave problem, since many of the economic changes that had contributed to planters' excess-slave woes also had created markets for slave labor elsewhere. Slave hiring in Virginia, then, emerged in part as a solution to whites' problems. Ultimately, however, slave hiring proliferated throughout Virginia's economy and society to become a fundamental facet of Virginia slavery by the turn of the nineteenth century, and it remained so through the Civil War.

Slave hiring impacted Virginia hired slaves' lives in numerous ways. Women's experiences as hired slaves, in particular, merit scrutiny on several levels. Contrary to historians' assumption that most hired slaves were men, this study finds that Virginia slave owners hired out slave women in large numbers for agricultural labor and as house servants, and that they usually did so with little difficulty. White Virginians routinely hired out pregnant slave women and women with young children when those women were seen as an expense, or what one white Virginian described as "unproductive consumers" of food and clothing. White Virginians who hired out slave women as a way to shift the expenses of the women's upkeep to others abdicated any paternalistic pretensions they may have harbored. For many slave women, therefore, child-care duties did not keep them from being hired out, as previous historians have assumed, but they actually made it far more likely. This is but one aspect of slave hiring in Virginia that shows that the practice was not an irregularity but a routine part of slavery in a region with a diversified economy and a rapidly increasing slave population. Finally, many slave women fell under greater white scrutiny than did hired slave men, and Virginia slave women's experiences as hired slaves illuminate the unique ways in which they resisted the bondage they shared with men.[6]

Although hired slave women's experiences were unique in various respects, all hired slaves were affected by the separation of family members and friends from one another. Usually the result of white Virginians' economic concerns, separations affected slaves of both sexes once they were considered old enough to work and so be hired out apart from their parents. Separation by hiring out, as opposed to separation by sale, is of special significance. The hiring out of slave children once they reached working age rendered such family separations a routine occurrence in Virginia, and slaves hired out for several years to a different person each year suffered the pain of separation repeatedly.

For decades, historians have debated the question whether slave hiring was advantageous or detrimental to hired slaves' well-being. This investigation moves beyond traditional analyses of slave hiring to consider Virginia hired slaves' experiences as affected by variables including the slaves' place of occupation, sex, and nature of occupation; the attitudes of owners and hirers about how slaves ought to behave; and considerations ranging from whites' financial circumstances and personal perspectives to crop prices. Examination of all types of hired slaves, rather than only urban males, produces a picture of slave hiring radically different from any yet advanced. In Virginia, the story of hired slaves is much more complex than the one that emerges from several decades of polarized debate among historians who have written either of nearly free hired slaves or of abused and exploited hired slaves. Virginia hired slaves' status and experiences usually were neither defined precisely nor fixed over time, but rather ranged along a continuum. While some hired slaves enhanced their agency as a result of being hired out and others did not, the lives of most hired slaves in Virginia encompassed the full range of experiences from nearly full autonomy to harsh exploitation. More specifically, contrary to many historians' contentions, most Virginia hired slaves' lives and work experiences did not differ appreciably from those of nonhired slaves.

Connections between slave hiring and white Virginia society were one reason for this. While some hired slaves exploited increasing hire rates and demand for hired slaves by pressing for discretion over hirers and working conditions, numerous threads in the fabric of owner-hirer racial unity often precluded hired slaves' ability to manipulate owners and hirers against each other. Specifically, far from creating "nearly inevitable" conflict and "guarantee[ing] constant disputes" between slave owners and slave hirers, as Jonathan Martin asserts in *Divided Mastery: Slave Hiring in the American South*, most hired slaves found that white Virginia slave owners' and slave hirers' actions, undertaken as various forms of mastery that was *transferred* in *reality* rather than *divided* in *theory* between white Virginians repeatedly, reflected their racial solidarity in support of slave control. In Virginia, slave hiring illuminated the fact that neighborhoods that included slave owners, non-slave-owners, journeymen, tenants, merchants, and a host of other economic and occupational groups were, at bottom, communities whose members saw themselves as white first and foremost; all of them might control hired slaves in one manner or another. Specifically, white laborers wielded authority over the hired slaves with whom they worked, and other whites controlled hired slaves in their performance of the logistical tasks necessary to transport hired-out slaves from owners to hirers and oversee them in the process. Also, slave owners who hired out significant numbers of slaves throughout their communities, the principal lessors of slave labor, served as hubs of white societal linkage by facilitating the hiring of slaves by large numbers of whites, who thereby became linked to slave owners because both groups held slaves. Ultimately, slave hiring diffused power over slaves to potentially all Virginia whites, and so it created a white web of responsibility for slave control, a society-wide white involvement with slave hiring far wider than the very narrow "triangular" interactions of owner, hirer, and slave that Martin describes in *Divided Mastery*. Whereas some historians suggest that more slaves hired out meant unsupervised, out-of-control slaves and slavery's institutional weakness, the fact was that, in Virginia, more hired slaves also meant more white involvement in their transfer, surveillance, and employment, that is, an extensive and united net of white control over the hired-slave population. As a result, slave hiring helped to strengthen white solidarity and Virginia slavery, rather than weaken them, on the eve of the Civil War.[7]

Among white Virginians, slave hiring's logistical inner workings illuminated notions about antebellum southern gender-role identities for both women and men. Specifically, the hiring-day sites to which slaves-for-hire were brought and auctioned off became white male public domains where all types of white men governed slaves, public domains from which white women were excluded. Slave-hiring days served as hubs of white masculinity because they brought together numerous white men regardless of occupation, economic class, or slave-owning status and gave those white men opportunities to surveil and otherwise master hired slaves and so display their masculinity to each other. Additionally, white women retained their ladyhood by virtue of their absence from the public, hiring-day sphere. White women were masters, too, however: they owned the slaves white men hired out for them, and their slave-owning status always was the basis upon which they told white men what to do with respect to their (the women's) hired-out slaves.

The lives of hired slaves who worked in Virginia's urban and industrial areas sometimes differed considerably from the lives of those who labored in rural and agricultural regions, but often they differed very little. The distinctive nature of many urban and industrial employments sometimes made slave hiring itself unique in them. Frequently, those differences offered urban and industrial hired slaves opportunities to enhance their agency, independence, and self-esteem, which made their experiences stand out among those of other slaves, hired and nonhired. Such hired slaves often were highly visible to contemporaries, and so they also later captured the attention of historians who transferred their experiences to those of hired slaves everywhere. Certainly, many urban and industrial hired slaves were able to derive advantages from their unique employments, such as overwork payments and board money, which they utilized to feel and to assert their humanity. Other hired slaves in Virginia's urban and industrial sectors, however, found that whites often limited their assertions of independence, that profit-driven hirers often opted for the whip over incentives, and that dangerous and unhealthy working and living environments often were their lot. Consequently, urban and industrial slave hiring in Virginia was, for hired slaves, a complex story, much as it was for rural and agricultural hired slaves. Ultimately, as an institution, urban and industrial slave hiring was effective both in sustaining Virginia's development in those sectors and in strengthening slavery itself there as a whole.

By 1860 absolute numbers of slaves had declined in Delaware and Maryland, but the slave population of Virginia had *increased* from 293,427 in 1790 to 490,865 in 1860. Also in 1860, more slaves lived and worked in Virginia than in any other southern state, including states of the Lower South, even though Virginia was a slave-exporting state. These developments are explained by slave hiring's strengthening of Virginia slavery. Specifically, whites' web of control over hired slaves was complemented by a host of other factors that also served to sustain Virginia slavery during the antebellum period. The proliferation of markets to absorb surplus slaves continued to make slave hiring feasible, as well as profitable, for white Virginians who wished to hire out their superfluous slaves to other white Virginians. This was especially the case when, even in the face of slaves' rapid natural increase, intense competition for hired-slave labor among several sectors of antebellum Virginia's diversified economy continued to push slave-hire rates upward. For this reason, many Virginia whites hired out their slaves within Virginia, rather than sell them to the Lower South. Slave hiring therefore kept large numbers of slaves out of the interstate slave trade and so reinforced slavery in antebellum Virginia.[8]

CHAPTER 1

THE ORIGINS AND PROLIFERATION OF SLAVE HIRING IN VIRGINIA

Following the end of his presidency early in the nineteenth century, Thomas Jefferson focused his attention on Monticello, his estate in Albemarle County, Virginia. At that time, Virginia was in the midst of an economic transformation, and Jefferson noticed one of the changes. "Tobacco," he observed in May 1812, was "very much abandoned." Jefferson's remark was a bit overdrawn for Virginia as a whole, yet his exaggeration reflected the fact that in some areas of Virginia, tobacco cultivation had declined significantly. Whereas Virginia tobacco producers had exported annual averages of approximately 110,000 hogsheads between 1790 and 1792, exports soon fell dramatically. During most of the first two decades of the nineteenth century, Virginia tobacco growers shipped averages of less than 10,000 hogsheads each year. Yet this was merely one of many changes that Virginia experienced during the eighteenth and early nineteenth centuries. Together, these changes brought about and proliferated slave hiring in Virginia.[1]

For most of the Virginia colony's first century, tobacco dominated the export trade. Yet by the late seventeenth century, tobacco production declined in some areas as the primary regions of tobacco cultivation moved westward. In 1687 Northampton County, on the eastern shore, produced only 4.2 percent of Virginia's total tobacco output, and by 1695 one observer noted, "In some places on the Eastern Shore they plant no tobacco, not finding a market for what they have." In Northampton County, the shift away from tobacco was nearly complete by the end of the seventeenth century.[2]

During the eighteenth century, international developments began to pull other Virginia planters away from tobacco. In Europe, population growth outpaced food supplies, and Spain and Portugal, in particular, looked to the Western Hemisphere for their needs. West Indies plantation owners, too, sought grain from the British colonial mainland. New demand for grain in both Europe and the West Indies soon led many colonial Virginia planters to grow wheat instead of tobacco.[3]

Other factors also persuaded Chesapeake planters to focus on grain. Decades of intensive tobacco cultivation had exhausted the soil and rendered tobacco production difficult. Additionally, the War of the Austrian Succession made it difficult for Chesapeake producers to export tobacco to England in any event. Shortly after the outbreak of hostilities in 1739, Spanish privateers and warships seized numerous cargoes of Virginia tobacco in Chesapeake coastal waters. By 1741, after the French allied with Spain in the conflict, Chesapeake tobacco planters began to lose dozens of tobacco shipments. Consequently, higher insurance rates were attached to tobacco vessels bound for England, increases that were absorbed by planters. Ultimately, losses at sea combined with mounting costs to push Virginia planters away from tobacco and toward wheat.[4]

Grain brought better returns than tobacco, too. Despite the large volume of grain Virginians produced, prices of wheat and flour advanced between the 1740s and the Revolution, an increase that reflected significant international demand for American grain. The price of flour, for example, rose from three to four dollars per barrel in Virginia port towns by the middle of the eighteenth century, and it remained at that level through the Revolution.[5]

Export figures for Virginia wheat illustrate the change. From 1737 through 1742, Virginia's wheat exports to southern Europe, the Wine Islands, and the West Indies, along with the coastwise trade, totaled 35,428 bushels. About thirty years later, between 1768 and 1772, Virginians shipped 254,217 bushels of wheat out of the colony. The figures are even more revealing of the change given that Virginia's rapidly growing population consumed most of the colony's grain output.[6]

The agricultural diversification in Virginia was paralleled by a rapid increase of its slave population. Importation of Africans to Virginia contributed to an increase in their population in the colony from 950 in 1660 to 16,390 in 1700. Natural increase, too, sustained the growth rate of Virginia's

African American population. In the Chesapeake region, that population doubled in every decade but one between 1650 and 1690, and its growth rate surpassed that of the white population. By the Revolution, African Americans outnumbered whites in several counties of the Virginia Tidewater, and they constituted more than 60 percent of the populations of James City and York counties. In the Northern Piedmont, Loudoun County's slave population rose from 998 in 1760 to 6,078 in 1800, and Virginia's total slave population increased from 293,427 in 1790 to 383,000 in 1810.[7]

Virginia planters' increased wheat production within the context of a growing slave population created slave surpluses. The reason was that the amount of labor required to produce wheat was less than that demanded by tobacco. Tobacco cultivation involved much time, care, and diligence throughout the year. Wheat required little attention until harvest.

Virginia planters and other observers noted the surplus-slave problem. At Mount Vernon, George Washington complained, "It is demonstratively clear . . . that on this Estate . . . I have more working negro[e]s by a full moiety, than can be employed to any advantage in the farming system." A British traveler reported that Virginia planters were "overstocked" with slaves and that slave surpluses constituted a "circumstance complained of by every planter." Another observer recognized, "Since the cultivation of wheat has excited the attention of farmers in the northern neck of Virginia, the hoe has been exchanged for the plough, consequently the same number of hands are not now requisite, to work the same quantity of ground, as when tobacco was the chief crop." In 1798 Virginian William Fleet asserted, "Something should be done with the negroes who are not employed in making the Crop." Many eighteenth-century Virginia planters had too many slaves, and they began to seek ways to resolve their problem.[8]

Possession of too many slaves made it easier for some white Virginians to act upon Revolutionary rhetoric concerning liberty and equality and set their slaves free. Consequently, Virginia's free black population rose from about 12,000 in 1790 to 20,000 in 1800 and to approximately 30,000 in 1810. Other white Virginians with extra slaves sold their surplus hands. After the turn of the century, the cotton gin pushed cotton prices upward, prompting slave-owner settlement of new western territories in the Lower South. These developments, together with the banning of legal importation of Africans in 1808, created enormous demand for slaves in the Lower

South. As a result, whites in Virginia and other Upper-South states sold some 750,000 of their extra slaves to the Lower South between 1790 and 1860.[9]

Slave hiring, however, became another solution to Virginia planters' surplus-slave dilemma. Beginning in the eighteenth century and continuing throughout the antebellum period, Virginia slave owners had little difficulty locating markets for their extra slaves in various economic sectors. Coal, salt, and gold mine operators; iron producers; and railroad companies and other industrialists, as well as tobacco manufacturers and other urban whites, for example, hired the surplus slaves. Slave hiring, in fact, facilitated urban and industrial development in Virginia. White Virginians also hired slaves out for agricultural work. Unable to afford slaves of their own, tenants hired slaves from slave owners who had too many on hand. Following the Revolution, tenants and small farmers formed the bulk of Elizabeth City County's population, and they were the largest group of slave hirers in that county. During the 1780s, almost 90 percent of Elizabeth City County taxpayers were involved in slave hiring, a system that became "an integral part of the institution of slavery" in the county.[10]

Rural white Virginians who wished to establish new plantations also found it expedient to hire, rather than purchase, slaves. In Chesterfield County, William McKean was employed to establish James Dunlop's plantation early in the nineteenth century. McKean hired slaves to drain land and clear it of trees, build a house for a gardener, build slave houses and horse stables, construct a corn crib, and raise sheds for wagons, carts, oats, grain, hay, and cows. Ultimately, the slaves McKean hired established Roslin Plantation.[11]

In Virginia, those who hired slaves by the year executed a slave-hiring bond for the transaction. When James Twyman "Hired of Frances A Michie four negro girls (to wit) Delia Fanny Amanda & Sophia for $35" in December 1849, Twyman "executed [his] Note payable on or before 1st January 1851." Two days later, Twyman "Hired of Alfred C Wood one negro man (Peter) and executed [his] bond for [$]65 payable on the 31st [of] Dec[ember] 1850." In addition to slave owners' and slave hirers' names, the names of slaves hired out, and the execution and due dates of the hire, most slave-hiring bonds stipulated the clothing the hirer was to provide the slave. Some Virginia slave owners also insisted upon security on any slave-hiring bonds they took in, and one claimed he "would not hire a Negro to any man without it."[12]

Virginia slave hirers retrieved their retired bonds at the end of the year. The bond's retirement was noted across its face, or the signatures of the persons who had executed the bond either were crossed out or torn off to signify payment. After John Fitzgerald paid off his bond for a slave he hired in 1856, for instance, Fitzgerald's signature at the bottom of the bond was crossed out, and "Paid in full" was written across the bond's face. Similarly, the signatures of Isaac and John Fletcher were crossed out after they paid their bond to Henry Dulany, from whom they had hired "negro woman Beck" for 1859. One year later, after the Fletchers paid their bond to William Childs for their hire of Childs's slave Wesley during 1860, the Fletchers' signatures were cut out completely. The removal of slave hirers' signatures following payment of their slave-hiring bonds was a routine practice. Elizabeth Feutress, in her deposition for a chancery cause in Princess Anne County, declared that after she and her son paid off a slave-hiring bond, "the signatures were torn off," and Feutress further affirmed that it generally was her "practice and was the practice of [her] Son, after paying a note to tear off the signatures."[13]

Virginia slave owners who took in slave hirers' bonds benefited from slave hiring in many ways. In Elizabeth City County, thirteen male slaves hired out as a group near the end of the eighteenth century brought hires that ranged from 7.3 percent to 23.7 percent of their appraised value. Slave owners' profits on female slaves were slightly lower but still significant. Seven slave women hired out at the same time as the men brought hires ranging from 5 percent to 17.1 percent of their appraised value. Even after the costs of supporting pregnant, sick, and infant slaves were deducted from slave-hire receipts, the slave owner made a handsome profit, and other Virginia slave owners in the same area benefited likewise. Consequently, "hiring out slaves was a profitable venture in Elizabeth City County at the end of the eighteenth century."[14]

The profitability of slave hiring made it an attractive way to secure an income for white Virginians incapable of supporting themselves. During the 1820s, York County resident George Smith, deemed "an Idiot," was supported by slave-hiring income collected by white fiduciaries who hired out Smith's slaves Sam and Lowther on his behalf continuously from 1820 through 1829 to several different hirers. Similarly, Halifax County resident Mary Hall was judged incapable of handling her own financial affairs, so

Beverly Fleming hired out Hall's slaves for her. Fleming hired out Hall's slaves, Granville, Mary, Chloe, and Moses, to numerous different persons from 1845 through 1849.[15]

Slave-hiring income sustained Virginia's minor orphans, too. Specifically, guardians hired out orphans' slaves "for the annual board, clothing, and tuition of [the] children" following the death of a slave-owning parent. In Virginia, the guardianship system was initiated during the seventeenth century, and guardians were required to submit to the county court clerk an annual account of receipts and expenditures on minor orphans' behalf until the orphans came of age. Guardians' accounts show that slave-hiring income for minor orphans was substantial. In Essex County, the seven slaves whom guardian Christopher Newbill hired out in 1856 brought $311.50 for orphan Edwin Hunley's support. A group of Sussex County slaves hired out annually from 1836 through 1843 generated $2,310.75 in income for orphans. Indeed, the Sussex guardian referred to his slave-hiring records as an "Account of the Annual Profits of the Negroes."[16]

Slave-hiring bonds and other records reveal additional benefits Virginia slave owners derived from hiring out their slaves. Slave owners escaped responsibility for hired slaves' clothing, a cost slave hirers assumed beginning in the eighteenth century. When Fauquier County farmer Peter Hitt hired Milly in 1777 and 1778, for example, he paid for Milly's clothing. In 1797, the two whites who hired "Negroe Man Bob" executed a slave-hiring bond for "the delivering up [of] the said Negroe Man Bob well Cloth[e]d with a Du[t]ch Blanket & Hatt" at the end of the year. Elsewhere, after James Moore hired a slave from Levi Gilliam, Gilliam filed a complaint against Moore to recover clothing costs, a complaint reflecting the expectation that hirers would pay for hired slaves' clothing.[17]

Virginia slave owners who hired out their slaves avoided tax payments on those slaves, too. Slave hirers' responsibility for taxes on slaves they hired is shown by slaves' rotation on and off annual personal property tax records in the years after the Revolution, and on slave-hiring bonds. In 1794, for example, when the hirers of "Negro Girl Anacai" promised in their slave-hiring bond to return the slave girl clothed with "a Jackett petticoat Blankett and hatt Two good shirts a good pair [of] shoes and stockings," they also assumed responsibility for "all Taxes" on Anacai during the year.[18]

Slave owners, guardians, managers, and others in Virginia who hired out slaves usually were responsible for medical expenses for the slaves they hired out. Consequently, physicians who treated hired-out slaves at hirers' residences billed the slave owners for medical services rendered. Slave owner Henry Carrington received doctors' bills for the medical treatment of his hired-out slave Ephraim. Sally Hunter's accounts from the late 1830s and early 1840s reveal payments to a Dr. Garnett and a Dr. Rennolds for medicines and treatments for slaves she hired out. Elsewhere, guardian William Macon made an account book entry for "cash paid Doctor John Adams for attending negroes . . . who were hired out including the boy Oliver that died." Macon also noted other medical expenditures, including "sugar & rum for sick negroes" and "3 bushels salt—bottle wine—salts for sick negroes." Several years later, Macon recorded payments to another physician "for attend[in]g . . . boy Charles" while Charles was hired out. Similarly, Lewis Burt assumed medical costs for Beverly, a slave he hired to John Hogg, and he recorded a payment to "Dr. Taylor's accounte for attending Negro man Bev[er]ly" and another payment for "necessaries furn[i]s[hed] sa[i]d Negroe while sick." Slave owners' specific responsibility for medical expenses sometimes was addressed in slave-hiring bonds, as in 1859 when James Maynard and William Coughlin "hire[d] a Negro boy named Henry Corbin." The bond stipulated that Henry's owner was "clear of all expence Doctors' fees excepted."[19]

Virginia slave owners' responsibility for medical expenses led them to assert their authority over medical matters. Frequently, slave owners demanded that hirers consult them concerning their slaves' treatment, and they often indicated which physician they wished to treat their hired-out slaves. In 1843 Lewis Hill specified that slave hirer William Gray employ a Dr. Carmichael should Hill's slave "require medical aid during the . . . year." Sometimes, slave-hiring bonds required that hirers call on slave owners' preferred physicians and added that "no other Physician, [was] to be employed." In medical matters, slave owners' instructions to slave hirers were shaped by their desire to avoid unnecessary charges and by their wish to protect the value of their slave property.[20]

Although Virginia slave owners normally paid medical bills on their hired-out slaves, any negligence on slave hirers' part rendered them liable for hired slaves' medical expenses. This occurred when hired slaves worked in dangerous employments and when hirers punished slaves in their charge. Hirers of seven of Benjamin Jackson's slaves for railroad work in 1853, for example, bound themselves to pay all doctors' bills for the slaves. And Thomas Chrystie assured Philip Croxton, who had hired and beaten Chrystie's slave Bob, that he would "make [Croxton] Pay for [Chrystie's] attention in curing [Bob]." As a physician, Chrystie treated slaves regularly, but he now threatened to extract medical costs from a hirer who had beaten one of his own slaves.[21]

Yet the numerous benefits of hiring out slaves more than outweighed any medical and other expenses, leading many Virginia slave owners to decree slave hiring in their wills. Judy Saunders directed that her "Negro man Will should be hired out by [her] executor for seven years, the first three years hire [she] [gave] to [her] son Robert Saunders towards boarding, clothing and schooling him." Richmond resident Bolling Starke also willed that his slaves be hired out following his death. Drawn up in 1787, Starke's will directed that his executor hire out his slave sawyers George and Daniel. Hire collected for George and Daniel during the first year after Starke's death was "to be considered (for that year) as *assets* in the hands of [his] Executors for payment of debts." If Starke's wife chose to reside elsewhere, Starke directed that his son Belfield run the plantation and "cultivate the same with common labouring negro fellows three of which kind [he expected could] be got for the hire . . . [the] sawyers [George and Daniel] [would] command." "Those three," Starke asserted, "with the aid of Charles and little Will will be full sufficient [to run the plantation] especially if aided by a ploughboy." Starke saw slave-hiring income as sufficient to support his heirs, purchase additional slaves, and sustain plantation operations following his death.[22]

Virginia slave owners also utilized slave hiring to extricate themselves from difficulty while they lived. Whites in need of money, for example, frequently mortgaged their slaves to others. In Sussex County, slave owner Nathaniel Green was "much pressed on . . . and obliged to raise a Sum" of money, and so he mortgaged his slave Cain to John Maclin, of Brunswick County, who "had heard of [Green's] Necessity for Money." Maclin agreed to advance Green the cash he required if Green "would mortgage a Negro Fellow" to him. Green's hiring of Cain, "who was very valuable," to Maclin was to remain in effect "till the Money was paid" back.[23]

Levi Gilliam, too, hired out a slave in order to deal with financial problems. A Charles Moore had won a monetary judgment against Gilliam at court, and to avoid an execution of the judgment against his other property, Gilliam "was induced to bargain & agree with . . . Moore that . . . Moore should receive a negro slave belonging to [Gilliam] named Ben, and should enjoy the labor & use of the . . . slave in lieu of interest on the . . . debt until [Gilliam] should be able to pay [it] when [Moore] was to re-deliver the . . . negro to [Gilliam]." Gilliam further was "induced to execute to [Moore] an unconditional bill of sale for the . . . negro" as security on the agreement, and "Moore . . . accordingly received the Negro and a Bill of Sale for the . . . Negro into his possession." In this case, Gilliam employed slave hiring to shield his other property from legal action.[24]

Slave hiring also rescued rural Virginia farmers from common agricultural problems of the early nineteenth century. In 1818 Joseph Lewis of Culpeper County complained to his brother about poor crops of wheat and corn caused by bad weather and disease. Lewis wrote that he was "disgusted with the heartless, hopeless, profitless, cultivation of poor land." Initially, Lewis saw no other "hope than a removal to the Western or Southern country [w]here [he] hear[d] of the immense proffits the cotton planters reap[ed]," as he pondered "the inconveniencies & anxieties [he] suffer[ed] [in Virginia] for a *little* money." In 1819 Lewis complained of a severe "drought and its consequences [which were] really alarming," and 1820 brought another disappointing crop. "We are suffering our annual fate," Lewis wrote, and he noted that little rain had fallen for three weeks. "My crop," Lewis lamented, "the best hitherto I ever had languishes accordingly." Yet slave hiring offered Lewis hope. "If I do not succeed" in selling my land, Lewis told his brother, "I shall hire out two or three of my hands and adopt some other plan of culture, for to subsist as I now go forward is impossible." In 1821 Lewis hired out slaves for the first time. The following year, still in Virginia, he informed his brother that half his receipts for 1821 "ar[ose] from hire of negroes" and that until he hired out slaves, he "never knew what it was to have 110$ surplus in [his] life." Lewis calculated that not hiring out slaves in 1821 would have left him only ten dollars ahead. Slave hiring enabled Lewis to remain in Virginia and to turn a profit far better than any he had known previously. In 1822 Lewis was more optimistic about crops; in a reflective letter to his brother, he wrote that "the whole mistery of [his] poverty [was] ... that [he had] rested all [his] hopes (until last year) ... on a small & poor farm." Lewis recollected his recent reliance on slave hiring, which saved him from poverty, allowed him to stay in Virginia, and enabled him to retain ownership of his slaves.[25]

White Virginians also depended upon slave hiring to survive the economic fluctuations that increasingly punctuated their diversified economy of the early nineteenth century. Late in the 1830s, an economic depression fell upon Virginia farmers. "I am really unhappy about the state of my bank business," Fauquier County farmer Edward Carter Turner declared in October 1839. "A great pressure is coming over the country again," Turner wrote; "the money market is deranged & the Banks have nearly all suspended specie payments." Turner was in debt for cattle, and he spent much of 1839 trying to scratch up the money he owed. Meanwhile, Turner killed beeves and sheep because he was "sorely pressed for something to eat," and he worried endlessly in his diary. After he got out of debt in November 1839, he vowed to avoid it in the future: "I have been fortunate enough to escape my protest in Bank & hope that the trouble which it cost me to do it, will teach me here after to shun Bank obligations." Accordingly, Turner decided to hire, rather than purchase, slaves at the end of 1839.[26]

In Southampton County, farmer Daniel William Cobb also pondered his economic fortunes in the grip of the economic downturn. In 1842 Cobb noted, "All property is quite low & people mightily in debt &c. . . . Grate many little folks has already been broak up. . . . We are almost in a horable situation in the United States." Cobb and his neighbors were pinched by declining prices of Virginia tobacco, wheat, and corn, a circumstance they believed was made worse by poor crops. Prices of Virginia's agricultural products dipped to lows approximating those that followed the Panic of 1819 and, with minor fluctuations, remained low for the balance of the 1840s.[27]

By May 1846, Cobb's economic circumstances had not improved. On one occasion, he fell into a despair that led him to write in his diary about being "Alone & Lonesome" and to complain about his financial situation and his crops. "I am as well off as I ever shall be," Cobb confided to his diary. "That is [I] shall all ways be in debt." In June, poor weather and crops kept him despondent for several days. "I am much in the suds as one may say low spirited & dejected of mind nothing to briten my hopes or to Chere me up," Cobb wrote. "My crop of Corn is sorry & the prospect for . . . next year is dull," he observed, "& all partes of the Crops is in bad order & seriously injured by the large quantity of rain which has fell. . . . My corn is tremmendious sorry owing to the glut of rain which fell during the last 8 or 10 day[s]." As he pondered the upcoming year, he predicted, "Times will bee cutting & pinching."

Cobb's concern about the future led to caution in all matters, including slave labor. On December 29, 1846, he attended a slave-hiring auction and noted prices, but he "did not hire [any slaves] [him]self." The next day, Cobb rationalized his decision in his diary. "I am going to let hiring alone," he wrote. "I am going to see what I can do alone." Cobb's labor force for 1847 included five slaves and the five whites in his family, and he determined to acquire no additional hands. "This year I have fell back in every thing undertaken so I am going to try our own power as hirelings is so high &c.," Cobb wrote confidently. For Cobb, slave hiring offered options with respect to the size of his labor force in times of economic uncertainty.[28]

Slave hiring not only helped white Virginians deal with their problems; it also facilitated their routine endeavors. Slave-hiring income sustained slave owners who traveled far from home for extended periods, for example. During the late 1830s and early 1840s, Virginian Benjamin Nalle was a cadet at Norwich University in Vermont. Like other white Virginia farming families, Nalle's family hired out slaves to contend with agricultural problems. In one of his letters to his mother in Virginia, Nalle wrote how happy he was to hear that the family's slaves had been hired out for the year and, in the same sentence, how "sorry [he was] to hear that the prices of produce [were] so low and that the times [were] so hard." Yet, slave-hiring receipts also supported Nalle while he was away at college. "The five dollars you enclosed came safely to hand," Nalle informed his mother in 1841 after a discussion of slave hiring. Nalle also advised his mother on the best way to forward slave-hire money to him in the future, about how much money he expected to owe Norwich University, and about "wood and oil which is something of an item in my bill here." Nalle's letters to his mother reveal that his family hired out its slaves regularly and that his support while away at college in New England was but one benefit they derived from doing so.[29]

Similar circumstances pertained to non-Virginian slave owners. Louisiana senator Ebenezer Cooley relied upon money raised by the hiring out of his slaves in Louisiana while he was in Philadelphia in 1829. Cooley arranged matters such as "to prevent any possible way of charging [him] with any expenses" connected to his hired-out slaves and to "be punctualy paid, without delay, or difficulty; when their hire should become due." "My being abroad and depending on the result of the labour of these few slaves," Cooley explained to his son, was why he desired that his agent "be more tenacious of [his] specific conditions" for his slaves' hire. At one point, Cooley was "full of anxiety" when one of the persons who hired his slaves failed to pay up. "A stranger in a large city, who falls short in paying his board," Cooley wrote anxiously, "falls into . . . contempt."[30]

Regardless of the circumstances under which antebellum white Virginians hired out slaves, slave hiring had proliferated throughout their society by the early nineteenth century such that the practice was a common subject in letters. "I was glad to hear how nicely you were to be fixed next year," Anna Hoge wrote her sister Susan Noland in 1849 concerning Noland's family's slave-hiring arrangements for 1850. Anna also expressed her expectation that Henry, Susan's hired-out slave, would be home at Christmas, but she also assumed that Henry would be hired out again the following year: "Where is Henry to go next year?" Anna inquired. Elsewhere, William Day wrote Ann Nalle, mother of cadet Benjamin Nalle in Vermont: "I expect you will have some two or three persons to See you to morrow who wants to hire hands." In 1832 John Nash wrote William Howard "to let [him] know that [he could] take Amy at Eight Dollars." Anxious to hire a slave in January 1848, Tom Ford made an inquiry to slave owner William Gray concerning one of Gray's female slaves. "If you wish to hire Jenny Ann out," Ford wrote, "I will . . . hire her if your terms be reasonable." In December 1858, slave owner Robert Cole responded to an inquiry about hiring his slave Martha for the following year. "In reply to your note in reference to the hire of Martha," Cole wrote the prospective hirer, "I am willing you shall keep her for the year 1859 at $55." In Northampton County, North Carolina, William Boone was so pleased with the hire of his slave Moses to William Drewry in Southampton County, Virginia, that Boone wished to hire Moses to Drewry again. "I have received one Hundred & twelve Dollars which you sent me," Boone notified Drewry. "Please accept my thanks for your attention to Moses." He added that Drewry would "confer a great favour by attending to [Moses] for [him] the ensuing year in the same way." Almost invariably, slave hiring was a topic of conversation during visits, particularly during slave-hiring season around the turn of the year. In Lunenburg County, for example, Robert Henderson Allen hired a slave woman with her young children from a guest who visited his home on Christmas Day, 1858. A little over a year later, Allen hired a slave girl from a visitor to his house one January evening in 1860.[31]

Whether cut by exchange of letters or during living-room conversations, many white Virginians' private slave-hiring deals also supported the agricultural activities central to their everyday lives. Neighbors, especially, hired out their slaves to one another regularly. On February 9, 10, 12, and 13, 1849, John Martin sent his slaves Sam, Vilet, Amanda, and Ann to Joseph Penney's place to work. Afterward, Martin sent the three women, Vilet, Amanda, and Ann, to Penney's place again, and on February 20 Martin returned Sam to Penney along with the slave women. Penney paid Martin eight dollars' hire for Martin's slaves. The slave exchange went both ways, as in July 1850 Martin paid Penney $1.25 "for his man Joshua cutting wheat 1 1/4 days." Throughout the 1850s, Martin hired slaves from anyone who could spare one to assist him with his summer harvests. Martin paid "W[illia]m Jourden for 2 hands William & Albert cutting wheat one day" in July 1852, for instance, and in July 1856 he paid "Turner Clay for his boy James raking wheat half day & aiding in getting out wheat one day." In Amherst County, Sarah Waller described one season's neighborhood slave-hiring activities. "I believe no one has finished planting corn," Sarah wrote. "Mr. Mitchel is trying very hard to get through this week, I am helping him with Charlott and Frances." On another occasion, Mitchel had "not finished sowing wheat but expected to go through next week." Although for "some time he [had] had Mr. Lovings hands for several days," he was going to be "the last to finish in the neighborhood."[32]

Neighborhood slave hiring was central to white Virginians' livestock production, too. When Daniel Cobb butchered his hogs, for example, his neighbor "Mr Little sent [him] two hands" to assist with the job, and later Cobb "sent [Little's slaves] home." The following year, Cobb's "help was [his] own hands [along with] 4 men from Mr. Littles and 3 women of Mr Littles." Cobb returned the favor when he "promise[d] 2 hands to help Mr. Little kill hogs"; he "sent a man and 1 woman to help Mr Little" perform the task. In another instance, Cobb "sent 1 hand to help H. Whitehead Cut out and salt up his pork." With many hogs on antebellum Virginia farms (about a quarter million head by the 1850s), white Virginians hired out many slaves to one another by the day to butcher hogs each year.[33]

Short-term slave hiring in Virginia also was common among relatives, especially when someone required an extra hand or two in a hurry. This was Benjamin Nalle's predicament one summer following his return to Virginia from Norwich University in Vermont. Caught short of hands in the middle of his harvest, Nalle borrowed slaves from his mother. "I lack a boy or two," Nalle informed his mother on August 15, "& if you can send George down immediately you will oblige me very much [as] I hope to finish befor[e] I stop." "Please send him *now*," Nalle implored, "if you & Brother Albert can spare him." In white Virginians' neighborhood and family networks, a hired slave at the right time could save a crop.[34]

Short-term slave hiring was pervasive in rural Virginia. In Elizabeth City County, Carter Crafford hired out a "Negro man" from October 28, 1827 through January 1, 1828. In the same county in 1827, James Phillips hired out Jane Cooper's slaves Miles, Warwick, Rachel, and Judy for two-thirds of the year. Also in Elizabeth City County, Teackle Savage hired out Edward Laws's slave George for six months in 1827 and for nine months during 1828. Sometimes, short-term slave hiring meant that white Virginians moved individual slaves from one hirer to another during the course of a single year. This was Leannah's experience. Leannah's owner hired her out at the rate of four dollars per month in 1846, and Leannah's first hire payment fell due on July 18. Leannah's owner then shifted her to another hirer, whose account became "Payable the 21st of August." Finally, Leannah's owner hired her out to a third person, whose monthly hire for Leannah fell due September 25, 1846. Monthly slave-hiring arrangements, much like daily ones, sometimes were determined by the seasonal rhythm of labor demands on Virginia farms. Crop schedules affected Thomas Calvert's slave-hiring plans, and he acted accordingly. "I will hire you Peter until Christmas after my corn is housed," Calvert assured James Massenburg in 1829, "so you can take him as soon as my corn is put up."[35]

White Virginians also hired slaves on a short-term basis for tasks that they themselves lacked the skills to perform. Early in the nineteenth century, John Porter of Orange County paid $7.50 for the "Hire of Stringfellow's Billy a fortnight to build a house for McClorny (Overseer)." Similarly, Walker Carter and Larkin Stanard arranged for Stanard's slaves to build Carter's family "one house of . . . two rooms sixteen feet square and . . . set twelve feet a apart . . . under one roughf . . . to be bui[l]t of hewed logs."[36] White Virginians who hired slaves on an annual basis, rather than for a short term, usually did so within an elaborate system that had developed for that purpose. For several days around the turn of each year, rural white Virginians converged upon stores, courthouses, taverns, and crossroads for slave hiring. On January 11, 1828, the slaves Dick, Isaac, Lizzy and her child, Mat, and Belinda and her two children, all of whom belonged to Thomas Walton's estate, were hired out at "Moores old Ordinary" to four different persons. Daniel Cobb attended the hiring days held regularly in the tiny villages scattered throughout Southampton County. On December 31, 1842, Cobb "was at a hiring at Little Town." A few years later, on Sunday, December 26, 1847, Cobb showed up at "a hireing at Vicksvill," and in December 1849, Cobb again appeared "out at the hireing at Vicksvill," and he noted the occurrence of another hiring at "Drewsvill." Four days later, Cobb made reference to a slave he hired "at Court." Several years later, Cobb continued his annual routine: "went to Franklin to the hireing and devision of [the] Vaughan nigross," he reported in his diary on December 28, 1857. At an otherwise quiet, rural crossroads on January 1, 1858, B. H. Walker of King and Queen County noted that "the Extreme beauty of the day was frequently the subject of remark at Stevensville . . . [where there was a] Large n[umber] of persons out at the hiring." In the private spaces of letters and living rooms, and in the public spaces of taverns, crossroads, and courthouse doors, rural white Virginians hired slaves by the day, month, and year under a multitude of circumstances. In all facets of Virginia's economy and white Virginians' lives, slave hiring was everywhere.[37]

The proliferation of slave hiring in Virginia was reflected in changes in the language contained in slave-hiring bonds. Eighteenth-century Virginia slave-hiring bonds' references to clothing, for example, were relatively detailed. When James Sneed and William Parker hired "a Negro Man Named Ned" in 1772, they agreed that Ned would be "Cloathed according to agreement, To Wit, two good shirts, a good Jackcoat & Britches, shoes stocking[s] & Boots." In 1783 William and Stephen Jordan hired Sarah, and they bound themselves to provide Sarah with "the Necessary Clothing one Jacket, two Pettycoats, two shifts, one pair of shoes & stockings, and a blanket double wove of Five Yards." Two years later, Drewry Partin and John Selby agreed to provision Toney, the slave they hired for 1785, with "two shirts one Pair of summer breech[es] one pair of boost or stockings one pair of good strong double sole shoes one Vestcoat [illegible] and breeches of Negro Cotton or Plain."[38]

By the late eighteenth century and afterward, however, the language in slave-hiring bonds became more general, a change that reflected white Virginians' familiarity with a practice that had become widespread. Thomas Mitchell and John Beddingfield, for example, agreed to provide "a summer suit and winter suit as Usual," along with a "Hat and Blanket," when they hired George in 1792. Similarly, Burrell Wilkerson and his associate were obligated to give "Negro Woman fortune" the "us[ua]l good negro clothing" when they executed their bond for Fortune's hire in 1798. Many Virginia slave owners required only that hired slaves were to be "well clothed," and they often made reference to "usual" clothing, vague language signifying white Virginians' familiarity with slave hiring. As early as 1785, Alexander Harrison and Francis Thompson were bound such that Dick, a slave they hired, would be "Clothed as usual." In 1802 Jesse Wallis executed a slave-hiring bond that specified that he give hired slave Billy clothing "as [was] usually given negroes," and in 1806 slave hirer Mary Wilkerson agreed to provide a slave clothing "as is usual for negroes to have." Elsewhere, Robert Magee executed a bond for "the hier of a negrow man named baley" in 1820, and Magee agreed to give Baley the "ushal Clothing." Similarly, the slave whom Phillip Long and William Williams hired from Fanny Judkins for 1841 was "to be clothed as usual for hirelings." In another locale, the hirer of Elizabeth McDowell's "servant Girl Eliza" was to return Eliza to McDowell "at Christmas 1851, well clothed in the usual way that slaves are returned." In 1856 John Fitzgerald and Sam Scott hired David from Patrick Foster. In their bond to Foster, Fitzgerald and Scott agreed to clothe David "in the usual manner of Clothing hired negroes." The hirer of a slave girl in 1860 was to return the slave "clothed as hirelings usually are." Slave-hiring bonds with specific, highly detailed clothing stipulations continued to appear around the turn of the century and afterward, but white Virginians' use of general language in their bonds reflected the rapid proliferation of slave hiring across Virginia. Revealingly, when James Miller and John Singleton hired "Umphry for 1849," they bound themselves to the condition that

Umphry was to be "well clothed according to the custom of the County," in this case, Gloucester. Such language reflected a by-then widespread expectation that all Virginia whites knew the manner in which hired slaves were to be clothed and that those who hired slaves would clothe them accordingly. This was the context in which a slave owner reprimanded a slave hirer who failed to provide hired slaves with proper clothing. Clothing for hired slaves, Ida Dulany insisted to slave-hirer John Fletcher, "is an understood thing." In Dulany's view, Fletcher's failure to give hired slaves appropriate clothing was due to something other than Fletcher's ignorance regarding the sort of clothing slave hirers were expected to provide hired slaves.[39]

In addition to the other circumstances in which slave hiring occurred, white Virginians' familiarity with slave hiring stemmed from the spread of the practice into local barter economies by the early nineteenth century. In Lancaster County, customers regularly paid their accounts with a merchant with hired slaves. Hill Hutcherson, for example, credited his 1800 tavern account, as well as his account for bacon and general merchandise, with "hire of [his] negro Will" to the merchant in 1802. Charles Lattimore hired his slave Peter to the merchant to pay off a cash advance and for some merchandise, and William Taylor hired his slave Spencer to the merchant as payment for corn, tobacco, stamp paper, and merchandise. The merchant also occasionally hired out his slaves to his customers, an activity that complemented his sale of crops and merchandise. In 1800 John Henry hired James from the merchant, who also rented Henry a house and lot, sold Henry corn and merchandise, and kept a tavern account for Henry. Similar transactions occurred throughout the antebellum period. Fauquier County resident Elias Edmonds paid for cotton, sugar, tea, coffee, brandy, candles, molasses, nutmeg, ginger, cheese, and nails, among other merchandise, with the hire of his slave Dinah to the merchant from whom he purchased those items in 1838 and 1839. Slave hiring also facilitated transactions for a sawmill owner in Powhatan County. In 1854 customer John Lawton paid for sawing with the hire of his slave Henry. The same year, the sawmill owner hired out his slaves Nelson and William to Thomas Munford and also sold Munford sheeting plank and weather boarding. Elsewhere, a slave owner put up cash as well as "Billy Jones hire to pay [his] insurance on [his] house." Slave-hiring bonds and notes themselves circulated as media of exchange, as when Samuel Shield used "Blair's note for hire of Sam" to pay for "Board washing mending &c." for 1819. White Virginians' use of hired slaves and slave-hiring bonds as media of exchange in local barter economies demonstrates the rapidity with which slave hiring expanded throughout Virginia to facilitate transactions between whites in the countryside. White Virginians' consequent familiarity with slave hiring, therefore, is of little surprise.[40]

By the 1850s, slave hiring had become so central to white Virginians' lives and activities that slave-hiring bonds were manufactured and preprinted. Information including dates, amounts of money, and names of slaves, owners, and hirers was written in by hand in spaces provided within pretyped, general statements of the sort white Virginians knew well, including "customary summer clothing" or lists of items that were to be "good [and] customary" or simply "good." In the last few years before the Civil War, slave hiring was a pervasive and familiar feature of white Virginians' slave society.[41]

Slave hiring was so common in antebellum Virginia that many whites were able to make their living solely by hiring out others' slaves. One slave-hiring agent, Lucien Lewis, printed and distributed business cards identifying him as an "agent exclusively for hiring out negroes," and Lewis promised slave owners "hires collected quarterly, and returns made promptly." Lewis sent slave owners a preprinted letter of introduction in which he informed them that he was "still in the business of hiring out negroes, and to respectfully solicit [their] patronage for the ensuing year." In his 1860 letter, Lewis stated that he had been in the slave-hiring business for eight years and that he had "design[ed] to confine [himself] exclusively to it." Like other businesspeople who sought clients regularly, Lewis provided a list of references, which included attorneys, merchants, county clerks, an army colonel, and other slave owners. Slave hiring was so widespread in Virginia that large mercantile firms found it worthwhile to hire out slaves on slave owners' behalf, too. In addition to selling real estate, household and kitchen items, lime, and plaster, for example, Branch & Company of Richmond hired out slaves for their owners during the 1840s and 1850s. Each year during that period, Branch & Company hired out slaves for many different slave owners, sometimes in excess of four dozen slaves per year.[42]

Slave hiring was everywhere in antebellum Virginia. Because it was an integral and permanent aspect of Virginia slavery, slave hiring had a profound impact on many, if not most, slaves in Virginia. For slave women, slave hiring shaped many facets of life while it also illuminated white Virginians' perceptions and expectations of them.

CHAPTER 2
HIRED SLAVE WOMEN

On December 27, 1809, John Wrenn and Richard Grigg executed a slave-hiring bond "for the Hire of a negroe woman" for 1810. Wrenn and Grigg promised to give the slave woman "good and substantial Clothing as usual," vague language that reflected white Virginians' familiarity with slave hiring, which had spread throughout Virginia by the early nineteenth century. Wrenn and Grigg's action in rural southeastern Virginia also highlights a little-noted aspect of slave hiring: the hiring of female slaves, a routine aspect of slavery in a region with a diversified economy and a rapidly increasing slave population.[1]

Virginia slave owners hired out women and girls as often as they hired out men and boys. In Essex County, for example, Warner Lewis hired out Sarah, Eliza, and Matilda along with two male slaves in 1842, and Samuel Bell hired out Maria, Phillus, Betty, Lucy, and Sarah in Augusta County in 1852. Advertisements to hire out female slaves filled the pages of local newspapers. In Loudoun County, J. W. and C. B. Wildman offered "A NUMBER of MEN, WOMEN, BOYS and GIRLS, for Hire for 1859." The 1860 slave schedules, too, reveal that large numbers of hired slave women labored in rural Virginia. In Loudoun County alone, Virginians hired out 360 female slaves age twelve and over in 1860, and the total number of female slaves hired out there that year was still higher, since many slave girls below the age of twelve were hired out also.[2]

Nineteenth-century white male Virginians believed that household domestic chores, including child-rearing, cooking, and other tasks, required a woman's attention, which meant that many slave women worked as house servants. This occupation limited slave women's mobility, because house servants normally were required to remain on call at all times, including Sundays. However, the household context offered Virginia's hired slave women unique opportunities to resist their enslavement. Hired slave house servants' access to food consumed by white families, for example, placed them in a favorable position to poison their hirers. James Sullivan's slave Louisa took this action as a hired house servant in the home of George Waddey in 1853. Court papers reveal that on July 13, Louisa "mingle[d] a certen Poison With . . . a parsel of Rice prepared for dinner at . . . Waddey's." The rice was meant for Waddey, members of his family, and several guests.[3]

House servants elsewhere in Virginia took similar actions against their hirers. In Southampton County, hired slave Tempe was hired out as a house servant, but she was dissatisfied at her hirer's residence. Tempe's manager deemed her "a woman of bad character, headstrong & ungovernable—and lately, was subjected to strong suspicion of being of an effort to poison, the family with which she lived." As a result, Tempe's manager determined "to sell her and send her away from this part of the country." Hired slave women who engaged in such aggressive forms of resistance, or were suspected of it, incurred the risk of drastic reprisals.[4]

White Virginians hired out pregnant slave women, too, usually for purely economic reasons. When Elizabeth Skinker hired out Delphia and Nutta to James Phillips for 1826, Delphia was of childbearing age, if not already pregnant. "If Delphia at any time of the year should have a child born alive and should suck the mother," Skinker and Phillips concluded, "there will be a deduction of five Dollars made" from the original hire of $47.50 for both women. In 1829 Joseph Carter of Lancaster County hired out Patty to Charles Ingram "for victuals and clothes she being pregnant." Patty was pregnant again in 1831, and Carter hired her out again on the same terms. In York County in 1830, Delaware Bryan hired out a "woman & 2 children for vict[ual]s & clo[thes] ([she] being pregnant)." In Virginia, slave owners hired out their pregnant slave women precisely because of the women's diminished labor capacities and consequent increased expense, which meant that hirers secured them at relatively low cost.[5]

Across Virginia, many pregnant slave women gave birth at hirers' residences. In Fauquier County, for instance, Tilghman Weaver hired out Hannah and Lucy to N. B. Butler in 1853. At Butler's place, Hannah gave birth to a son, Austin, in August, and Lucy delivered a daughter, Martha, in September. Shortly afterward, another hired-out slave woman delivered a son "at A. Manyett's" in 1854. In 1858 the Fauquier County Commissioner of Revenue noted that Horrace Weaver and R. Tripletts had "Hired the Mother" who gave birth to slave children at their residence. Meanwhile, a slave infant born "at Westley Riley's" farm the same year was the child of a slave woman Riley hired from Polly Ann Moffitt.[6]

In Loudoun County, the pattern was similar. Lucinda, owned by Margaret Beavers and hired out to A. F. Osburn, gave birth to a son at Osburn's place in 1856. The same year, Lucy, whom Ignatius Elgin hired from Edmund Berkley, had a daughter at Elgin's residence. In 1857 James Simpson's slave Julia gave birth to a son, Willis, while she was on hire at D. F. Gulick's place. Also in 1857, Marshal and Mahlon Carpenter's slave woman Caroline delivered a son, Nelson, at the residence of William Reader, who held Caroline on hire. Hiring out slave women was a very common practice among Virginia slave owners, and far from being an obstacle to the hiring out of female slaves, pregnancy *increased* a female slave's likelihood of being hired out by whites who sought to get relatively unproductive, and relatively costly, slaves off their hands. Contrary to assumptions that most hired slaves were male and skilled, the fact is that the hiring out of pregnant slave women, and slave women generally, was an inherent and routine feature of slave hiring, and of slavery generally, in Virginia.[7]

Because slave women who gave birth at hirers' residences were expected to be less productive than other slaves, Virginians who hired out birthing women normally granted hirers a deduction from the original amount of the hire. In Accomack County, John Turlington allowed a deduction for hired slave Mary, who had a child in 1834. Turlington also provided that "Cash [be] deducted from hire of Britania, in consequence of her having a child, [in] the year 1834." Britania then had another child while she was hired out in 1836, and Turlington once again allowed the deduction. In Halifax County, Fanny's manager noted sarcastically in his memorandum book a deduction "inconsequence of Fanny's having a child which was agreed upon at the time of hiring in the event of such a National Calamity." The deductions owners allowed hirers reflected white Virginians' recognition that newborn children reduced hired slave women's capacity for labor and, therefore, their value to a hirer.[8]

Hired slave women faced possible complications associated with childbirth, and they never knew what sort of medical care awaited them at hirers' residences. Responsible hirers of slave women took appropriate steps in response to the women's medical needs. "The girl Lavinia I hired . . . is I think in a bad situation and requires the attention of a Physician," Jordan Taylor informed Iverson Twyman in 1859. Taylor requested that Twyman take the slave girl back for treatment, concluding, "It [is] more than probable she has the '*bad Disorder*' at any rate she has some venerial desease." Shortly afterward, however, Taylor reported to Twyman: "Your woman Lavinia was confined last knight. She gave burth to a fine Daughter and her Condition is as well as could be expected."⁹

Other white Virginians who hired slave women were far less prepared for medical emergencies. This was made worse by the fact that male hirers of slave women were less likely than female hirers to even recognize slave women's special needs related to childbirth. Such was hired slave Rosetta's experience in Lancaster County. Rosetta's owner, John Towles, hired her out to Pharoah Douglass for 1855. "Great with child" while hired out to Douglass, Rosetta's troubles began when a panic-stricken Douglass placed Rosetta in a buggy at the very moment she was "in the act and article of parturition." Douglass intended to travel some eight miles with Rosetta to a person Douglass believed might be of some assistance, but on the way, Rosetta gave birth to a son. Though born alive, the boy, "while still connected with the mother by the umbilical cord . . . for want of the proper assistance, and by reason of the improper situation of the mother . . . [from] bruising, marking, choking, suffocating and strangling . . . then and there died." Rosetta's experience illustrates that some of the dangers hired slaves faced were peculiar to hired slave women and that some hired slave women were worse off for want of someone who had some idea of what to do when they went into labor.¹⁰

Most Virginia hired slave women's birthing experiences, however, were characterized by neither the attendance of a physician nor a dangerous ride in a buggy. Several considerations determined the amount and nature of the care slave women received for medical needs associated with childbirth. Some whites believed that slave women required less attention in childbirth than white women, because, they reasoned, regular exercise in the fields conditioned slave women for the task. Also, most white Virginians preferred to avoid paying the prices physicians charged for slaves' medical care, and the rural isolation of many farms and plantations often precluded physicians' visits in any event.[11]

Frequently, white Virginians' solution for slave women's medical care was the employment of midwives, who were available in greater numbers, and at lower cost, than were physicians. In Virginia, though white women sometimes served as midwives to slave women, slave midwives often served other slaves, and their owners hired them out specifically for that purpose. In many instances, slave women were hired out as midwives to other slave women who were themselves hired out. White Virginians like Daniel Cobb recognized and accepted slave women's role as midwives to pregnant slaves, as on the night of December 2, 1857, Cobb "had a nigrow woman . . . Call out for a Mid wife . . . so [he] sent for her."[12]

Many white Virginians respected hired-slave midwives' services and paid them directly, as was the case with "old Catey." Judy and "old Catey" were separated from one another when Judy was hired out to John McGill. When Judy prepared to give birth at McGill's place, however, Catey was permitted to travel to Judy to render her midwife's services. Catey's role as a hired-slave midwife commanded considerable respect, as shortly after Catey performed her services, hirer McGill was notified that Catey awaited payment for her services to Judy. "Old Catey's fee for attending Judy in her confinement is too dollars," McGill was told, "& she wishes you to send her the Munney [as] she is in great want of it." Elsewhere, a similar pattern prevailed in the summer of 1855, when John Martin paid "James . . . Shaddock's Hager for attention to negro woman Ann, as midwife."[13]

Many Virginia hired-slave midwives, however, did not receive cash for services rendered slave women at other farms. Instead, many Virginians who hired out slave women as midwives charged owners or hirers of pregnant slave women directly and then pocketed the cash. In York County in 1802, for instance, a Mrs. Mitchel hired out a slave woman to give midwifery services to a slave woman in the charge of William Macon, and Macon paid Mitchel four pounds, four shillings "for services of [Mitchel's] old Woman." Similarly, the slave woman Betty, in the custody of Robert Waller, received the aid of John Lee's hired-out slave midwife, and Lee charged Waller two dollars "for services of his woman to Betty." In another instance, Waller paid a slave owner four dollars for the slave owner's "midwife to 2 women" he held. Elsewhere, Molly, a slave owned by a Mrs. Baytop, was hired out as a midwife in 1848 and again in 1850, services for which Baytop received payment. In 1854 James Thomas hired out his slave woman Ellen for "services as midwife to Big and little Nancy," slave women owned by William Perrin, and Perrin paid Thomas four dollars for Ellen's services to his slave women. In Orange County, guardian Lancelot Burrus paid a slave owner $2.50 for "furnishing a woman to wait upon [his ward's] woman in child bed" for one month.[14]

Hired-slave midwives' importance in Virginia cannot be exaggerated. Unlike most slave women, hired-slave midwives had some mobility, which they used to create important communication links between slaves on different plantations. These channels complemented general interplantation visiting during the holidays and interplantation visits made by male slaves who ran errands for their owners or visited their wives. The mobility of hired-slave midwives, coupled with the fact that many of the midwives commanded enough respect to be paid for their services, enabled them to forge a special niche for themselves within Virginia's slave-hiring system.

Virginia whites' awareness of, and respect for, hired-slave midwives' special role was reflected in their hiring of slave midwives to attend to birthing white women in their own families. In the spring of 1863, Daniel Brady, manager at William Weaver's Buffalo Forge iron works, sent for the slave midwife Aunt Phillis to assist his wife, Emma, with the birth of the Bradys' new daughter, Wilhelmina. Brady had previously paid Aunt Phillis for midwifery services to slave women, and he recognized and valued her skills sufficiently to call upon her to aid with Emma's delivery, for which he paid Aunt Phillis ten dollars. In Hanover County, Mildred's owner hired her out as a midwife to assist area white women regularly. "Whenever any o' de white folks 'roun' Hanover was goin' to have babies," Mildred recalled, "dey always got word to Mr. Tinsley [Mildred's owner] dat dey want to hire me fer dat time." Mildred was hired out as a midwife to white women, sometimes more than one at the same time, at all hours of the day and night, and she recalled that her owner gave her a portion of the money he collected for her services. Hired-slave midwives' assistance to birthing white women shows that black and white women, though divided by their status as free and slave, often experienced one of womens' most wonderful life events together.[15]

In the case of hired-slave midwives' attendance on other slave women, the new slave children became white Virginians' object of complaint. In Stafford County, although William Gordon collected twenty-five dollars "for keeping an infant of Amy" (Amy had died at Gordon's place) from February 1851 through the end of the year, Gordon quickly complained that caring for Amy's infant child had been "attended with much trouble." Patrick Catlett wrote his wife to inform her that he had hired a house servant to cook while she was away. Catlett told his wife that he was pleased with the slave, who "so far . . . has done very well . . . is obedient and semes disposed to do her duty In fact she dose better than . . . expected." "There is one objection to her however," Catlett continued, "And that is, she has a young child." Catlett quickly added, however, that "we must try and put up with that inconvenience [as] Negroes are hireing very high this year." These comments reveal hirers' impatience with slave women rendered less productive by virtue of their possession of infant children and hirers' expectation that hired slave women would work for them as well as care for their children.[16]

Newspaper advertisements reflected Virginia hirers' wish to avoid slave women with young children in order to get some work out of them. G. B. Cooke, for example, wished to hire only "a good female house servant, who is without incumbrance." Elsewhere, Joseph Toy declared his intention to hire "a good Cook, Washer and Ironer, without any incumbrance." Many advertisements also revealed that Virginians who hired out slaves knew of prospective hirers' concerns. In Loudoun County, G. W. Ball boasted that one of the three slave women he offered for hire for 1859 was "entirely unincumbered," while two others, he conceded, had "one child a piece." In January 1859 L. W. S. Hough, also of Loudoun, offered for hire "a young woman unincumbered, accustomed to Cooking and Washing." Because they knew that many would-be hirers considered hired slave women with young children as troublesome, inconvenient, and less able to work, Virginia slave owners emphasized that their slave women did not have children, when that was the case, in order to make them appear more attractive to hirers who wished to get as much work out of the women as possible. Yet a slave woman's possession of young children did not preclude whites' desire to hire them when they expected to get some work out of some of the children themselves. Charles Washington made this clear in a letter to his father in 1847. "I hired from Lorenzo Lewis a Woman with five children the oldest of which is a Boy large enough to plow with a one horse," Washington explained, and "the second is also useful in making a fire in the house and setting the table." "But the balance" of the slave family, Washington continued, "have to be supported the woman is very awkward I do not think she could have ever seen the inside of a house before, for the family I have to pay 38$."[17]

Virginia whites sometimes were not able to hire out slave women who were pregnant or had infant children. In Lancaster County, a young slave woman, though "valuable intrinsically," in her manager's estimation, "from the fact of her being a breeding woman she does not hire out." In Accomack County, Thomas Joyner noted that he did not succeed in hiring out "negroe Patience for the year 1847 because she had a child in the beginning of the year and no hire could be obtained for her." Elsewhere, Southampton County Court papers reveal that "negroe woman Charry was kept by Elizabeth Doles, [but] belonged to Rebecca Doles," Elizabeth's daughter. Elizabeth kept Charry because Charry "had one [child] that lived, and one miscarriage . . . was . . . very sickly, and confined a long time when she miscarried," and therefore could not be hired out.[18]

An individual slave woman's value changed over time as her situation changed with respect to pregnancy or young children. Records kept on hired slave Rose, of Princess Anne County, reveal the wide fluctuations of slave women's value on the slave-hiring market as affected by pregnancy and the presence of very young children. Rose's manager hired Rose out each year from 1842 through 1852. During that time, Rose gave birth to three children, one in 1843, another in 1844, and a third in 1848. Also during that time, two of Rose's children died, one in 1847 and another in 1850. There is a clear pattern between these births and deaths, on the one hand, and the prices recorded for Rose's annual hire, on the other. Following the birth of a child, Rose's hire value went down, and each year after the death of a child, her hire value went up. The unavoidable conclusion is that additional young children decreased slave women's value on the slave-*hiring* market (in contrast to the slave-*selling* market), and fewer children enhanced it.[19]

Virginia slave owners' utilization of slave hiring to shift childbearing slave women's expenses to hirers, coupled with prospective hirers' reluctance to hire such slave women, meant that many whites *paid others* to hire slaves they deemed insufficiently productive to feed and clothe. "As to

Henrietta," Samuel Cooper wrote to Sarah Maria Cooper, "I think I shall have to furnish board for her somewhere . . . as I do not think it likely I can hire her out even for only her food, with the incumbrance of her child." Elsewhere, Lucy's manager offered to pay T. S. Stubbs to take Lucy in 1802. Stubbs accepted, and he noted afterward his receipt of "Eight pounds nineteen shilling. & six pence for the keeping of Lucy & her children for this present year." In 1844 Middlesex County slave-hiring agent Robert Trice paid William Hackerey "a liberal price," in Trice's estimation, of twenty dollars to feed and clothe Betsy and her three children for the year. Trice's "reason for doing so," he explained in clear reference to Betsy's having small children, "is, that . . . her situation this year peculiarly requires that." In Southampton County, Daniel Cobb's observation at "a hireing of negrows" in 1846 reflected how frequently white Virginians paid others to feed and clothe slave women with young children: "Women and Children was kept for some [$]2 to [$]5 per head," Cobb reported. Virginia slave owners paid other Virginia whites to hire slave women with young children in order to escape the costs and troubles they associated with relatively less productive slaves. These actions constituted a routine aspect of slave hiring, and of slavery itself, in antebellum Virginia.[20]

With or without young children, hired-out female slaves in Virginia were more likely to fall under close white male supervision than were hired-out male slaves. This applied not only to women hired as house servants, but also to most hired-out slave women who were surveilled by whites when they were transported between owners, hirers, and hiring-day sites. "I have sent my wagon in for China and her children," John Alston wrote Asa Dupuy in December 1827, as China's slave-hiring year was about to end. Similarly, James Carr informed Dabney Carr that "the wagon for the servants will leave Charlottesville tomorrow." James hoped that the slaves would be prepared to leave at the appointed time so that the wagon would not be kept waiting. "It is impossible to hire [a wagon] for less than $5 p[er] day," he complained. The expense of transporting hired-out female slaves influenced whites' decisions as to how much hire to offer when a slave woman had to be conveyed from a considerable distance away. "I did not think at that time," Patrick Catlett explained to his wife about a particular slave woman, "that I should be justifyable in giving more than 16 or 18 [dollars hire for her] as I should have had to send 23 miles after her." White Virginians' insistence that hired-out slave women be transported and surveilled on their journeys by white men attached yet another expense to the slave women in white Virginians' eyes.[21]

Yet white Virginians usually shouldered expenses associated with transporting hired slave women from one place to another, often by various and elaborate means. In 1827 Samuel Hannah's "Girl Martha" was placed upon "David Staples Boat," and Hannah was assured that "Mr. Staples promis[e]d to take good care of her." Martha's transportation arrangements were made on short notice, because Martha's hirer, a Mr. Anderson, had "found some fault [with Martha] & sent her home before her time was out." Frequently, several white men were brought into the plan to transport a hired-out slave woman. In 1858, for example, Mary was conveyed first by boat in the custody of two white men, then transferred to a train, "under the care of the conductor on the cars," and brought to William McGuire, who had arranged in advance for Mary to have a note to "show to the Clerk on the Boat, and also at the wharf when she reaches Alexandria." Elsewhere, in 1857 Lydia's owner hired her out with a note addressed "To The Conductor of the B & O Railroad." Lydia departed Harper's Ferry with her owner's note, which outlined the several stages of her journey to her hirer, James Markell, a merchant who resided in Jefferson County. Lydia's owner informed the railroad conductor that "Lydia, the bearer hereof [the note, was] . . . put . . . on the cars to go as far as Kerneysville, thence by stage, to Shepherdstown & then to her home," that is, to hirer Markell's residence. Lydia, like other hired-out slave women, traveled to hirers under the surveillance of one or more white men along a preplanned route that often involved more than one means of transport, including railroads that other hired-out slaves had built. The participation of numerous white men in the transportation and surveillance of hired slave women took white involvement with slave hiring in Virginia far beyond white owners and white hirers alone.[22]

Regardless of the precise nature of logistical arrangements, Virginia slave women and their children frequently were hired out as family units over periods of several years, particularly when they were under the management of a guardian of minor orphans who sought to keep the orphans' expenses as low as possible. From 1839 through 1845, guardian Washington Perkins handled the financial affairs of Essex County orphans John, Thomas, William, and Ellar Ann Fisher. Like other guardians, Perkins managed the assets bequeathed to his wards to yield an income to cover expenses the orphans incurred during the years before they came of age. The Fisher siblings had inherited a diverse array of slaves, including full working hands, elderly slaves, and several families of women with their young children. One of those women was Julia Ann and her children.[23]

Julia Ann and her children spent at least six consecutive years out on hire during Perkins's guardianship of the Fisher orphans. Julia Ann and her children did not, however, bring a cash hire for any of those years. Rather, as was the case with so many other slave women and their children, guardian Perkins paid someone to hire Julia Ann and her children. For Julia Ann's family, the hiring-out experience began in 1840.

On December 31, 1840, Perkins paid Robert Moody $25.00 for hiring Julia Ann and her family for that year. In 1841 Julia Ann had four young children, and Perkins again paid $25.00, this time to John Tune, to hire them for the year. During her time at Tune's place, Julia Ann had an additional child, so Perkins paid Tune a larger sum, $29.50, to hire Julia Ann along with five children the following year, 1842. The amount Perkins paid to hire out Julia Ann and her children fell to $22.00 in 1843; Mary Ann Clarke, whom Perkins paid to hire them for that year, was given care of Julia Ann and only four children. As for the fifth child, the record is silent. Most likely, either the child had died, or one of the other children had been deemed old enough to work and bring a small hire separately from the rest of the family and so was hired out elsewhere. In any event, Mary Ann Clarke again hired Julia Ann in 1844, this time with five children, and the higher number of children was reflected in the increased cost of $30.00 to Perkins. Clarke also was paid midwife's fees of $4.00, indicating that the new child was born while Julia Ann's family was hired out to Clarke. The final entry in Perkins's accounts concerning Julia Ann and her children is another payment to Clarke to hire them for 1845. Perkins did not note the number of children with Julia Ann that year. For several years, Perkins carried out his primary responsibility as a guardian: he kept the Fisher orphans' expenses connected to a slave woman and her children as low as possible.[24]

The management of slaves bequeathed to York County orphan John Chapman also illustrates how hiring out slave women and their young children as family units enabled white Virginians to cut financial corners connected to "unproductive" slaves' upkeep. Chapman's guardian, Benjamin

Wootten, hired out several of Chapman's slaves from 1814 through 1822, including the slave woman Sally and her children. In 1814 Wootten recorded his own expense of $50 for "supporting Sall[y] and five children." In 1818 Sally and her children remained with Wootten again, at a cost of another $50. In 1820, however, the experience of Sally and her children took a drastic turn when Wootten decided to hire them out and thereby shift their expenses over to someone else. That year, Wootten recorded that "Sally & 4 Children [were] set up [to the] Lowest Bidder" at a cost of only $4, a full $46 less than the cost Wootten had incurred in keeping the slaves himself. The following year, 1821, Wootten managed to hire out Sally and three children to John Powell at a cost of only fifty cents. Wooten's actions concerning Sally and her children show that he succeeded in keeping his orphan's expenses as low as possible by hiring out the relatively unproductive mother-child slave family unit. Because guardianship entailed financial responsibilities, white guardians often viewed slave women and their children in economic terms, as expenses to be reduced, if not avoided entirely.[25]

Many white Virginians saw slave women this way, and they paid other white Virginians the lowest price possible to hire slave women at auction on hiring days. In York County in 1821, for example, Amy was "let to the lowest bidder taken by John Culley for [$]3.00." In 1822 "Amy & child [were] put up to the lowest bidder and taken by Robert Billups at $10.50." In Gloucester County in 1852, "old Tabby . . . was put up & taken by [John Catlett] being lowest bidder." Hiring out rural Virginia save women to the *lowest* bidder meant that slave owners cut their expenses down to the lowest level possible, placing a higher priority upon the bottom line than upon any paternalistic pretensions.[26]

Some white Virginians found a different way to avoid the expenses of women with young children. In Stafford County, John Moncure faced the prospect of supporting a slave woman with young children in 1827. "This woman has 3 children," Moncure grumbled, "& I believe she could be supported cheaper by giving her a little and occassionally than by paying any person to take her with her children." Elsewhere, another white Virginian also opted to send a slave out to fend for herself when in 1845 he rented a room for Hester and her children and placed them there to live.[27]

Virginia slave owners also hired out slave women with young children for their food and clothing only, without a cash payment. In Gloucester County,

John Perrin did this on a regular basis. In December 1801, Perrin hired out Dido and her three children to George Bristow for their "Victuals & Cloaths," as well as Cloe and her three children, Sophia, Jenny, and Hannah, to Robert Shackelford on the same terms. One year later, Perrin hired out Judah and her children Bob, Tom, and Thacker to James Thomas for their "Victuals & Cloaths," and he later hired out Cloe and her children to Shackelford again under the same arrangement. In 1803 Perrin "hird [out] several women . . . this year for Victuals and cloaths each [of whom] had four children." Many white Virginians hired out slave women they considered unproductive, if only for their food and clothing, as a calculated plan of action. In Henrico County, Maria Gooch made a note in her slave lists to "hire some of the young females out & put out others for their victuals & cloathes." Similarly, Robertson Coons's slave records reveal that during the 1820s he hired out some slave women, kept some at his place, and hired out still others along with their "children for their victuals & cloathes." A Gloucester County resident's record of "Negroes hired out for the present year 1848" in an account book also shows the routine manner in which white Virginians hired out different types of slaves simultaneously, on various terms. Amy, Bob, Plato, George, and Kit were hired out to work, and cash was collected for them, but Sally, Nelly, and Dinah were hired out "to be clothed"; a relatively low hire was collected for Sally, while Nelly and Dinah were hired out for their clothing alone. Clearly, white Virginians employed various forms of slave hiring to enjoy maximum return and minimum expense for the several different slaves they owned and wished to hire out.[28]

White Virginians' efforts to escape expenses of slave women and their children paled in comparison to the daily struggles of the slave women themselves. Hired slave women with young children in Virginia everywhere faced arduous days, and they were forced to divide their time between care of their children and labor for the white family that had hired them. Frequently, there was not enough time for both responsibilities to meet whites' satisfaction. "I have not a creature who I can have a bout me," Elizabeth Carter complained in 1834, as "all mine have young children." Carter's slave women were occupied constantly with the needs of their own children, and Carter knew it.[29]

In Lancaster County, hired slave Fanny was frustrated by the simultaneous demands of her hirer and her children. Fanny, said her manager, "will not work [while hired out], has children frequently but will not take care of them and they all die for want of proper care and attention she now has one child about five months old." John Williams, who hired Fanny in 1857, echoed her manager's sentiments. Williams considered Fanny "a negro of bad character." He found her "idle and inattentive to her work and . . . very insolent and abusive." Said Williams, "She has had several children none of whom are living but her last who is about five months old." Upon the insistence of both Fanny's manager and hirer Williams, the court ordered that Fanny and her children be sold.[30]

In Scott County, hired slave Letitia also endured the experience of balancing child-care duties with laboring for a hirer. Letitia's owner, Henry Kane, hired her out in January 1857 to John Rutter for the "kitchen and [to] obey the order[s] of [Rutter] and his familey." Kane claimed he initially "was assured that [Rutter's] family was small and that the task of labour assigned [Letitia] would not be heavy," but Kane later discovered that "after he hired [Letitia to Rutter, Rutter] took in boarders making the labour of [Letitia] quite onerous." Furthermore, Rutter "ascertained that [Letitia] was pregnant and advised Mr Kane of the fact," and Letitia delivered her child in March. Consequently, Letitia suddenly was in the position of having to labor for a larger number of white people and care for her new child at the same time. With these pressures, it is little wonder that Letitia became involved in a violent confrontation with Rutter's wife early in the fall. As a result of the incident, Letitia was whipped and ran away from Rutter.[31]

Tension in white Virginians' households where hired slave women lived and worked may have been somewhat common. In 1817 Nancy Conn, of Washington County, filed a petition for divorce from her husband, William. She did so because she had "observed an unusual intimacy between" William and the slave woman she and William had hired. The "little indiscretion of conduct" Nancy was "determined to bear in silence till [William and the hired slave woman's] intimacy became so mark'd, his attentions to her so conspicuous" that the affair became the talk of the neighborhood. Ultimately, the "illicit intercourse" between William and the hired slave woman prompted Nancy to move out and live with her father.[32]

Yet whites, including those in Virginia's urban centers, always desired to hire, and hire out, slave women as house servants. As early as the Revolution, Virginia hired female slaves for "women's work," while it hired male slaves to produce war material. The Quartermaster's Department, for example, compelled the two slave women it hired to wash officers' laundry for the duration of the war. At foundries, while hired slave men produced cannon and the like, hired slave women labored to "answer the purpose for which women are wanted . . . to cook and wash for the tradesmen." In the decades following the war, the trend continued. In Norfolk G. B. Cooke offered to hire out "several NEGRO MEN and WOMEN," and another Norfolk resident advertised "For Hire, A LIKELY Mulato Girl, of unexceptionable character." Some slave women were hired out to work in the city by owners who resided in adjacent rural areas. Hired slave Maria, for instance, worked in Richmond but belonged to John Anderson of Hanover County. In Alexandria one resident offered "To Hire . . . A WOMAN who has been accustomed to house work of every description," and another wished "to Hire, A NEGRO GIRL, AS a Cook" and promised "liberal wages" to any owner willing to hire out such a slave. In the Norfolk-Portsmouth area, S. W. Paul sought to hire "a Cook that understands her business well; also Two Female House Servants" in 1839. Elsewhere, Sarah Clayton hired out her slave Nancy in Richmond to David Hardy, who "st[oo]d as master for her . . . while she . . . work[ed] in part of [his] house." In contrast to these slave women, urban male hired slaves commuted to or from factories and warehouses on foot, repaired streets and dug sewers, and drove wagons about the city. This meant that the lives of slave women who worked as house servants in Virginia's cities were characterized by far less mobility than were those of their urban male counterparts. With some exceptions, such as urban slave women who were hired out as midwives or sent on errands, the lives of hired slave women who worked as house servants in Virginia's cities were much like those of most hired slave women who labored as house servants in rural areas, both hired and nonhired, with respect to their relative lack of mobility. Being a hired slave, therefore, conferred no special status upon most slave women. During the antebellum period, most hired slave women in Virginia's cities labored as house servants, and in 1860 more than fifteen hundred slave women were hired out in Richmond's first and second wards alone.[33]

Divergent levels of mobility between male and female slaves hired out in Virginia's cities raises the question of hired slaves' family integrity in urban bondage. Hired slaves' efforts to remain physically close to loved ones in the city met with mixed success. In some cases, urban slavery's unique character facilitated hired slaves' ability to be with family members, as when hired slave Pleasant was able to leave his hirer at the end of the day and sleep at the residence of his mother's owner in the evening. Other hired slave women in Virginia, however, were not as fortunate as Pleasant's mother with respect to visits from loved ones and other slaves in the city, because some hirers did not permit such visiting.[34]

Yet hired slave women who labored as house servants in Virginia's cities resisted hirers' efforts to prohibit their socializing with male slaves who tried to visit them. At five o'clock on the morning of February 4, 1849, Richmond resident Emanuel Seaman discovered a fire in the basement-level coal house of the Masonic lodge that he was responsible for. Suspicion fell immediately upon Fanny, whom Seaman had hired as a house servant from a Mr. Hill. In the alley adjacent to the coal house, along with "charcoal and pieces of broomhandles, used to light the fire," Seaman found the matches he had given Fanny the previous evening to light a candle while she ironed. Fanny recently had slept with her clothes on, and Seaman also discovered matches in her bed. The kitchen where Fanny slept was "separated from the coalhouse by a plank partition," and Seaman found a hole in the partition near Fanny's bed.

Before the fire, after Fanny had lived at Seaman's place for only one week, Seaman had refused to allow other slaves to visit Fanny at his house. Fanny had then told Seaman that "she did not like to stay" with him. Fanny also had complained to Hill, her owner, who declared that "he could not take her back, and that [Seaman] must keep her and make her work." She did not succeed in her attempt to play her owner and hirer off against each other. Fanny remained with Seaman "and seemed content, until she was told that she must not have persons to visit her [and] she seemed to be dissatisfied with this prohibition." Shortly afterward, the fire broke out. In the end, Fanny was "Tried & convicted & sentenced to be hanged on the 30th March, [1849]."[35]

A similar case involved hired slave Frances. Elenor Robinson, Frances's owner, hired Frances out to the Coopers in Richmond. Marmaduke Cooper returned home from church one evening to discover that "his house had been set fire to," and he found a candlestick belonging to Frances "setting immediately under the burnt place." Significantly, another witness in the case testified that three days before the fire, Frances had declared "that she liked Mrs. Cooper very well, & the only thing which she did not like was that she could not have company."[36]

During the summer of 1850, hired slave Mary, owned by Elizabeth Winfree of Chesterfield County, worked as a hired house servant for John Bransford in Richmond. The night of July 28, a fire engulfed Bransford's house, and a succession of witnesses testified that the fire had originated in the interior of the residence. Because Mary worked and lived in the house, she was accused of having set the fire. Mary attempted to escape her impending arrest, but she was apprehended. During the course of the case, Bransford himself pointed out that his house had been set afire two months earlier, though from the outside, after he "had ordered the husband of . . . Mary, to go off his lot, and he has never been allowed to come on the lot since." Sometime before the second fire, Mary had confided to Tarlton, a slave, "that she did not like to live at [Bransford's] house," and Tarlton "heard Mary say, that she wished the house would burn." As with other urban Virginia conflagrations, the fires at Bransford's place were the consequence of Bransford's attempts to control hired slaves' personal lives.[37]

The commission of arson by these urban hired slave women is of special significance. In the hired slave women's eyes, hirers' refusal to permit them visits with loved ones amounted to nothing less than a denial of the most cherished aspect of human dignity slaves sought to preserve within the context of their enslavement: their families. Urban hired slave women, enraged at this assault on the very fabric of their humanity, may have felt they had little left to lose, and so they responded by attacking and attempting to destroy the symbol of their *hirers'* family lives: their homes. Quite possibly, their anger led them to reason that destroying at least this symbol, something that was within their power to do, was a fair repayment for their hirers' destroying the hired slaves' family lives.

Urban hired slave women resorted to arson as a form of resistance for a variety of other reasons, too. In 1848 hired slave Maria, owned by John Anderson of Hanover County, "set fire to and burn[ed] the house of Moses Middledoffer" in Richmond. In 1849 William Clopton's slave Nancy worked as a hired slave for William Gibson in Richmond. When Gibson's house caught fire, Nancy was accused of setting it. Gibson admitted that Nancy, "the day before the house was set fire to, had been slightly whipped by him." The evening following the fire, Thomas White appeared at Gibson's place, where he found Nancy tied up. After White untied Nancy, Nancy told him that she had set Gibson's house afire "because Mr. Gibson had whipped her and she wanted to be sent away." Nancy's attempt to be sent elsewhere, however, did not succeed, as court papers show that Nancy was "tried and convicted and sentenced to be hanged on 24 August 1849."[38]

In 1852 hired slave Lucy set fire to the house of James Peay, who held Lucy on hire in Richmond. Thirteen-year-old Lucy, who had lived and worked at Peay's house for some eighteen months at the time of the fire, once received from Peay "a whipping, for improper and unruly conduct." Afterward, Peay's house caught fire. Following the fire, Peay, incensed and frustrated with Lucy, took her "to her master and asked him to sell her." At length, Lucy was tried and discharged. Even when family matters were not the issue, house servants' close proximity to hirers often caused them to be whipped for "improper" words or looks, and hirers were the judges of what was "improper."[39]

Slave hiring in Virginia enabled white owners and hirers to mesh their perceptions and expectations of slave women as property and as women, and their hiring out of slave women became an integral facet of Virginia slavery, often to the detriment of the slave women themselves. Because of its routine nature, and because it frequently involved slave children with their mothers as family units, slave hiring presented Virginia slave families with significant challenges and difficulties.

CHAPTER 3

SLAVE HIRING AND HIRED SLAVES' FAMILY AND FRIENDSHIP TIES IN RURAL AREAS

In York County about 1811, James Temple described his disposition of the slave woman Milly and her family: "They are out for their victuals & clothes with . . . Spencer where they will be taken care of & honorably dealt by." Significantly, Temple added that Milly's "fine family of children . . . will begin shortly to hire." Temple perceived that the value of each of Milly's young children on the slave-hiring market increased as they grew older. Temple's economic assessment of Milly's children within the context of slave hiring warrants an investigation of slave hiring's impact upon slave family and friendship ties.[1]

The relative stability of Virginia slave children's ties with their mothers while hired out as family units diminished with each passing year. As slave children approached laboring age, their slowly increasing value on the slave-hiring market captured their owners' or managers' interest. Countless slave families hired out as mother-child units across Virginia, therefore, faced an uncertain future. Consider a slave family owned and hired out by the Briery Presbyterian Church in Prince Edward County from 1840 through 1847. Much like other such slave families, Mary and her daughters Louisa and Martha began their hiring-out experience in 1840 with all members of the family hired out to the same place, because Louisa, age ten, and Martha, age seven or eight, were deemed too young to work and bring a return on their own. In 1841, however, Louisa, at eleven, was judged old enough to work and so was hired out apart from her mother; Martha, too, was hired out separately the following year, when she was about nine or ten years old.[2]

Elsewhere in Virginia, the pattern was similar. One slave owner in York County hired out many of his seventy slaves once they were nine years old, with "the smaller ones . . . kept home"; that is, the slave owner hired out his slaves as soon as they were old enough to bring a hire apart from their parents. As a result, the York County census enumerator noted that "many of th[o]se negroes ha[d] no permanent home." Kenneth Stampp points out, "The master, not the parents, decided at what age slave children should be put to work in the fields," and the same applied to hiring them out.[3]

The hiring-out system separated Virginia slave spouses from each other, too. "As to the place you propose respecting the men that are advanced in years," one overseer wrote his absentee employer, "the great objection is their having wives from home." The slaves' desire to remain at home had the overseer's sympathy, and he hastened to convince his employer that "they are all well treated [and] I never put . . . any of the old men to a piece of work but such as I know they are fully able to accomplish." "I have endeavoured & will continue as long as I have the charge of them," the overseer assured his employer, "too make them happy." These "old men" fared better than Zek, a slave in Augusta County. During the final days of 1863, Francis McFarland arranged with Zek's owners to hire Zek. A few days later, however, McFarland was notified that Zek was "unwilling to live so far from his wife." McFarland considered the entire situation "an embarassing affair," but he remained determined to hire Zek nonetheless. The very next day, January 7, McFarland "went . . . to see Zek, who after much trouble to persuade him agreed to come & live with [him]; & he came & began to work." The nature of McFarland's persuasion is unknown, but Zek's owners hired him out away from his wife against his wishes. McFarland, meanwhile, thought only of his own trouble in the matter, occasioned by Zek's strong desire to remain with his wife. After he hired Zek, McFarland proclaimed in his diary: "Glory to God, the perplexity is ended."[4]

Virginia slave owners separated hired-out slaves from not only family and friends who remained at the home place, but also from each other, because they usually hired out individual slaves to different farms. Ambrose Madison of Orange County, for example, hired out six slaves to six different hirers in 1835. The following year, Madison again hired out the same six slaves in six different directions. In 1839 Henry Layton of Middlesex County hired out seven slaves to six different hirers. The following year,

Layton again hired out the same seven slaves, this time to seven different hirers.[5]

Virginia slave families' hiring-out experiences over periods of several years reveal the many ways slave hiring affected individual family members, and they illuminate the economic considerations that usually motivated white Virginians' slave-hiring decisions connected to slaves' families. In Keysville, Prince Edward County, the Briery Presbyterian Church hired out slave families each year from 1840 through 1847.

The church utilized slave ownership as a source of income from its inception during the eighteenth century, when its purchase of slaves was incorporated into a "plan for establishing the gospel at the head of the Briery River, for the benefit of the adjacent inhabitants in Charlotte & Prince Edward Counties." In 1766 several subscribers pledged money to purchase "6 slaves . . . 3 men & 3 women . . . [who along with] their increase [were to remain] in the care of the Trustees to raise money forever [t]hereafter, for the benefit of a regular Presbyterian minister." By 1781, including births and other purchases made in the interim, the congregation owned fifteen slaves.[6]

In the 1830s, the slaves and the matter of what to do with them became an issue within the congregation. When in 1835 the congregation "met to take into consideration the propriety of selling the slaves belonging to them," it instead passed several resolutions providing for the slaves to be retained and hired out. It was decided "that in hireing out the slaves of the congregation, the trustees [would] consider as of first importance the comfort and moral condition of the slaves, and the price of the hire as of second importance." This resolution appeared to signal the congregation's departure from most white Virginians' economic concerns connected to hiring out slaves. Another resolution provided "that the trustees themselves [would] choose the persons to whom the slaves [were] hired, and that they [would] not set them up to the highest bidder." This resolution represented a deviation from the common practice in Virginia of hiring out slaves by auction. The final resolution granted the trustees "discretionary power to sell any of the Slaves for viscious conduct." Convinced that its resolutions constituted the best course of action as concerned the slaves as well as the congregation, the committee held prayer and adjourned the meeting.[7]

One of the slave families the Briery Presbyterian Church hired out from

1840 through 1847 was Jincy and her children. In December 1841, when the congregation made a list of its slaves and their ages, Jincy was forty years old, and she had three children, Frank, Mary, and Bill, ages eight, six, and four, respectively. During 1840 and 1841, Jincy and her children were hired out to Isaac Duffie. Duffie paid five dollars to hire for them the first year, but in 1841 the congregation paid him ten dollars to hire Jincy and her children, because Duffie also hired seven-year-old John and three-year-old Pamelia, young orphans of another of the Briery Church's hired-out slaves. The church paid Duffie to hire the slaves in 1841 also because Jincy gave birth to a son, Charles Anderson, who was seen as a greater expense.[8]

The following year brought changes for these slaves. The Briery congregation decided that John, who was "about 7 or 8 yrs old" as of December 1841, was old enough to be hired out to labor apart from his sister, Pamelia, as well as from Jincy and her children, and thereby bring additional hire for the congregation. So, while Pamelia was hired out to Isaac Duffie again along with Jincy and her children in return for their food and clothing, John was hired out to William Watkins, who paid ten dollars for him. John's hire alone enabled the church to recover the ten dollars it had spent the previous year for the upkeep of both John and his sister, Pamelia, along with Jincy and her children. Despite its resolution stipulating that financial issues were not its highest priority in hiring out its slaves, the congregation's hiring out of John away from the family shows that economic considerations *were*, in fact, paramount in its slave-hiring decisions.[9]

For 1843 the congregation took John from Watkins and hired him out to William Flowers, and Pamelia "was kept by R[ichard] Robertson." Meanwhile, whereas all four of Jincy's children had been with her at Isaac Duffie's place in 1842, only three of them remained with her in 1843. The reason was that Frank, Jincy's oldest child, was about nine years old, and he was judged old enough to work on his own. Frank was hired out to Hiram Hawkins for fifteen dollars, while Jincy and her other three children were taken from Isaac Duffie and shifted over to Richard Robertson, who was paid ten dollars to hire them. Even after paying Robertson to hire Jincy and her family in 1843, the congregation placed itself ahead by five dollars by hiring out Frank separately from the other members of his family. Once again, the congregation's actions revealed that money was the chief criterion in its slave-hiring decisions.[10]

The following year, 1844, the congregation hired out Frank to Hiram Hawkins again. Neither John nor Pamelia, however, went to the same person to whom they had been hired the previous year. About nine or ten years of age in December 1843, John, who had been with William Flowers in 1843, brought a hire of five dollars from Littleberry Rutledge in 1844. Isaac Duffie, meanwhile, was paid seven dollars for hiring John's sister, Pamelia, because she was only five years old in December 1843 and was not yet considered old enough for work that would bring a hire. Finally, Jincy and her other children were hired out to William Waddill for 1844 for three dollars because the two oldest children were eight and six years old, respectively, and were deemed capable of performing light chores.[11]

The congregation evaluated Jincy's family once again in preparation for the hiring year 1845. That year, Jincy and her children were hired out to B. Foster for 1845 at a cost to the congregation of $16.75. At first glance, it is unclear why the church was able to get $3.00 for Jincy and her three children in 1844, yet had to pay someone to hire them one year later, with the same number of children, each one year older. The birth and death list kept by the congregation for its slaves yields the explanation. The birth of a daughter, Nancy, to Jincy in 1845 shows that both hirer Foster and the church anticipated the birth and consequently saw Jincy's family as an expense for 1845. Meanwhile, Frank was hired out to William Clark for $27.00, Pamelia was again hired out to Isaac Duffie at a cost of $4.00 to the church, and John was taken from Littleberry Rutledge and hired out to Joseph Dickinson for $7.50.[12]

The next year, 1846, brought significant changes for Jincy's family. Although Jincy had borne a new daughter in 1845, she was hired out in 1846 to Roger Thackson along with only three children, because yet another of her sons was considered old enough to be hired out away from her. Specifically, the church noted that Jincy's son Bill was eight years old, so it hired him out to Thomas Cox for two dollars. The church's opportunity for profit led to the family's separation once again.[13]

The final year the congregation recorded the hiring out of its slaves was 1847, and records for that year reveal the continuation of past patterns. The church paid Samuel Legrand nine dollars to hire Jincy and three of her children. Meanwhile, Bill brought three dollars from James Haley, and Frank, Jincy's other son, brought a hire of twenty dollars from John Preddy. At the same time, Pamelia was hired out to Isaac Duffie for her food and clothing, and Pamelia's brother, John, was hired out to A. Webb for ten dollars.[14]

Another slave family owned by the Briery church was that of Frank and Vilet. In December 1839 Frank and Vilet had two sons and one daughter. Their oldest child, Spencer, was about five years old in 1839, Brister was about three, and Catherine, the youngest, was about two years old.[15]

The hiring-out experience of Frank, Vilet, and their children began in 1840, when the congregation hired them out to John Hawkins for sixty dollars. In 1841 the church took the slaves from John Hawkins and hired them out to William Hawkins for just forty dollars, because a new daughter, Amy, was seen as an additional expense. Frank, Vilet, and their children were moved yet again for 1842 when they were hired out to Creed Jenkins for forty-five dollars; there, the family's third home in as many years, Vilet gave birth to another child, Frank Jr. The following year, 1843, the church shifted the family to Joel Webb, the fourth person to hire Frank, Vilet, and their children in four years. In 1844 Spencer, the oldest of the five children, about ten years old, was judged old enough to bring his own hire apart from the rest of the family and was hired out to S. D. Stuart for four dollars. The church therefore hired out Frank and Vilet with only some of their children to Creed Jenkins the same year for twenty dollars. As the value of slave children as laborers increased with age, the church took the children from their parents and hired them out to work separately for their own hire.[16]

In 1845, because Spencer was a bit older, he brought ten dollars' hire from S. D. Stuart. Brister, meanwhile, was about eight years old, and the church hired him out to John Carter for his food and clothing; the congregation realized that if fewer children were hired out with Vilet, it would reduce the cost of paying someone to hire her along with her children, particularly since Vilet had given birth to a new daughter. Ultimately, the church paid John Merryman just ten dollars to hire Vilet and the children who remained with her in 1845. Vilet's husband, Frank, was hired out to Creed Jenkins for forty-five dollars and thereby separated from his family.[17]

The reason Frank was separated from his family is revealed in the slave-hiring records in the church treasurer's book. Each year beginning with 1840, the church received a hire for the family, but the *amount* of hire declined every year from 1841 through the time Frank was hired out away from his family in 1845. The amount of each of these decreases, moreover, ranged from five to fifteen dollars, and the church recognized the downward trend. Consequently, the church separated Frank from his family in 1845 precisely because it could collect fifteen dollars more by doing so than it could take in by hiring out the family members together. As a result, for the first time since the beginning of the decade, the amount of hire brought by this family in a particular year was greater than it had been the year before. The church's calculated decision to reallocate Frank in 1845 was motivated by the opportunity to fetch a larger hire by splitting the family up even more than it already was.[18]

In 1846 A. G. Green hired Brister for $2.50, and Spencer remained hired out to S. D. Stuart. Meanwhile, the church received $65.00 hire for Frank from William McCormick, less $10.00 it paid him to hire Vilet and her young children, for a net hire receipt of $55.00 from McCormick. Frank and Vilet thus were afforded a chance to be together again for 1846, and they no doubt welcomed it. Their reunion was bittersweet, however, as Brister and Spencer, their other sons, had been hired out elsewhere by the church.[19]

The church's hiring-out arrangements for 1847 illuminated the ongoing uncertainty that characterized its slaves' lives. Spencer went to S. D. Stuart again, and Brister was taken from A. G. Green and hired out to James Foster. Foster's payment of $3.25 for Brister, a figure $1.25 higher than Green had given for him the previous year, reflected the fact that Brister's value as a laboring hand had increased slightly with his age. As for Frank, Vilet, and the young children, the church once again sought a greater return by hiring out Frank apart from his family: while it paid Creed Jenkins $15.00 to hire Vilet and her children, it received $50.00 hire from A. Webb for Frank. This left the church with a net hire of $35.00 from these members of the family alone, which did not include the proceeds of hiring out Spencer and Brister apart from the rest of the family.[20]

The Briery Presbyterian Church's hiring out of its slaves broke up slave families annually for its own financial advantage. As an institutional owner of the slaves it hired out, the church's goal was to generate an ongoing income, which meant that its slaves were hired out for the duration of their lifetimes. This represented a significant difference from slaves hired out by guardians of orphans or by individual slave owners. Slaves might expect to avoid being hired out once they reached majority, and a slave owner sometimes opted to retain slaves in response to market fluctuations. Furthermore, despite the church's resolution of the 1830s stipulating that it would not hire out its slaves at auction, it did just that. This meant that the church intended to derive maximum monetary benefit from the hiring out of its slaves, and it also made familial separations of the slaves much more likely. The result, according to a study of slave-owning Presbyterian churches in Virginia, was that the church found itself "in the awkward situation of fostering marital infidelity among its slaves," who, being hired out to different places each year, had little hope of maintaining monogamous relationships.[21]

As for any slaves hired out at auction rather than to specifically selected hirers, the Briery Church slaves' pain of family separation sometimes was compounded by poor treatment in the hirers' custody. Because hirers lacked long-term interest in the church slaves' welfare and sought to derive as much work as possible from them during the year, hired slaves' experiences included poor medical care, lack of adequate food and clothing, and overwork of both pregnant and nonpregnant hired slaves. Such things became more likely when slaves were hired out to relatively poor hirers, who sought not only to squeeze as much labor out of a slave as possible but also to do so on the cheap, avoiding any expenses. The result for hired slaves was even higher rates of disease and child mortality than those that attended nonhired slaves in their owners' possession. Yet even relatively wealthier hirers did not promise humane treatment. Hilery Richardson, the hirer of some of the Briery church's slaves and the wealthiest slave owner in the area, subjected his slaves to such cruelty that he was murdered by one of them in response. The slave who killed Richardson was transported out of Virginia rather than executed, an action reflecting the white community's awareness that Richardson was an abusive slave owner. Revealingly, however, despite Richardson's reputation, the Briery church hired out its slaves to him, since income was its top priority and Richardson could outbid everyone else. Along with the annual prospect of family separation, therefore, the Briery church's hired slaves lived with the annual fear of being hired out to someone like Richardson. For the Briery Presbyterian Church, as for other institutional owners of slaves, slave hiring's impacts upon its slaves removed any basis for paternalist pretensions and meant that institutional slave hiring was "the worst kind of slavery."[22]

In the face of routine fears, difficulties, and dangers, the Briery slaves and other Virginia slaves hired out apart from family and friends attempted to ease their burdens by creating new ties at the places where they were hired out. One of the clearest indications that some rural hired-out slaves created new ties at new places is that in Loudoun County, for example, several slave women gave birth more than nine months into the year during which they were out on hire. Penolope Tyler's slave Emily for instance, gave birth to a daughter, Frances, on November 7, 1853, while she was hired out to Dennis McCarty. Similarly, John Harrison's slave Maria gave birth to a daughter on November 25, 1853, while she was on hire at Thomas Littleton's place. Sally McNealy's slave Mary gave birth to a daughter, Rebecca, on December 18, 1853, while she was hired out at John Moran's residence. These children may have resulted from the rape of the slave women, and it also is possible that the births were the result of contact with partners the slave women knew who either were at the place where they were hired or visited them while they were there. Yet Emily, Maria, and Mary may have met new partners at the farms to which they were hired out.[23]

Some Virginia hired slaves, however, found it difficult to establish new ties because they failed to get along with slaves who lived at the residences to which they were hired out. When asked what price he would give to hire a particular slave, a Fairfax County slave owner responded that he "would not be willing to have him at all." "If I had no blacks," the slave owner explained, "I might be willing to have him, but [my slaves] would bother him & [the hired slave then] would do nothing for me." Similarly, the atmosphere among the slaves at James Dunlop's Roslin plantation shows that relations between owned and hired slaves on some farms were not cordial. William McKean, Dunlop's overseer, managed Roslin during Dunlop's residence in Europe early in the nineteenth century. In 1816 McKean explained to Dunlop his reluctance to hire additional slaves to work on the place. "I want nothing now to make the Estate productive but 8 or 10 able negroes," McKean informed Dunlop, but "there is continually a jealousy between [the hired slaves] & the family negroes." Though aware of Dunlop's determination "not to purchase [slaves]," McKean advised him that doing so would be "to the satisfaction of the people at home." The precise nature of the animosity between the owned and hired slaves at Roslin is not clear, but they did not enjoy relations conducive to the formation of positive ties.[24]

What McKean characterized as jealousy between owned and hired slaves who lived and worked together on a farm sometimes developed into violence. In Southampton County, hired slave Mike was wounded by another slave at the farm where he was hired out, so his owner removed him from the hirer's possession. Similarly, at John Marshall's place in 1856, "seven of [Marshall's] negroe men [took hired slave] Billy and stripped him and whipt him." According to Marshall, his own slaves "charged [Billy] with several things as the pretence" for whipping him. As part of his study of honor in the slave community, John C. Willis maintains that Marshall's slaves whipped Billy because Billy had violated the sense of honor, loyalty, and "communal solidarity" that Marshall's slaves had cultivated among themselves. The negative feelings between the owned and hired slaves at Roslin, Mike's experience, and Billy's treatment at the hands of Marshall's slaves show that some hired slaves did not get along with slaves they met at new farms and so found it more difficult to create new, positive ties with other slaves while out on hire. Hired-out slaves' experiences in Virginia reveal that the notion of the slave community had its limits.[25]

Even Virginia hired-out slaves who created good relationships with other slaves with whom they came into contact still faced a formidable obstacle if they wished to preserve those new bonds: the possibility that they would not be hired out to the same farm again the following year. Concerning the hired slaves at Roslin, McKean once complained to Dunlop that he had "a new set to teach every year, as it [was] hard to keep them more than one year or two at farthest," a remark that reveals a rapid turnover rate for hired slaves in rural Virginia. This was the case with Mary Hall's slaves Granville, Mary, Chloe, and Moses, who were hired out each year from 1845 through 1849. These slaves were hired out to different places apart from one another each year, and none of them were returned to a place of previous hire, where they may have established ties with other slaves. Mary, for example, was hired out to Nat Nelson in 1845, to Elizabeth Parker in 1846, to Edward Arrington in 1847, to Jackson Guthery in 1848, and to Eliza Throckmorton in 1849. Any new relationships that may have been created were sundered annually, over and over again.[26]

The experiences of two of the Briery Presbyterian Church's slaves, Charles and Reason, resembled those of Granville, Mary, Chloe, and Moses. During the eight years the congregation hired them out, Charles and Reason were hired out apart from each other, and each was hired out to a total of five different persons. Charles worked for William Watkins in 1840 and for Ezra Hawkins in 1841. From 1842 through 1845, Charles labored for Asa Dupuy, but in 1846, the congregation shifted him to James Dupuy. Finally, for 1847 the congregation took Charles from Dupuy and hired him out to Hilery Richardson. Reason had a similar experience. B. W. Womack hired Reason in 1840, and Creed Jenkins hired him for 1841. From 1842 through 1845, the congregation hired Reason out to Thomas Spencer Jr. For 1846 the church hired Reason to Isaac Duffie, and then it hired him to Wiltshire Cardwell Jr. for 1847.[27]

In some cases, high annual turnover rates stemmed from Virginia hired slaves' dissatisfaction at one place or another, which in turn precipitated hirers' dissatisfaction with the hired slaves. According to overseer William McKean, hired slave Sam Price did not care to remain hired out to anyone: "When I can get any person to hire him it is well enough," McKean observed, "but no person that hires him once will have him again." Similarly, in 1858 hired slave Richmond perplexed hirer Richard Douglass, who consequently wished to send Richmond away. Douglass evaluated Richmond this way: "[He is] a very indifferent hand idle . . . and rogueish, and insolent and so unmanagable that I determined to get him off my hands even if I had to pay the whole amount of his hire for the year and prevailed upon [Richmond's manager] early in the year to take him off [my] hands." Hired slaves' dissatisfaction at hirers' residences sometimes developed because family and friendship ties had been severed, and hired slaves' overt discontent usually led the person who had hired them not to want them back.[28]

Several members of the Briery Presbyterian Church congregation felt that the annual turnover was detrimental to hired slaves' family ties. During the 1840s, these members represented a minority of a committee charged to determine the disposition of the congregation's slaves; this minority wished to sell the slaves, rather than continue to hire them out, which the committee majority proposed to do. Significantly, in its dissenting report issued in May 1846, the committee minority charged that slave hiring so severely injured its hired slaves' family ties that the slaves actually would be better off sold than hired out annually. "The Condition of the slaves [owned by] good and humane masters would be better than at present," the report began. When the slaves were hired out annually, the report continued, their "family connections [were] formed one year in one neighbourhood and the next [the slaves were] removed so far [away] that they [could] but seldom visit or be visited by their families and in that way [they were] liable to . . . [be] broken up, and new connections formed," and so on, year after year. The disruption of the hired slaves' family lives in this manner, the committee minority declared, "we think is very unfavourable to their moral & religious charectors." Because of this and other considerations, the committee minority concluded, "[We perceive] no legal (and if their Condition is to be bettered) no moral objection to [the slaves'] sale." The committee minority's assessment was in keeping with the congregation's own resolution of the 1830s, which had placed hired slaves' welfare above financial considerations, and it recognized that, for several years, the Briery slaves had been hired out with money as the congregation's principal concern.[29]

While the committee minority believed that *annual* turnover harmed the Briery hired slaves' family ties, it is significant that many Virginia hired slaves did not even have the entire year to cultivate any new relationships they may have formed at the places to which they were hired out. Sometimes, for example, unanticipated snags in hiring-out arrangements suddenly removed hired slaves from hirers' possession before the end of the year. This occurred with Mary Hall's slave Sydnor. Beverly Fleming hired out Sydnor to William Morriss for 1849, but Fleming later noted that "Mr. Morriss fail[ed] to Comply with the terms of hire [so he] took Sydnor back on friday the 4th [of] May at ab[ou]t noon." Elsewhere, Willis Ashby hired Martha but later found the "Negro taken away before the end of the year." The hiring-out system's uncertainties prematurely severed any new ties of family and friendship Sydnor and Martha had created at the farms to which they had been hired.[30]

Premature removal of Virginia hired-out slaves from hirers also occurred at the whim of owners and managers and by sale under a variety of circumstances. In 1850 Alexander Findlay wished "to ascertain from the Gentleman that hire[d] Geo[rge] & Winston if they [would] give them up a month or six weeks before their time [was] out." In Essex County, Richard Eubank hired out Louisa and three other slaves in 1853. Eubank took Louisa away from the person who had hired her, however, after only "2/3 of the year [had passed,] she having been sold before the expiration of the year under a decree of the Court." In Northumberland County, a female slave remained on hire to William Hudwall only through May 15, 1848, "at which time [Hudwall] gave her up it becoming necessary that she should be sold for the payment of debts." Annual turnover and early removal from hirers' possession meant that many Virginia hired slaves suffered the pain of separation repeatedly.[31]

Some Virginia hired slaves tried to be hired out in the vicinity of loved ones in order to cushion the blow of separation from others. In Gloucester County, for example, Lucy and her young children, along with several other slaves, constituted a portion of a deceased slave owner's estate in 1803. Because she anticipated being hired out, Lucy endeavored to be hired out to John Crue, who either owned her husband or lived very near him. "Lucy informd me you would take hir and hir children," Lucy's manager, John Perrin, wrote to Crue, and Perrin offered Crue "Five Pounds for the[ir] maintainnance . . . for the insoing year." Perrin informed Crue of his willingness to forego a cash hire for Lucy and her children "as she [was] willing to live with [him] . . . conveneant to her husband." Perrin believed that Lucy was less likely to run away if she lived near her husband, and he felt that not hiring Lucy out for cash was well worth that expectation. In Lucy's case as in others, the presence of loved ones near the farms to which they were hired out provided hired slaves with an emotional buffer against the pain of being hired out away from other slaves.[32]

Other hired slaves in Virginia did not fare as well as Lucy. Slaves hired out at auction, for example, had little hope of being hired out in the vicinity of friends or relatives. Nancy Williams remembered "dem hirin' days" during her interview in Norfolk in 1937. "De young marsa hired you out for a year," Nancy said. "When dey put me on de block to 'cry me off,'" Nancy continued, "all de po' white bacy-chewin' devils [were] stanin' 'roun waitin' to get me." "[I] yells loud's I could, 'I don' wan no po' white man git me' [but] as de devil would have it, one got me." Hiring day differed little in Tennessee, where ex-slave Kelly also remembered hiring-day auctions very well. Christmas season, Kelly recalled, "was sho' nuf fine times . . . fine times for them" but, she insisted, "awful for us po' niggers." Before long, hiring day arrived, and then, said Kelly, "them red headed yaps would bid us off to the highest bidder and we couldn't do nothin' but pray." "They would cry you off to the highest bidder for the next year," she continued, and "one by one, we had to get up on that block, and he bid us off." Slaves often could not be hired out where they wished, and the successful bidder at any slave-hiring auction was not necessarily a person who owned, or even lived near, a slave's friends or relatives.[33]

Some white Virginians' pockets were not deep enough to hire slaves, and that, too, reduced slaves' chances of being hired out to a farm where their friends or relatives lived. In 1854 Joseph Halsey informed Andrew Grinnan that while he would "take Frederick at $75" for 1855, Halsey could not "nor [could] anybody Else stand [Grinnan's] price for William." Many whites' shallow pockets limited the range of prospective hirers to whom a slave might be hired, lengthening significantly Virginia hired slaves' odds of being hired out in the vicinity of friends or relatives.[34]

The fluidity of the slave population on many Virginia farms also dashed hired slaves' hopes of finding friends or relatives at the residences to which they were hired out. Several Fauquier County slave owners, for instance, hired slaves in and out simultaneously in 1860. Strother Colbert hired in a slave from William Smith, but he also hired one out to William Embry and another to Wellington Gordon. Similarly, Rice Payne hired in two slaves in 1860, but he also hired two others out. Loudoun County slave owners made similar decisions. Joseph Mead hired in two slaves and hired out six of his own. Likewise, William Chamblin hired in one slave in 1860 and hired out six others, too. Virginians' practice of hiring slaves in and out at the same time exacerbated the uncertainties that attended hired slaves' lives, because the particular persons slaves may have expected to see at the place to which they were hired out may have been hired out away from that place.[35]

Opportunities for visiting friends and relatives also shaped Virginia hired slaves' lives following their separation from loved ones. Other than the Christmas holidays, at which time hired-out slaves normally returned home at least "fer three o' four days," as Virginia ex-slave Horace Muse remembered, hired slaves' opportunities to visit with friends and relatives varied in accordance with several factors: physical distance, the nature of a hired slave's occupation, owners' and hirers' attitudes concerning visiting, and an individual hired slave's determination to visit loved ones by prodding a hirer or by running away.[36]

In Virginia, physical distance was one variable that determined how often, and whether, hired slave visiting occurred during the hiring year. Hired slaves separated from friends and relatives by shorter distances probably were afforded visiting privileges more frequently than those who lived farther away from each other. The circumstances of hired slaves who remained geographically closer to their loved ones probably differed little from those of spouses in an abroad marriage who, in part because they lived fairly near each other, saw each other on a fairly regular basis. In Loudoun County, for example, the thirteen-year-old girl Syddnah Williams hired out to Charles Paxson in 1860 remained within a feasible walking distance from home, since Williams and Paxson lived approximately two miles apart. Greater distances, however, lay between other hired-out slaves and their families. In 1860 James Sexton of Loudoun County hired a twenty-eight-year-old man from Benjamin Higs of Fairfax Courthouse, about twenty miles away. Still farther from home were some of the slaves hired by railroad contractor John Buford in 1854. For his construction operations on the Virginia and Tennessee Railroad that year, Buford employed hired slaves from Sussex and Southampton counties, located at the opposite end of Virginia.[37]

Virginia hired slaves' occupations, too, conditioned their ability to visit with loved ones. This was especially true of hired house servants. Based on B. H. Walker's observations in King and Queen County, rural Virginians hired a considerable number of house servants every year. On a slave-hiring day in 1859, Walker carefully noted that he had "heard of Cooks hiring for $50 & washerwomen for $40 & upwards." Because many house servants, hired and otherwise, remained on call at all times, they had limited opportunities for visiting, or for visiting with some measure of privacy. The experience of hired house servants in Virginia no doubt differed little from that of those in Tennessee, where one ex-slave recalled being hired as a house servant:

> [M]y owner hired me out to some poor people that lived in the country . . . [when] I was only about six years old. . . . They hired me to nurse, but I had to nurse, cook, chop in the fields, chop wood, bring water, wash, iron and in general just do everything. On Sundays they would go to church and leave me there to clean the house and cook dinner. . . . When they got back from church I always had the meal ready [because] [i]f it wasn't ready, I knew what was coming. I didn't get any whippings because I always did what I was told, in a hurry.

While hired field hands may have done some weekend visiting, hired house servants found it more difficult to do so, since they spent their Sundays laboring for their hirers.[38]

Some Virginia owners and hirers permitted hired-slave visiting. In February 1839 Gabriel and James Wren executed a bond "for the hire of negro boy Richard" through the following January. The hiring bond stipulated that Richard's "washing and mending [was] to be done at home if [he were] allowed to go home once a fortnight." Hired slave Warner's circumstances resembled Richard's. When Charles Faulkner hired "negro man Warner" from Mary Timberlake during the 1830s, Faulkner secured a "deduction . . . in hire for lost time in [Warner's] Going to see his wife every other saturday eve[nin]g five Dollars."[39]

Other Virginia owners and hirers, however, did not permit hired slaves to visit very frequently. This was true for the slaves Benjamin Jackson hired out to the Richmond and Danville Railroad on December 28, 1853. The railroad permitted the hired slaves, Bob, Patrick, Ben, Oscar, Stephen, Sidney, and Mortimer, to visit their wives only "once in two months" during 1854, the year the slaves were hired out to the railroad. Elsewhere, a slave owner stipulated that the seven slave men she hired out could visit their wives only twice during the year, not including Christmas.[40]

Some Virginia owners and hirers did not allow visiting at all. Circumstances in Virginia probably differed little from those in Kentucky, where ex-slave Sarah Grant recalled that her mother, a hired slave, "was only allowed to come home on Christmas eve and had to go back New Years." In Tennessee, ex-slave Kelly recalled that as a hired twelve-year-old girl, she was not permitted to return home. "I went in and asked the old white woman to let me go home." Kelly did not tell the woman why she wished to go home, but the woman "wouldn't let me leave," she said, adding, "o'course, cause I was hired out to her." Kelly's hirer's attitude concerning hired-slave visiting took precedence over Kelly's home being only "'bout four miles from . . . where [she] was hired out." Ultimately, Kelly took her leave anyway, but she reminded herself to return before very long.[41]

Virginia hired slaves who were not granted visiting privileges took action to make visiting arrangements for themselves during the hiring year. In 1854 Joseph Halsey complained to Andrew Grinnan about the slaves he had hired from Grinnan. "I really did not wish to keep Old W[illia]m & Mitchell another year unless they were very desirous to remain," Halsey confessed, as "the time lost by them in going to their wives houses at all seasons caused a serious interruption to business." It is not clear whether the hired slaves had prodded Halsey into allowing them to visit their wives or whether they had run away periodically and returned afterward. In either event, assuming Halsey wished to get some work out of the hired slaves, he could do little about their desire to see their wives. William and Mitchell wished to visit their wives as much as Halsey desired that they remain at his place, and William and Mitchell had made their sentiments known to Halsey, one way or another.[42]

Not satisfied with whatever arrangements Virginia whites made, or did not make, for their family lives, some hired slaves opted to run away in order to visit family members. This occurred with Peter, a hired-slave blacksmith of Fairfax County. In 1814 William Deneale, Peter's owner, willed "Peter and his tools," along with four other slaves, to his daughter Syble. Significantly, Deneale also had directed that Peter's father, Tom, "remain upon the plantation" in Fairfax County. Following their father's death in 1814, James Deneale, Syble's brother, became Syble's guardian. To generate an income for Syble, James began to hire out her slaves, including Peter.[43]

In the spring of 1818, Peter lived and worked as a hired slave at the residence of John Hopkins in Frederick County. Frederick County was located some forty or fifty miles to the northwest of Fairfax County. On March 29, 1818, Peter ran away from Hopkins, who several days afterward claimed in the first of several letters to James Deneale that Peter had "absconded from [his] farm . . . without any known cause, and certainly without any provocation." Hopkins immediately anticipated Peter's return to Deneale's place, as he let Deneale know that he had "no doubt [Peter was] in and about his old haunts in Fairfax and [would] probably come to [him]." Hopkins became impatient, and informed Deneale that "Peter [had] not . . . made his appearance, at [his] Farm," and he further complained to Deneale that his "utensils . . . [were] constantly wanting repair." At length, Hopkins discovered that Peter had "already been . . . with his Father," Tom, back in Fairfax County. The length of time Peter was away is not known, but he succeeded in his determination to see his father.[44]

Since Peter had been separated from his father by a considerable distance, he probably did not receive permission to visit his father regularly, which led him to run away from Hopkins. Yet Peter ran away also because he wished to absent himself from Hopkins, whose letters betray him as a person very easily agitated. Peter sensed Hopkins's admitted dissatisfaction with him, and he feared the "severe Chastisement" that Hopkins believed Peter deserved. Whether Peter ever was punished for running away is not known.[45]

At the end of each hiring year in Virginia, many hired slaves returned home for the December holidays and enjoyed happy reunions with friends and family who had remained behind at the beginning of the year, as well as with those who had been hired out to different farms. However, many other hired slaves returned to discover that those from whom they had been separated were gone. Each member of a group of six York County slaves hired out in 1810, for example, was hired out to a different person. Though separated, the slaves expected to see one another again during the December holidays. At the end of the year, however, only five of the six slaves returned home. According to Thomas Curtis, who had hired the sixth slave, Judah, "yong woman Judah . . . departed this life the 23rd of October 1810." A hiring year ended in similar fashion in Lancaster County a few years afterward. In December 1832 all the slaves Benjamin Walker had hired out returned home for the holidays with the exception of Aaron. On January 1, 1833, Walker noted unceremoniously that "Aaron died last year (1832)" while he was out on hire. Like Judah's friends and family, Aaron's loved ones never saw him again.[46]

The sudden sale of Virginia slaves from the home place while others labored out on hire also brought sadness during the holiday season. One year, Lancaster County hired slaves Edmond, Moses, and Eliza looked forward to seeing Ralph, a boy, when they returned home for the December holidays. When the slaves returned home, however, Ralph was gone. Ralph had been sold the previous August, according to his manager, "in consequence of his general bad conduct and its influence upon other Negroes on the farm." Even the *possibility* of the sale of loved ones during the year weighed heavily on the minds of hired slaves. Circumstances in Virginia no doubt resembled those in Kentucky, where one hired slave "used to cry when she had to go back to work," according to her daughter, "because she was always scared some of us kids would be sold while she was away."[47]

The thought of not seeing family and friends again pressed some Virginia hired-out slaves to desperation. In Stafford County, hired slave Willis, an elderly slave, ran away from the person to whom he had been hired out in 1826 or 1827. Willis, according to his manager, "remained out nearly 12

Months . . . was advanced far in life & had become verry dissipated." Willis's experience as a hired slave ended sadly and unceremoniously, for after his manager apprehended him and paid his jail fees, Willis's manager sold him for $250, "as the estate was in want of funds."[48]

In addition to the difficulties that slave hiring posed to their family lives, hired slaves found that a host of circumstances and developments over which they had little control confronted them at seemingly every turn.

CHAPTER 4
HIRED SLAVES, WHITES, AND SLAVERY

On Christmas Day of 1858, slave hirer William Cabell reported to Iverson Twyman on the conduct of a slave he had hired from Twyman during the year. "Your boy Anderson has behaved well during his stay with me," Cabell wrote, adding that Anderson "ha[d] not been whipped at all though has been continually reminded of the fact that he would *certainly get it* unless he walked *very straight*." Perhaps most significantly, Cabell then informed Twyman that he had "treated [Anderson] in every respect as [he] would [his] own negros and just as [he] would have [Tywman] treat [his] should [he] ever hire[d] [slaves] to [Twyman]."[1]

Cabell's remarks contain important clues about Virginia hired slaves' experiences. Clearly, Anderson's status as a hired slave did not eliminate, or even mitigate, the threats of force and violence that were inherent features of slavery; his remark shows that he saw Anderson as just another slave to be coerced. Cabell's viewpoint, shared by numerous other Virginia slave hirers, illuminates some key questions in historians' debate about slave hiring: Did being hired out enlarge slaves' opportunities for agency? Did hired slaves' experiences differ from those of their nonhired counterparts? and Did slave hiring represent a peculiarity, or was it an integral facet of Virginia slavery? In Virginia, hired slaves' lives varied considerably, both from one hired slave to another and over the course of a single hired slave's experience while hired out. Additionally, hired slaves usually found that their experiences were shaped by a host of factors and variables beyond their control.

Self-hired Virginia slaves, that is, slaves who hired their own time, led lives that differed considerably from those of nonhired slaves. Self-hired slaves were most numerous in Virginia's urban centers, although they were not entirely absent from rural areas. The self-hired were usually skilled males who made their own work arrangements and were paid directly for their labor. With their earnings, self-hired slaves paid their owners a fixed sum of money at periodic intervals, reserving the balance of their cash to find their own food, clothing, and lodging and otherwise to dispose of as they pleased. Self-hired slaves normally were those most trusted by their owners, since they had greater freedom of movement and control over their time than the vast majority of slaves. Ultimately, the practice of self-hire flourished to such a degree in cities that, in Richard Wade's view, "'hiring one's own time' became an inseparable part of urban slavery."[2]

For self-hired Virginia slaves, the hiring season ran from late December through early January, as it did for other hired slaves. In December 1853 out-of-town businessman John Gault observed the self-hiring process in Richmond. "The city is full of niggers from all parts of the country to let themselves for the coming year," Gault reported to his colleague in Boston. "At the Christmas holidays," another visitor remarked, "some of the Southern cities and towns are alive with negroes, in their best attire, seeking employment to come, changing places, and having full liberty to suit themselves as to their employers." Some slaves hired their own time for relatively shorter periods, but their experiences were similar. In Petersburg, Miles was given a pass in April 1848 "to Pass & Repass about Petersburg and get work wherever he can get and Receive the money for the sam[e] untill first day next month." Miles's owner gave him another pass at the beginning of May and another on July 17, this time "to pass & repass to Richmond V[irgini]a to get work there and rec[e]iv[e] The money for the same untill The 10th day of August and return on or before That time." Although self-hired slaves were far less common in the countryside, their degree of autonomy approximated that of their urban counterparts. In December 1845, self-hired slave Nick wrote his mistress to inform her of his plans for the upcoming weeks. Nick told his mistress that he would not come home for Christmas because he lacked the money to do so and that he expected to get different employment the following year. Nick begged his mistress to not worry about him, and he asked her to write him about the welfare of people back on the plantation. Many self-hired slaves decided when, how much, and for whom they would work, and they had some voice in determining the value of their labor services in their negotiations with prospective employers. Beyond that, self-hired slaves could travel and meet other slaves in the course of making their own arrangements.[3]

Yet most Virginia hired slaves' experiences show that their status, and their consequent capacity to exercise agency, was far more complex than is suggested by some self-hired slaves' experiences and also by some historians. Marcus, a sawyer owned by George Nelson of Middlesex County, was hired out in the area of Gloucester Courthouse during most of 1859. In January 1860 Marcus wrote his owner to inform him that he was nearing completion of his work. Marcus was a skilled slave who traveled on his own and reported directly to his owner about the progress of his work by letter, but nevertheless he had to ask his owner "what he shall do next, if [his owner had] engaged a situation for [him], after [he had] finished the job [he was then] about." On the one hand, Marcus resembled many self-hired slaves in that he moved about without white supervision and informed his owner about his work. On the other hand, because Marcus had to ask his owner "to write, informing [him of] any arrangements [his owner had] made" for him, Marcus was not a self-hired slave in the strictest sense, because he remained subject to his owner's authority. Marcus's opportunities for mobility, however, show that he was not a typical hired slave, either. In short, Marcus's status as a hired slave was complex and mixed; it rested on a continuum somewhere between most historians' characterizations of complete autonomy and ruthless subjugation.[4]

In Charlotte County, Ephraim's experience also reveals that Virginia hired slaves' lives did not fit neatly, if at all, into historians' characterizations and assessments of slave hiring. Ephraim's owner, Henry Carrington, hired out Ephraim, a skilled slave, in the Roanoke area during the 1840s and 1850s. Carrington allowed Ephraim to keep earnings in excess of a stipulated amount, and Ephraim traveled on his own with cash given him to do so. Ephraim's access to cash, and his ability to travel unsupervised by whites, may appear to place him in the ranks of self-hired slaves. Ephraim's ability to shape his circumstances, however, was limited, and it varied over time. In the first place, Ephraim did not make his own working arrangements. He was in the charge of Thomas Read, Carrington's agent, who hired out Ephraim, kept Carrington apprised of developments surrounding Ephraim's hiring, and forwarded Ephraim's hire money to Carrington. In other words, Read, as Carrington's agent, asserted his own control over hired slave Ephraim regularly, especially concerning to whom Ephraim was hired out. Read's detailed letters, including his complaints about the considerable time entailed by his management of Ephraim, show that Read was closely engaged in Ephraim's hire. Consequently, hired slave Ephraim was, at one time or another, under the thumb of any one of three whites: his owner, his owner's agent, and his hirer.[5]

Ephraim's capacity for autonomous activity was fluid, at best. In 1847 he requested that Read inquire of Carrington whether Carrington "would be willing for him to hire himself or not the next year [1848]," as Ephraim had learned of a job that would "make [him] the money to pay his hire long before Christmas." Ephraim's request amounted to a deviation from the regular routine, since, whereas Read normally made Ephraim's arrangements for him, Ephraim now pressed to decide for himself where he would work. Whether Ephraim succeeded in working at the place of his choosing in 1848 is not entirely clear from Read's letters to Carrington. Read's correspondence does reveal, however, that Ephraim was no more than partially successful. Even if Ephraim selected his 1848 hirer himself, Read informed Carrington that the hirer had paid only a part of Ephraim's 1848 hire by February 1849. Consequently, the hirer's shallow pockets meant that Read did not permit Ephraim to return to the same hirer, regardless of Ephraim's past or present preferences. Additionally, Read decreed that lawyers' fees incurred in forcing hirers to pay up would come from Ephraim's portion of his hire money, not Carrington's. Read viewed these costs as Ephraim's price for choosing his own hirers over Read's reluctance. Although Ephraim pushed Read and Carrington for an enlarged degree of autonomy, he was beset by numerous obstacles, parameters, and variables that prevented him from gaining any advantage whatsoever from his status as a hired slave. Specifically, Ephraim's hiring-out experience was conditioned by the combination of Carrington, Read, and some hirers' failure to pay up.

Still more uncertainty came into Ephraim's life in 1854. That year, Carrington insisted that Ephraim return to Charlotte County because of Ephraim's poor health. Ephraim refused to return, asserting that his health had improved such that he would shortly be able to work. The larger issue for Ephraim, however, was his reluctance to be pulled away from his wife, who lived in the vicinity of where he was hired out. Also, Carrington discontinued his previous practice of allowing Ephraim money above a stipulated hire amount; William Watts, Ephraim's new manager, inquired of Carrington in 1855 whether any "of this [hire] money is to be paid to Ephraim himself." Ultimately, Ephraim's success in exerting control over his circumstances changed over time. Whereas Ephraim selected his own hirer and work location and acquired access to cash during some years, the whites in control of his life withdrew their permission for such independence during others. Ephraim's experience reveals that hired slaves' status is most properly located somewhere between the extremes of full autonomy and harsh exploitation often described by historians, and it also shows that hired slaves' status changed over time in response to numerous variables over which they had little control. In these respects, hired slaves' experiences differed little from those of their nonhired counterparts.[6]

In Powhatan County, hired slave Fanny, too, encountered constraining variables. Fanny's owner, James Cooke, hired Fanny out under the management of Hezekiah Ford. Ford handled arrangements for all the slaves Cooke hired out, and he kept Cooke informed about matters related to his slaves from the late 1840s through the early 1850s. An elderly slave, Fanny did not wish to be hired out by Ford for 1851 and proposed instead to "secure to [Cooke] a fair hire for herself" in order to remain near her husband. Fanny endeavored to craft her own hire arrangements under Ford's management.[7]

Cooke accepted Fanny's proposal and a $15 hire amount, and Fanny and her husband "promise[d] to pay the hire." At the end of 1851, however, despite promises of assistance from two slave sawyers, Fanny was able to give Cooke only a part of her $15 hire. Fanny promised to "pay the bal[ance] as soon as she could ship out a little parcel of tobacco," but she complained that the low price of tobacco, along with the high rate of hire she had to produce for Cooke, did not "leave her anything to live on." Fanny received a bit of sympathy from Ford, who wrote Cooke that Fanny "begs that you will not be as hard with her the next year." Ford added that he believed $15 hire was "too high—Fanny is not able to do much." Fanny received $12 for some corn, fodder, and hay, but she found that her tobacco, which Ford initially "supposed wou[l]d certainly be worth $3 more" to cover her hire, turned out to be worth considerably less. Ford further reported that he "had to give the old cre[a]ture a dollar to help to buy her a winter coat, for after paying all she had, she was without a dress & other comforts." In the end, Fanny was able to pay only $13 of her hire, that is, two dollars short of the amount stipulated. The following year, 1852, Fanny was permitted to find her own hirer, and Ford "agreed to be security for her hire," but Fanny derived no financial advantage from the arrangement. This was partly because Fanny was too elderly to work hard enough to raise a sufficient hire and also partly because she remained indebted to Cooke from the previous year, 1851, when she was unable to pay Cooke her full hire. Ultimately, Ford informed Cooke that $8 was as much hire as Fanny would bring for 1852, "but as she falls short $2 for last year [I] shall make her pay ten dollars this year." In other words, Ford mandated a hire amount that he knew was beyond Fanny's reach.

Fanny's experience exemplifies the difficulties Virginia hired slaves encountered in their efforts to shape their own circumstances. Although Fanny obtained her owner's consent to choose her own hirer and hire her own time, she remained under the control of a manager and at the mercy of fluctuating crop prices. Fanny's hard work to produce crops to pay her hire did not result in any financial advantage for her and was not even sufficient to pay her hire. Her capacity to benefit from being a hired slave also was limited by her advanced age, which rendered her incapable of performing a level of labor that a younger slave might undertake if given the opportunity. This difficulty was made more insurmountable by the high rate of hire fixed for her, which she was unable to generate despite assistance from two slave sawyers. Fanny's experience does not fit within the array of advantages many historians assume hired slaves enjoyed by virtue of being hired out.[8]

Many Virginia hired slaves' opportunities to derive advantages from being hired out also were limited by the fact that their occupations were neither privileged nor permanent. Henry, Ellick, and Peter, for example, worked as hired slaves on a plantation in Chesterfield County. During their time on the plantation, the three performed work that varied widely, both over long periods of time and within the course of a single day. In 1829 Henry, a skilled slave, worked in the plantation shop, where he made plows and ox carts and repaired rakes and gates. He also worked in the carpenter's shop and built a cattle shed. Yet Henry's hired-slave status conferred upon him no special privilege stipulating that he labor solely in skilled occupations and be exempted from field work. During the year, in addition to his skilled labor, Henry also worked in manure; grubbed a meadow; hauled hay, oats, fodder, rails, and wood; cut wheat, hay, and brush wood; and worked in the garden. Ellick's experience was similar: in 1830 he cleared land, sawed planks, planted tobacco, weeded and shucked corn, assisted a carpenter, and worked in potatoes. Likewise, Peter worked in the garden, shucked and shelled corn, fetched ice, worked potatoes, plowed, worked with rails, tended hay, raked wheat, worked in oats, looked for hogs, wormed and hung tobacco, and weeded turnips. Daily work records for Henry, Ellick, and Peter reveal occupations that were the same as those of nonhired slaves in rural Virginia; their work carried no privileges, varied considerably, and changed frequently. Also like nonhired slaves, Henry, Ellick, and Peter were noted periodically in plantation records as being sick and as apprehended runaways.[9]

On Richard Cunningham's farm, hired slaves' occupational patterns were similar. In 1835 Cunningham employed twenty slaves on his place, eight of whom were hired. The hired slaves worked alongside Cunningham's own slaves at a wide variety of chores, including general jobbing, hauling wood and ice for the ice house, clearing a river bank, planting corn, working in rye, hoeing and plowing, and ditching. For his ditching, Cunningham hired Cyrus from a Mr. Ross in August "to ditch by the day for 1 month," and Cunningham noted that he had "3 hirelings ditching" one day in September. When Cunningham once put four slaves to ditching in a particular spot, he made a point of recording that "3 of them [were] hirelings." Shortly afterward, Cunningham shifted the hired-slave ditchers over to another job, and he noted the change in his diary: "all hands including the 3 hired ditchers clearing away Corn & Weeds from the piece of Meadow above the old mill." On Cunningham's farm, hired slaves did the same work as Cunningham's own slaves. Also, the labor duties Cunningham expected of hired slaves were changed from one day to the next, and they were no different from the types of work nonhired slaves performed on other farms and plantations across rural Virginia. Significantly, Cunningham's slave-hiring practices were an indispensable part of his ongoing operations. In 1836 Cunningham supplemented his own slave force with nine slaves hired from four different slave owners, and the year after that, Cunningham hired seventeen slaves from eleven different slave owners. Cunningham engaged in similar slave-hiring activities each succeeding year through at least 1842.[10]

In Fauquier County, Richard Buckner, too, owned several slaves, but he hired additional slaves regularly as supplemental labor. Like Cunningham,

Buckner put his hired slaves to a variety of chores. "We are stone fencing with two hired negro men & one cart hauling stone for them," Buckner wrote in his diary in January 1836. In July Buckner's hired slaves worked in his wheat harvest, and Buckner noted that of the six cradlers he set to work one day, one was hired. In August Buckner changed the hired slaves' work routine again when he "commenced a stone fence round the garden with 2 hired hands." On Buckner's farm, as on Cunningham's and countless others, the hiring of slaves was routine in nature, and the work hired slaves did was the same as that performed by nonhired slaves.[11]

Virginia whites' shifting whims and circumstances often affected individual hired slaves' lives over the course of several years. During the 1830s and 1840s, Socrates Maupin brought his slave Garland with him from Charlottesville to Richmond to work at the Richmond Academy, thus separating Garland from many relatives and acquaintances. Over the course of several years, Maupin had Garland wait on him, but he also hired out Garland to the Academy and to others in the area. Over time, Maupin's changing situations and sentiments altered Garland's hiring-out experience dramatically.[12]

Garland's hiring-out experience began at the end of 1836. Concerned that Garland's work for him personally might cause the Richmond Academy to pay only a portion of Garland's hire, Maupin concluded that he would have to hire out Garland elsewhere in order to obtain the full hire he commanded, or else send him back to Charlottesville. Maupin noted that "Garland did intend to go up home" to Charlottesville for Christmas 1836, just as numerous other hired slaves returned to their permanent residence for Christmas regardless of their work arrangements for the following year. Maupin, however, forced Garland to remain with him in Richmond. From there, Garland conveyed messages to his loved ones in Charlottesville in Maupin's letter to his brother: "Garland and I together a[re] sending quite a family letter," Maupin wrote from Richmond in Garland's company.

In 1843 Maupin hired out Garland as a house servant, but the hirer returned Garland to Maupin, saying that Garland knew "very little as yet about the duties of a house serv[an]t." Accordingly, Maupin took Garland back "to try to make a house servant of him." But Maupin's correspondence reveals that Garland did not care to be employed at occupations that involved close white scrutiny. Several months later, Garland had not yet improved his skills as a house servant to Maupin's satisfaction, but he nevertheless prepared to hire Garland out again. Maupin offered Garland to his brother, a merchant and keeper of a boarding house in Charlottesville, either as a dining room servant or as a gardener, but with less-than-glowing recommendations for those particular occupations. Maupin was well aware of Garland's work preferences, as he mentioned to his brother that Garland "would be very faithful I think in exerting any commissions upon which you might send him into the country." Maupin's brother declined to hire Garland, however, so Maupin gave Garland a pass to go out and find his own hirer in Richmond. Maupin, it seemed, would permit Garland to secure employment that suited his preferences.

A few years later, however, Maupin's attitude toward Garland changed. Maupin learned that Garland's hire arrangements for 1848 promised less money than Maupin expected, a circumstance caused, in Maupin's view, by Garland's failure to find a hirer soon enough in the hiring season. Consequently, Maupin recommended Garland to his brother as a good "gardener and market man," and he abruptly offered to sell Garland to his brother for "whatever price any disinterested person may say he is worth." By 1848, then, Maupin had become frustrated with Garland, and he was tempted to sell him.

But near the end of 1848, Maupin resisted his initial inclination to sell Garland; he tried to hire Garland out again instead. Maupin noted that he had been hiring out him for several years at the rate of seventy to seventy-five dollars per year, and he asked whether his brother wished to hire Garland, who by that time was "very well acquainted with gardening." Garland "is always at home," Maupin pitched, "having no disposition to run about." Maupin believed Garland would suit his brother "in taking care of [his] horses and cows, and going about the country to procure supplies." Maupin believed that Garland would consent to be hired by his brother because the work involved errands, which Garland preferred, and also because Garland would be nearer his family and friends in Charlottesville. Yet at precisely the moment that Maupin proposed to hire out Garland to his brother in Charlottesville under circumstances he *believed* would be to Garland's liking, Garland appeared and gave Maupin the distinct impression that "he did not seem very willing to leave Richmond."

After several years in Richmond, Garland's sentiments had changed. Garland had grown accustomed to being in Richmond and so preferred to remain there. Rather than heed Garland's preference to remain in Richmond, however, Maupin now tried to talk him out of it. Maupin told Garland to hire with his brother for a year in Charlottesville, and he promised Garland that if the situation did not suit him, he could return to Richmond. Garland relented. Maupin then warned his brother, "[Garland] is very averse to changing about from place to place, and as he has been a long time about Richmond I think he would prefer staying here." Maupin told his brother about these matters because of their potential significance connected to his brother's ability to control Garland should he hire him. Yet in the same letter in which he told his brother of Garland's disinclination to leave Richmond, Maupin wrote that he was "persuaded [that Garland] will be very well satisfied when once he makes the change of residence." Clearly, Maupin sought to persuade himself, as well as his brother, that Garland would offer no trouble. Significantly, Maupin then told his brother that he was "very anxious" that he hire Garland, "as it will be the means of paying the interest on what I owe you, in a way more certain and more convenient to myself under present circumstances than any other." Maupin's financial circumstances, therefore, had diminished Garland's opportunities for autonomous action, specifically in terms of Garland's desire to remain in Richmond. Previously, Maupin had accorded Garland latitude regarding selection of hirers in order that Garland might find the type of work he preferred, entrusted Garland with the conveyance of other slaves, and persuaded himself that Garland was a contented slave generally. Now, although he knew Garland wished to remain in Richmond, Maupin's economic situation led him to try to persuade himself that he could force Garland to hire with his brother in Charlottesville and that Garland would adjust himself to the change easily enough.

Maupin discovered, however, that Garland was not the sort of slave that Maupin wanted to believe he was. On January 1, 1849, Maupin reported to his brother that Garland had not yet agreed to leave Richmond, as Garland believed "Richmond a better market than the University [of Virginia in Charlottesville] for mats and baskets which he employed his spare time in making last year." Eventually, however, Garland left Richmond for Maupin's brother's place in Charlottesville for 1849, but he was not happy. Garland was quite troublesome to Maupin's brother; at the end of May, Maupin informed his brother that he was "vexed at the conduct of Garland, at the same time that I regret the annoyance which he appears to have given you." Maupin had had it with Garland, and he wrote his brother that he was "very sorry that you did not order [Garland] to be flogged." Also, Maupin was fully aware of the contrast between his previous attitude toward Garland and his new, changed one. In a revealing comment, Maupin told his brother that Garland "has wanted a master for many years," a statement reflecting the latitude Maupin had accorded Garland in the past, "and a good flogging would be of more service to him than any thing else that could be named." Maupin then wondered whether it would be best "to hire [out] Garland on the RailRoad between Charlottesville and the mountains," and, in contrast to his previous policy of allowing Garland to secure the sort of work he preferred, Maupin quickly added, "It makes no difference with me whether it pleases him or not [as] I am done with humouring him from this day forward." "Hereafter I will make him go wherever I deem it expedient." Maupin said, "[Garland] is disposed to pay no respect to my wishes or convenience, and [therefore] I will pay none to his." Maupin was now fully determined "to get rid of so great a nuisance as [Garland was] disposed to make himself," and he told his brother that any disposition he made of Garland would suit him. Maupin then asked his brother whether it would "be well to set [Garland] up at auction at June or July court and see what he would bring," as Maupin was "entirely willing that [his brother] should sell him at a fair price, nay at any price that a judicious man would say approximates his reasonable value."

Yet much as Maupin was tempted to sell Garland, rising slave-hire rates within the context of Virginia's diversified economy were too attractive to resist. "There must be a general demand for laborers about Richmond," Maupin observed, "and consequently a high price must be paid for them." The lure of slave-hire money, coupled with his desire to get Garland out of his sight, made Maupin determined to hire out Garland, since "gardeners and field hands must rise in value as the demand for labour increases on the public works." Maupin knew that Garland had brought between $70 and $75 hire per year during the 1840s and that he would command between $80 and $100 at the beginning of the 1850s in the midst of the competition and demand for hired slave labor sustained by Virginia's rising crop prices and internal improvements construction projects. In 1851 Maupin "hired Garland to drive a milk cart at 100$ for the . . . year," and he observed that "servants are hiring higher than last year." Garland was in Richmond, where he desired to be, and he was employed at a job that kept him on the move and out of regular, direct white supervision, a circumstance he always had preferred. Yet Maupin also got what he wanted: Garland was not around to annoy him, Maupin was taking in considerably more money for Garland's hire than he had during the 1840s, and he expected to take in still more in the future. Since Maupin collected Garland's substantial hire and did not have to be bothered with him during the year, hiring out Garland rather than selling him seemed a rational course in achieving his goals of making money from slaves without being troubled by them. In the end, Garland's work preferences coincided with Maupin's desires.[13]

Over the course of several years, Garland demonstrated just how troublesome a dissatisfied hired slave could be, but he also discovered that his ability to enhance his agency by being troublesome was limited by Maupin's whims and circumstances. Maupin granted Garland some discretion in selecting his own hirers, but only so long as Garland's work preferences happened to coincide with Maupin's needs and desires. Garland grew to prefer Richmond because of the business he conducted on his own time there, but Maupin's monetary concerns trumped Garland's work and location preferences. When Maupin hired Garland out to his brother in Charlottesville for financial reasons, Garland's manifestations of displeasure prompted Maupin's attitude toward him to change, which was reflected in Maupin's regret that his brother had not whipped Garland for the difficulties he had caused. Garland's experience reveals that although some hired slaves' work preferences were honored, their circumstances could, and often did, change dramatically on the heels of new developments related to their owners' changing attitudes and financial situations. For Garland as for other hired slaves, privileged status, autonomy, and opportunities to exercise agency were neither automatic nor permanent.

Hired slaves' clothing provisions varied no less than their other circumstances. James Cooke's slave John, for instance, claimed that hirer James Foster did not give him adequate clothing in 1849. "John has been to see me several times," Cooke's agent informed Cooke in November, "and begs that you will not hire him to Mr Foster and says [Foster] has not given him a rag of clothing or attended to him during the year." Elsewhere, hired slave Edmund's clothing awaited the working out of details between owner and hirer. "Your man Edmund being much in want of his winter cloathes has prevailed on us to request from you permission to receive such cloathing as we are granting our hired negroes," Edmund's hirers informed his owner, Jesse Nalle, "and from his good conduct feel disposed to gratify him, should we not receive contrary instructions by return mail." Edmund's hirers then assured Nalle of the high quality and low cost of the clothing. Significantly, however, although Edmund's hirers claimed to be "unwilling to suffer a man in our employ to return home so badly clad as [Edmund] is at present," they forced Edmund to await word from Nalle "respecting his cloathes by Sundays mail." Some hired slaves never received clothes for their return to their owner at the end of the year, which begs the question of whether they had received adequate clothing during the previous twelve months. This was especially true when slaves were hired out to persons of relatively modest means, as is shown in a notation made by an Essex County resident in 1840: "Clary and Children were hired to [tenant] C.B. Moss and returned to me without Clothes."[14]

Cases concerning exposure in Virginia's local court records reveal that hired slaves received inadequate shelter or clothing, or both, fairly frequently. In Princess Anne County, slave owner Henry Keeling charged that hirer Ezekiel Ewell had "greatly abused and injured by exposure to frost and fire" his two slave boys Frank and Davy. In Fairfax County, Samuel Coleman hired George Gunnell's slave George for three consecutive years during the late 1830s. George labored outdoors during the winter but did not receive proper clothing; he already "was very badly frost bitten" when he arrived at the residence of R. B. Darne, to whom he was hired out next. At Darne's place, George worked for about three months, and after five months at Darne's residence, George died.[15]

Virginia hired slaves suffered other types of physical injuries, too. In Sussex County, James Benford hired out his slave Peter to William Wilcox. The precise nature of Wilcox's occupation, as well as the work Peter performed, are unknown, but Peter "was very much burnt" while in Wilcox's employ. Wilcox employed his sister Ruth "to cure the hand of the . . . Negro which was so much burnt as to lay the Sinews bare." At length, Ruth "did every day for near three months dress the . . . Negro's hand & did at last cure it" with the aid of "Spirits of Turpentine & other Medicines from the Apothecary's Shop." It is possible that Peter harmed himself deliberately in order to gain some respite from his labor or to try to manipulate his owner's financial interest in his welfare and be removed from the hirer's employ. If so, the severity of Peter's wound suggests that the hirer and/or the work he did was so disagreeable that he was willing to go to great lengths to extricate himself from the situation.[16]

Given frequently poor material conditions and beatings at the hands of Virginia hirers, many hired slaves ran away from them. Some white Virginians, like James Harris, perceived the connection between whippings and running away. Harris related his understanding of these matters in a letter describing one hired slave runaway's actions in 1856. "I have been informed that Ned one of the hands hired from Miss Grace Austin," Harris wrote, "has Run away." Harris suspected that the slave returned to the place from which he had been hired out. "If you can ascertain that [Ned] is about the place of his nativity or hear of him," Harris continued, "please inform me." Harris stated that Ned had been away for several days, and that he had "heard nothing from him." Significantly, Harris "learned [Ned] ran off because the overseer threatened to whip him."[17]

Hired slave Ned's action was no peculiarity. Elsewhere, another white Virginian noted that hired slave "Amanda ran away was gone some time the length of time, not now rem[e]mbered." Some slave-hiring bonds show that many owners and hirers anticipated hired slaves' running away. When John Fitzgerald and Sam Scott hired David for 1856, they agreed "to loose the time that [David] may loose by . . . runing away during the year, and to pay all lost [illegible] that may be incured by his runing away." Hired slaves, like their nonhired counterparts, attempted to elude whites' authority whenever and however they could.[18]

Hired slaves who ran away from hirers did so at enormous risk. In Sussex County, for instance, hired slave Julius, a young boy, ran away from hirer Edwin Scott, but Julius did not make it back to his owner's place alive. An inspection of his body showed that "Julius came by his death by [his] attempt to cross [the] Nottoway River, by wading in the water and by the extreme cold weather." Significantly, the examination of Julius's body also revealed evidence of "a small sear under [his] left eye and some very slight marks on [his] back and shoulders apparently produced by whipping." The occurrence of this incident in the middle of January explains the cold weather, and it also indicates that Julius was not in the hirer's possession very long before he received the whipping that prompted him to run away.[19]

Some Virginia hired-slave runaways were overtaken by whites in pursuit of them. One Sussex County hired slave met up with other runaway slaves, and together they headed for North Carolina. The slaves crossed the border, but before long, local whites noticed that "several run-away negroes had been committing depredations in Halifax [County, North Carolina] and the neighbourhood" in the course of their flight. As a result, "some Gentlemen went in search of them . . . and fired upon them." The hired slave from Sussex County remained in hiding all night, and the next morning he appeared at the house of a local resident, "much wounded with shot." The hired slave explained that he had been "hired out, had been run-away some time, and was shot by the party the day before." The Halifax resident believed that the slave "appeard in much want of surgical assistance" and so directed him to the home of a physician nearby, who later reported that the hired slave "was badly though not dangerously wounded." The Halifax resident implored the physician "to take some care of the fellow for the sake of humanity" and assured him "that he did not doubt, but that the master . . . would cheerfully pay him for his trouble." The day after the hired slave was shot, the physician "assisted in extracting a number of shot from different parts of [the hired slave's] Body." This, coupled with the fact that the physician administered medicine and applied new dressings to the hired slave's wounds each day from May 17 through June 3 of the year in question shows that the hired slave's wounds were quite severe.[20]

Virginia hirers' physical violence upon hired slaves periodically brought owners and hirers into conflict with each other. Specifically, owners and hirers sometimes disagreed over whether hirers had the right to exercise violence upon the slaves of others. In 1857 Robert Carter hired out his slave Elias to Coleman Smith in King and Queen County. At Smith's residence, Elias wished to have a say in when he would work and what he would do. Elias soon found, however, that Smith's sentiments refused to permit him any discretion. Consequently, Elias ran away from Smith, who wrote Carter a letter describing his version of events. "Your man Elias left here on yesterday morning," Smith wrote, "without my leave taking his tools with him." Smith admitted that he "had to correct [Elias] for several offences & this is the cause of his leaving." Smith explained to Carter that "one offence was, [he] wished [Elias] to [work] . . . on a sunday & told him to get ready . . . & he took himself off and did not make his appearanc[e] again during that day." Smith insisted that he "intended to pay [Elias] for his days work but did not choose to make bargains with him." On another occasion, Elias refused to perform certain types of work. Smith told Carter that Elias ignored an order to help one of his other slaves carry a plank to his house, and that Elias had been "insolent" when Smith tried to compel him to obey the order. Smith "immediately chastised" Elias for his refusal, and Elias disappeared several days later during Smith's absence from home. Smith further expressed to Carter his expectation that Elias would show up at Carter's place, and he asked Carter to "be kind enough to send [Elias] back I shall offer a reward for him." Following his escape from Smith, Elias wrote a letter of his own to one of the other slaves at Smith's place. Elias described his experience at Smith's, as well as Carter's reaction to the whole affair following his return to Carter's residence. Carter called an overseer to witness Elias's physical condition, and Carter "sa[id] that he never seen no body whipt in such away in his life." Smith had whipped Elias so severely that Carter told Elias that "he would have been much better . . . satisfied If smith *hader* [had] brought [him] home and put [him] down & told [Carter] that he would not pay [Carter] for [his] hire, [rather] th[a]n to whip [him] in the way that he did & [Carter] told his overseers that any man that *wood* whip a hired servant . . . was a Dam *raskell* [Carter] did not car[e] who he was." Ultimately, Smith intercepted Elias's letter, was offended by Carter's objection to his violent punishment of Elias, and declared his readiness to "prove by respectable gentlemen that [he] did not give [Elias] as much as [he] was advised by those who own slaves & know how to use them."[21]

Elias's experience represented a conflict between his determination to have Sundays off and to exercise other discretions and agency to which he was accustomed at Carter's place, on the one hand, and Smith's conviction that slaves—even male, skilled, hired slaves—should not be permitted any discretion or agency and must submit themselves to *all* whites' authority, on the other. Smith's belief that he had the right to whip Elias was based on the notion that slaves should submit themselves to white men's control, and he was the white man who had control over Elias during the year.[22]

Other Virginia slave owners, too, retained their hired-out slaves following their escape from violent hirers. In 1811 Hanover County slave owner and physician Thomas Chrystie hurled a lengthy admonition at hirer Philip Croxton, who had beaten Chrystie's slave Bob. "My Servant Bob got home yesterday morning in Such a Situation, that nothing but the dread of a repetition of the crulty exercised on him by you could have given him sufficient energ[y] to perform the walk." Bob, Chrystie observed, had "been beaten about the Head, arms, & Hands with Sticks or billets of Wood so as to render his arms entirely useless for the present." "In addition," Chrystie went on, Bob "has been whipt with a . . . Cow Hide, so as to leave Upwards of one Hundred cuts on his back & Belly—which has brought on Fever, & much Inflamation." "I give you notice," Chrystie informed Croxton, "that Bob shall not return to your Services [and] that I Shall immediately sue you in damages for the improper beating and that I shall make you Pay for my attention in curing him." Chrystie suspected that Bob might die from his beating, and whether Bob recovered is unknown. Elsewhere, hirer George Johnson "shot twice at [hired slave] John," whom Johnson had hired from James Coleman for 1855. Following John's return to Coleman's place, Johnson showed up there with another man, determined to regain John. Johnson and his friend spoke with Coleman about John, but Coleman told Johnson that "he could not get the boy," because he "can't have [his] boy shot." Virginia slave owners often refused to return their slaves to violent hirers when they saw evidence of hirers' beatings on hired slaves' bodies.[23]

Some Virginia slave owners also held their escaped slaves if they suspected hirer violence was imminent, as was the case with "Peter the Blacksmith." Peter's manager, who resided in Fairfax County, had hired Peter out to John Hopkins of Frederick County. Hopkins's letters to Peter's manager reveal that Peter sensed Hopkins's dissatisfaction with him and that Peter ran away back to his manager's place in Fairfax in order to avoid an anticipated punishment from Hopkins. In a letter to Peter's manager, Hopkins described his view of events:

> Peter the Blacksmith absconded from this farm . . . without any known cause, and Certainly without any provocation. I have no doubt he is now in and about his old haunts in Fairfax [County] and will probably come to you. I

write now to desire that you may be informed of his absconding and that he may be apprehended & put in Jail or sent to me. This fellow has been giving himself for nearly a year very impertinent airs, and has so often neglected his duty that I did intend if he would not mind his manners to Correct him, which has never been done since he was on the Farm. He has become lazy, impertinent and insolent in the extreme & I must desire that you will interest yourself in having him apprehended and delivered here without any extraordinary expence on my part, and I trust you will do so.

Like other slave hirers, Hopkins contemplated whipping a hired slave. Hopkins next informed Peter's manager that he "had heard nothing of peter" and then accused Peter's manager of harboring Peter in Fairfax:

There is no doubt he is in your neighbourhood, and I do supppose could be apprehended at any time, and I hope you will cause it to be done, and the Fellow sent to me or put into Jail so that I may send for him. This wanton and unprovoked Conduct of the fellow merits severe Chastisement, and the longer he stays away, subjecting me to loss and expence will only agravate his Crime and render his punishment (which I could wish to avoid) more exemplary.

Hopkins's letters were enough to persuade Peter's manager not to return him to Hopkins.[24]

When Virginia whites decided against returning their slaves to violent hirers, they did so because they feared losing the value of their slaves, either through physical injury or by the slaves' running away entirely. Hired slaves who escaped hirers' beatings by running to their owners did so because they knew that their owners had an interest in their monetary value, which their owners sought to preserve and protect, and many hired slaves exploited that interest successfully when their owners refused to return them to abusive hirers. Hired slaves' success in this respect amounted to protection of themselves from further physical harm, which was but one form of disagreeable working conditions, and that ultimately meant that they also had succeeded in exercising some choice as to which hirers they would not work for.

Hired slaves' ability to select hirers and craft better working conditions for themselves was enhanced by the context of increasing slave-hire rates and demand for hired slaves during the antebellum period. In the face of competition for hired slaves in several sectors, individual hirers were anxious to secure hired slaves, which entailed special efforts on their part to do so. Specifically, in addition to combing vast areas of the Virginia countryside in search of slaves to hire, hirers often then had to persuade slave owners and slaves alike to hire with them rather than with others. Prospective hirers' persuasion was necessary partly because competition for hired slaves placed slave owners in a position to choose a hirer from among numerous applicants. In particular, slave owners knew that rising hire rates meant that they could fetch a considerable sum from any of a number of hirers, and they knew that threats posed to their slave property by dangerous occupations and abusive hirers often compelled hired slaves to run away. All this meant that many slave owners, with the value of their slave property on the line, felt that they had to be selective about hirers as concerned their workplace conditions and personal reputations respecting hired-slave treatment, and competition for hired slaves meant that they were able to be picky. Aware of their owners' concerns and sentiments, hired slaves could express, and push for, their own preferences as to working conditions and hirers generally, and they often succeeded when their feelings about particular working conditions and hirers were in alignment with those of their owners.

Slaves' success in determining for whom they would or would not work and influencing their working conditions is revealed in hiring agents' letters. In 1830 one of William Weaver's agents informed Weaver that Isaac, whom Weaver had hired previously, refused to return to Weaver. Another slave, Sam, Weaver was told, "also was unwilling to return, but says he would have no objection, provided he could live at your establishment." The agent explained to Weaver the fear that the slaves might run away if compelled to do something against their wishes. For this reason, Isaac attained his preference for not returning to Weaver, and it also was the basis for the agent's hope that Weaver would "grant [Sam's] request" to live where he wished at Weaver's place. Hired slaves' views with regard to previous hirers and working conditions, especially sentiments of dissatisfaction, spread among slaves in areas that were prime hiring markets. Another hiring agent, for example, informed Weaver that he had "not been able to get [him] any hands in consequence of their being unwilling generally to go over the mountains (as they call it)," because several hired slaves, upon their return to the area, had "made somewhat an unfavorable impression on the negroes in the neighborhood as to the treatment at the place for which they were wanting." As it turns out, the conditions to which the slaves objected returning were food and clothing shortages, as well as disease. Ultimately, throughout the area, slaves' preference to avoid such conditions was in alignment with their owners' desire to protect the value of their slave property from harm or from total loss as a result of their slaves' running away from a disagreeable situation. And because owners knew that competition for hired slaves meant that they could secure other hirers in any event, the slaves got their way.[25]

Slave owner Mary Gregory's communication to Weaver regarding the possibility of his hiring her slaves illuminates the connections between rising hire rates, competition for hired slaves, slaves' preferences, and slave owners' monetary concerns with respect to their slaves. Gregory told Weaver that she was "willing [he] should have" her slaves and, in a direct reference to high hire rates and competition, added, "I know we can get good prices for them on this side of the mountain." With numerous prospective hirers competing for slaves, Gregory knew she did not have to select Weaver, yet she offered her slaves to him because "they [were] willing to live with [him] again," a preference in line with Gregory's own wish to hire out her slaves "in the Country" and not to railroad contractors. Gregory, like other slave owners, could hire her slaves to any number of persons, given the demand for them, but she hired them out to Weaver because she felt that, since Weaver was their expressed preference, her slaves would not run away from him and cause her loss. From the interconnected circumstances of competition, handsome rates of hire, and slave owners' concerns, hired slaves sometimes extracted some measure of discretion as to where they were hired out.[26]

Fully aware of the larger circumstances, hired slaves sometimes merely had to pressure their owners into granting their preferences as to hirers. In 1830, for example, a slave owner bowed to his slave's "recent declarations," which convinced him that his slave "wou'd make an effort to reach the State of Ohio" if sent to a particular hirer against his wishes, which would "be the means of [the owner's] loosing the fellow entirely." Accordingly, the slave owner did not compel his slave to go to that hirer, whom he informed that his slave's sentiments on the matter were "the reasons which have influenced this cours[e]"; the slave owner likely also was confident that he could hire out the slave elsewhere. In another case, would-be hirer John Tomlin admonished Benjamin Brand, the owner of slave Lewis, to allow Lewis to pick his own hirer. "Lewis says he will not hire with me, but will run away if I attempt to keep him," Tomlin wrote, and Tomlin further declared, "[Since Lewis] appears to be an impertinent & obstinate fellow, I am willing to have nothing to say to him." "Suppose you let him apply to some of those who want him," Tomlin advised, "which may save some trouble, & satisfy the fellow." In this instance, Lewis threatened to do what he knew whites feared, and the whites gave in. Elsewhere, another Virginian perceived considerable benefit in allowing a hired slave to choose his own hirer. "As the negro wishes to go to [hirer] spencer, he will be less likely to run away from him, and cause greatly less trouble and vexation" for his owner. Clearly, hired slaves knew what whites were thinking and understood that the right kind and amount of pressure might enable them to get their way.[27]

In a tight hiring market where hired slaves were increasingly scarce and expensive, prospective slave hirers were compelled to exert efforts to assure that slaves they hired would not complain about them to their owners and to other slaves in the area. Reliant as he was on a steady supply of slave labor, William Weaver's efforts to secure hired slaves amid the stiff competition for them included offering relatively better working conditions, which he hoped would assure that slaves he hired would wish to hire with him again. Specifically, Weaver's reliance upon overwork payments and an "allowance" for hired slaves, along with the opportunity these offered hired slaves to enhance their self-esteem and make them feel more like men than slaves, led many slaves to express a preference for Weaver over numerous others who wished to hire them and made the slaves willing to return to him for another year. Ultimately, the overwork system, within the contexts of considerable hire rates and competition for hired slaves, represented hired slaves' successful efforts to compel a hirer to institute better working conditions for them.[28]

Yet despite some successes in influencing whites as to hirers and working conditions, many Virginia ex-slaves did not recall slave hiring fondly at all. Virginia ex-slave Sister Carrie related a verse that she and a group of other Virginia ex-slaves sang for an entire day following their emancipation:

> Tain't no mo' sellin' today,
> Tain't no mo' hirin' today,
> Tain't no pullin' shirts off today,
> Its stomp down freedom today.
> Stomp it down!

Sister Carrie's equation of slave hiring with sale and whipping speaks volumes about what many Virginia slaves thought of slave hiring. To them, it was not a pleasant experience, and specifically, it was as fundamental a facet of Virginia slavery as were sale and whipping, occurrences to which all Virginia slaves, hired and nonhired, were subject. In addition, all hired slaves in Virginia experienced the many ways slave hiring and white society shaped each other and how Virginia's white society as a whole was a world in which all whites were masters.[29]

CHAPTER 5

WHITE LADIES, WHITE MEN, MASTERS ALL: SLAVE HIRING AND WHITE SOCIETY

In the summer of 1857, slave owner Martin Webb wrote a hirer concerning his three slaves who had run away from the hirer. "I am sorry to hear that Peter has run away from you," Webb stated and added that he had "been on the watch for Ned & William but [had] been unable to hear any thing from them." Peter, Ned, and William had little hope of playing Webb off against the hirer, and they knew it. Webb's letter to the hirer explains why that was the case: "When Ned & William were apprehended and brought to me before, I whipped them severely and told them if they ran off again and were brought to me, or came to my house, I would give them a thousand—I do not think, therefore, that they will come to me. Peter will learn from them the Course I pursued with them and he will not come to me." Unlike some other slave owners, Webb was not swayed by the relative ease with which, especially by the 1850s, he could fetch a considerable hire from numerous others who competed for hired slaves, hirers from whom his slaves might be less likely to run away. Webb had transferred his slaves to a white hirer, and he expected his slaves to submit to that white hirer without question. White racial solidarity of owners and hirers behind slavery was Webb's paramount concern, a fact known to his slaves, who therefore stood little chance of manipulating Webb's financial interest in them to their advantage.[1]

Elsewhere, hired slave Maria also found whites' power arrayed against her. In 1856 Maria, "a perfect devil . . . ha[d] been whipped most unmercifully" by a hirer, from whom she had run away "with a chain around her neck and fastened with a pad lock to keep her from running off but by some means she got loose." Maria's owner then placed her in jail "to let the people [i.e., the hirer] know she would not harbour or screen" Maria. Maria's owner recognized the hirer's right to punish Maria and further punished her for running away from the hirer by putting her in jail. Maria was not able to exploit her owner's financial interest in her welfare by lodging complaints about a hirer's treatment, for example, in order either to remain at home or to be sent to another hirer. For Maria's owner, the chief issue was unity of white owners and hirers behind hired slave control, a sentiment communicated to the hirer by placing Maria in jail.[2]

Many Virginia slave owners did, of course, investigate hirers' treatment of their slaves when they ran away from hirers or lodged complaints upon their return from hirers. One slave owner looked into such matters because he feared possible financial loss; his policy was that "if the negroes' complaint was just [he] would not send them back" to the same hirer the following year. Because many hired slaves complained, and because many slave owners were concerned about their hired slaves' monetary value, slave owners in many locales across Virginia at the end of each year awaited the views and sentiments of their returning hired-out slaves. One group of hired-out slaves who returned to their owners in Southampton County in December 1854 complained of cruelty and mistreatment and expressed their unwillingness to return to the same hirer for 1855. A white observer informed the hirer that "the hands came back very much dissatisfied. . . . you never herd such complaint lodged in your life." The slaves' fate for 1855 hinged upon their owners' determination of whether their slaves' complaints were "just."[3]

Slave owner Samuel Drewry was suspicious of the slaves' complaints. Speaking for himself and others, Drewry addressed the "manner our servants was treated dureing the last year." "As I stated to you in my note," Drewry informed the hirer, "the statement of my servants had no effect on me." "I talked with them seperately," Drewry went on, "and satisfied myself they had misrepresented things." Like other slave owners, Drewry rendered his decision not upon hired slaves' words, but upon the basis of evidence he could see for himself, that is, the condition of the hired slaves' bodies. Drewry informed the hirer that the hired slaves' "appearance belied the story of hard usage cruelty &c." and that "they all returned looking well and comfortably clad."

Other slave owners took the same position. According to Drewry, the slaves of two other slave owners "also did not wish to return [to their hirers] but it had no effect on [their owners]." "They both had taken the same view as myself," Drewry assured the hirer, "believing the negroes statem[en]t to be incorrect." When the other two slave owners inquired as to whether Drewry intended to send his slaves back to the same hirer the following year, Drewry "told them [he] expected to do so." Without evidence of physical abuse, hired slaves' verbal complaints often were not sufficient to avoid being sent back to the same hirer.[4]

Another slave, Charles, knew that he required evidence of cruelty in order to persuade his owner to refuse to send him back to the same hirer, and so he attempted to feign evidence of such. At first, Charles's owner had "believe[d] the statement" about mistreatment made by Charles and his other slaves upon their return from a hirer, and Charles's owner "looked on [Charles as] being valueless had the appearance of hard usage &c." Yet Charles's owner eventually saw through Charles's attempt to trick him. Another slave owner who had caught on more quickly explained: "About ten days afterward I inquired after [Charles's owner's] hands told me [that they] had [been] hired . . . out at $160. I told [Charles's owner] I thought from what he said about one of them [Charles, that he] never would be of any more service. [Charles's owner] laughed and remarked it turned out as I had said to him a few days before it was a concocted plan with the negroes to tell the tales they had [told] to prevent their being sent back." Although Charles initially "had much deceived" his owner into thinking that "he could not hire [for] a great while," Charles suddenly "dureing [the] xmast hollidays . . . got as well as he ever was." In the absence of any objective indications of hirer abuse, and especially given whites' general suspicions concerning their slaves, white slave owners often sided with white slave hirers against their own slaves' words and preferences.[5]

Still more white Virginians refused to allow hired slaves to select their own hirers in the first place. The ever-suspicious Samuel Drewry insisted, "It is true there is two much attention paid as I think to gratifying servants in choosi[n]g their homes." Drewry's and other whites' attitudes and personal convictions kept them from giving in to their slaves' pressures. In Lancaster County, Robert Dunaway hired out Dennis, Davy, and Vincent "after selecting as good homes for them as could be procured," yet the slaves expressed their dissatisfaction with Dunaway's selection. "At the time of hiring them out," Dunaway related, Dennis, Davy, and Vincent "refused to live at the homes thus selected for them . . . and stated that they would not go to those homes." Dunaway, however, did "not regard [the slaves'] refusal, knowing the homes he had selected to be proper homes for them he of course did not change them." Yet the slaves did not go to the hirers, but ran away and remained out for some time. Shortly afterward, the slaves appeared at Dunaway's place, but they still refused to go where they had been hired. The slaves, Dunaway maintained, had "all taken it into their head that [they] must oyster, that they are not willing to do any thing else and will only live where they please to live." Yet Dunaway still refused to budge on the matter. Citing past problems of management, including Davy's theft and sale of a load of posts, and Dennis's being "a very shrewd inteligent negro," Dunaway determined to sell the slaves. For Dunaway, there remained no other options. Dunaway rejected the notion that the slaves should have their way in the matter, and he also realized that "if [the slaves were] forced to go [to the hirers] under the circumstances . . . they [would] again run off, and . . . be an entire loss . . . either by death from lying out at this inclement season of the year or by making their escape to some of the free states." Dennis, Davy, and Vincent failed to succeed in their attempt to pressure Dunaway, and their efforts in fact resulted in Dunaway's decision to sell them.[6]

Hired slave Dick, also of Lancaster County, had a similar experience. Like Dennis, Davy, and Vincent, Dick refused to work where he had been hired out. According to his manager, Dick had "become unmanageable and [was] not disposed to perform his services," though hired out, in his manager's estimation, "to a good home." Although Dick had "already run off some two or three times" from that home, Dick's manager allowed Dick no discretion as to where he would be hired out. Rather, Dick's manager determined to sell him, lest "he . . . be lost . . . either by sickness and death produced by lying out or by attempting to make his escape to a free state." Like Dennis, Davy, and Vincent, Dick derived no privileges, discretions, or enhanced agency from his status as a hired slave, because his efforts to do so were blunted by his manager's power to sell him.[7]

Hired slave Hannah did not succeed in choosing her own hirer, either. Court records show that Hannah was troublesome at home, where Ralph

Chilton claimed that her refusal to labor to his satisfaction, her "misconduct," rendered her "of little or no value." As a result, Chilton felt "compelled to hire her out having no other means of taking care of her, and no other means of supporting her & her children, or making them valuable." Accordingly, Chilton hired out Hannah to Leroy Beane. Beane, Chilton claimed, offered "a good home where [Hannah] would be taken care of." Hannah, however, disagreed. Chilton soon reported that Hannah "ran away from [Beane] and refuse[d] to go back to him," which convinced Chilton that if he tried "to force her [to] live with [Beane] or with any other person except where she may think proper to live, or to perform any labour, that she [would] run off [again] and . . . be lost . . . either by making her escape to a free state, or by contracting disease, by lying out which may cause her death, or render her an invalid for life and a charge." For Chilton, the only solution remained "selling her and investing the proceeds of sale in the purchase of other slaves."[8]

Virginia slaves often tried to select their own hirers, but many slaves found that whites refused to allow them to do so. Virginia whites' decision to sell slaves who pressed the issue was a common way to control the slaves and still eliminate the risk that hired slaves would run away from hirers the slaves had not selected themselves. Virginia hired slaves, therefore, had no hope of manipulating whites when those whites were willing to sell them. Such whites exercised very successfully the prerogatives of whiteness, reflecting their conviction that whites told slaves, both hired and nonhired, what to do, not the other way around.

White Virginians' solidarity often was sustained by their community ties. In 1850 Edward Carter Turner reported in his diary that Peter, a slave his mother had hired out to a Robert Beverley, had run away from Beverley. Turner took it upon himself to "see after" Peter. Turner found that Peter had run back to his mother's place, where Turner discovered him "complaining to his mistress," whereupon Turner took Peter back to Beverley. Revealingly, several days later, Turner and Beverley rode to church together. Such neighborhood connections enhanced the unity crafted by white skin and made it that much more difficult for hired slaves to play whites off against each other.[9]

Virginia whites also were united by fear. Several hundred slaves were hired out each year in Fauquier County, where Turner's comments in his diary reveal local whites' anxieties about slaves generally. Turner expressed astonishment that so many voters in Fauquier County had been "made by intriguing demagogues to believe" that one of the candidates, "who is himself a slave holder is an abolitionist acting with the people of the North to put a knife into the hands of his own slaves to cut the throats of his own wife & children." Similar anxieties prevailed among whites in neighboring Loudoun County, where hundreds of slaves also were hired out each year. On December 29, 1856, at the height of slave-hiring season, Elizabeth Noland wrote her daughter, Ella, concerning whites' fears of slave insurrection activities in her neighborhood. "There has been such a terrible excitement here ever since xmas that I did not feel much in the spirit of going from home," Elizabeth wrote, as "several fires have occurred," including at "Mr Sanford Roger's fine barn and stables and all his grain, supposed to have been set on fire by his own servants." "A few nights previous" to that, Elizabeth continued, "Mr Green a very peacible and inoffensive man, and a good *humane* master was horribly murdered and then burnt up in his house and by his own servants." Those slaves, Elizabeth reported, were in jail, and she also noted that one of her neighbors "keeps a man at his barn every night with a loaded gun." Elizabeth then admitted that "no one feels safe in his own *house,* every body has provided themselves with firearms—what do you think? of a gun and revolver kept loaded in this house and a Bowie knife," she asked. In rural Virginia neighborhoods, white racial solidarity was rooted partly in white fear of the slave population.[10]

The white fear betrayed by Edward Turner's and Elizabeth Noland's remarks characterized not only northern Virginia, but the entire slave South in the fall and winter of 1856. The presidential election of that year created rumors of slave revolt among whites that, when circulated across the South, led to a panic. Specifically, the rise of the Republican Party as a significant contender for power in 1856 placed abolitionism as a major threat in the forefront of white southerners' minds and persuaded them that the slaves in their midst were rising, or were preparing to rise, in bloody revolt against the white population. As a result, panicky whites across the South jailed, whipped, and shot numerous slaves and placed a number of controls, restrictions, and prohibitions upon them. Turner's and Noland's comments about abolitionists and barricading oneself in a house with a loaded gun, therefore, were manifestations of the fear that gripped the entire white

South at that time. The fires, at all times occurrences that created white suspicions of slave arson, further fueled whites' fears, as did the relative proximity of northern Virginia to free soil and the fact that slave-hiring season meant large numbers of male slaves were on the move throughout the countryside. As with the panic in other areas of the South, however, talk of abolitionists and loaded guns in northern Virginia were indicative of "white hysteria rather than a black plot" among large numbers of slaves who were about to slaughter the white population at the behest of their abolitionist allies. In short, it was all in whites' minds, and it was placed there by the ascendancy of the Republican Party, which precipitated "the overheated atmosphere surrounding the presidential election of 1856."[11]

White racial solidarity and desire to control hired slaves also was reflected in the fact that white men of Virginia other than owners and hirers captured runaway hired slaves. In Fairfax County, a landlord offered his tenant, James Harrison, one hundred dollars to "go after" a runaway hired slave. Elsewhere, Zachariah Austin collected sixteen shillings "for taking up Cato a runaway [hired] Negro" in York County in 1803. At Roslin Plantation, hired slave Henry ran away on Thursday, March 19, 1829. By March 24, plantation records listed Henry as "Not found," but by the beginning of April, Henry had been brought back to Roslin by the white men who had apprehended him. Roslin's daily work records show that Henry remained at Roslin for the balance of the year. In Essex County, several hired slaves had run away repeatedly during the 1850s, but they were taken up by various white men and then hired out again. In 1855 Franklin Taylor caught Booker, and Thomas Schuse brought in Henry. Another hired slave, Laurence, ran away twice in 1855, but he was apprehended first by James Rogers and the second time by James Matthews. Laurence again ran away on two occasions in 1857, but white men captured him and returned him in both instances: John Coleman apprehended Laurence the first time he ran away, and William Trice brought Laurence back the second time. Booker, too, absconded once again in 1857, but he, too, was captured and returned. Essex County records reveal that all of these escape attempts resulted in the hired slaves' apprehension by white men other than their owners and hirers. The white men who brought in runaway hired slaves shared several things in common: they were nearby, they were available, and they were white. In rural Virginia, these were the only prerequisites for mastering the slaves of others, and they transcended any other occupational, slave-ownership-status, or class distinctions between the men.[12]

The slaves hired out to Virginia hotel keepers James Deshields and Charles Tavenner in 1860 also found many white men in their immediate vicinity. White men of various occupations resided in Deshields's and Tavenner's hotels, including a gentleman, a head gardener, a preacher, a physician, and two dry goods clerks. Such white men helped to control the slaves hired out to Deshields and Tavenner by virtue of their presence as potential surveillers and apprehenders, regardless of their occupation.[13]

Indeed, Virginia slave owners expected other white men to exert authority over their hired-out slaves. One hirer who applied for a slave owner's permission to whip a hired slave received this reply: "I received your [letter] stateing the misbehaviour of Nead & your wish to correct him. [W]henever [Nead] acts in the like maner again nothing would give me greater satisfaction than for you or aney other person in town to give him a pretty severe correction every time he is caught in Town of a sunday evening. [T]here is two maney negroes resorting that place of a sunday & I think there o[ug]ht a stop be put to such conduct." The slave owner had transferred white racial prerogatives to the slave hirer as well as to "aney other person in town." Similarly, slave owner Joseph Hiden recommended that a hirer punish his slave Delpha, to "cure" her behavior:

> I am sorry to hear that Delpha is so impudent but glad to be able to recommend a cure which I have often tried with certain success. Let the overseer take Delpha and give her fifty lashes, on her bare [back?] and repeat the dose morning after morning. . . . God . . . commanded his household. Delpha is a [part?] in corporal dimensions no inconsiderable part of your household and I humbly suggest that it is your duty to command her that she may keep the way of the Lord, to do justice and judgments (see Genesis 18 chap.) What is due from Delpha to you? Service, labour—ready, willing, faithful service unquestioned obedience. If she fails in this she keeps no[t] the way of the Lord to do justice and judgment.

Elsewhere, slave owner Nelson Hicks told a hirer to "not send for the Dockter any more" to visit his hired-out slave, and insisted instead that the hirer "must whip her and make her do her work." For these slave owners, control of hired slaves by men with white skin took priority over any concerns about the potential lost value of injured or runaway hired slaves; thus the hired slaves' chances of playing whites off against each other were reduced.[14]

Virginia whites took measures to assure that control of hired-out slaves involved all whites in the community. In 1804 hired slave Charles ran away from his hirer, a Mr. Clarkson, and appeared at the residence of George Twyman. At Twyman's place, Charles spoke of Clarkson's "over-seer having struck him and that he had Flung the over-seer Down and run off." Charles also complained to Twyman of insufficient food at Clarkson's place and indicated that he had refused to obey an order to burn brush along with Clarkson's slaves because he wished to go "git something to eat." Even though Charles had been struck by an overseer and had never received enough to eat, Twyman told Charles "to go and submit himself" to Clarkson. Twyman chose this course despite his having "reason to think from [Charles's] own Discourse that [Charles] [had] a thought of making an[other] elopement" from hirer Clarkson. Accordingly, Twyman requested other whites to "keep a strict watch of [Charles's] movements" and to notify Clarkson "on the first knowledge[e] of a Brake" from him. For Twyman, the entire white community's inclusion in the mastering of Charles was of the highest importance. Even though Twyman knew Charles might run away, he simply arranged for more whites to keep a close eye on him, rather than give in to Charles's attempt to exploit the situation to his advantage.[15]

White solidarity made repeat hirings, that is, slave owners' transfer of their slaves to the same hirers over a period of years, pervasive. In Norfolk, slave owner Sarah Shepherd sent many of her slaves to the same hirers from the mid-1850s through the Civil War. Shepherd's papers indicate, moreover, that she had been hiring out slaves since the 1840s. In Sussex County, hirer Henry Parker offered slave owner Henry Blunt extra money in an attempt to hire the same slave from Blunt again. Hirers' satisfaction with hiring-out transactions was sufficient for many of them to hire slaves regularly over lengthy periods of time. In Essex County, whites who hired slaves for three or more years during the 1840s from estate sources alone included Wiley George, William Gravatt, William Sadler, Polly Sale, Thomas Shearwood, and Zachariah Williams. This does not include the large number of persons who had hired slaves for different periods of time from Essex County estates during the 1830s and 1840s, nor does it include the many persons who hired slaves from sources other than estates, which, 1860 slave schedules show, were but a tiny fraction of hired slave sources. The same pattern prevailed throughout Virginia. In Middlesex County, John Pippin hired slaves in 1829, 1830, 1831, and 1832, as did John Seavill. John Orrill hired slaves in 1829, 1830, 1831, 1832, and 1833. In the Shenandoah Valley, S. F. Taylor and John Bumgardner were but two persons who hired slaves from Folly Farm Plantation for several years throughout the 1850s. Elsewhere, slave owner William Wirt thanked Sam Washington for Washington's "promptness in paying" a hire, and Wirt expressed his "particular desire that [Washington] should take any and all [of Wirt's slaves for hire] before any one else" for the next year. Accordingly, Wirt enclosed with his letter to Washington "a list of those that will be offered for hire." Significantly, although Wirt acknowledged some of the slaves' family connections and indicated his willingness to hire out those slaves in a manner that would keep them near their loved ones, he told Washington, "[I] would prefer that you should be satisfied before any one else," including, therefore, the slaves themselves. Clearly, slave owner Wirt's relationship with slave hirer Washington was extremely cordial. Such slave-hiring patterns across antebellum Virginia show that the practice was not an institutional irregularity but a routine aspect of Virginia slavery that brought all whites into contact with slavery on an ongoing basis.[16]

Because slave hiring was an integral feature of Virginia slavery, certain logistical activities were integral facets of slave hiring, and they also involved Virginia whites in addition to owners and hirers with slavery. York County guardian William Macon, for example, recorded seven pounds in "expences incurred in travelling to hire out the Negroes & other Services for the Estate" in 1807. Macon engaged in such activities during his guardianship period, which ran from 1803 through 1809. In 1820 York County guardian Gavis Dean paid Thomas Billups "wages & horse hire" to bring a slave family back to him at the conclusion of a hiring period. In addition to Billups's pay and the costs to rent Billups's horse, Dean recorded other "Traveling expences going after & bringin Armistead his wife and 4 Children from Linchburg to Gloucester Cart hire &c." This hired-out slave family spent ten days traveling from central Virginia to the coast under the paid surveillance of a white man. Loudoun County resident John Beale incurred expenses in 1829 and 1830 for his personal surveillance and transportation of slaves to hiring day. In Middlesex County, Benjamin Robinson paid a neighbor one dollar "for carrying Lucinda and old Milly to [the] hiring grounds" in 1839. In 1845 Thomas Baytop earned the same amount "for bringing [a] negroe to [a] hiring" in Gloucester County. Guardian Thomas Gee recorded "expenses of sending negroes to hiring" in Sussex County in January 1846 and again in January 1847. In Fairfax County, John Carter spent several dollars each year during the early 1850s for a "wagon to take negroes to [the] hiring." At the hiring grounds, still other white men were employed to hire out the slaves at auction. Such persons included Southampton County resident Isham Newsum, who "was call[e]d on by Geo[rge] Gurley & Henry Thomas to cry up a parcel of negroes (for one years hire)." In Lancaster County, Edward Payne was paid "for Crying negroes to hire" during the 1830s, and M. G. Wood of Essex County earned cash "for crying hire of negroes" in 1857. When the slave-hiring year concluded, slave owners often paid still other white men to bring their slaves back from hirers. In 1849 Nelson Hicks paid Weldin Parks $1.50 "for fetching Julia from the Natchal bridge home to Amherst county the negro which Mr. G. W. Taylor hired of Nelson Hicks." The language on Parks's receipt emphasizes the point: slave-hiring's logistical activities, which were necessary for slave hiring to occur, represented a transfer of power over hired slaves to many white men in addition to slave owners and slave hirers in Virginia.[17]

In Virginia, hiring days were held around the turn of each year at central, public locations familiar to the white population, including market houses, taverns, courthouses, and crossroads. In addition to the white men who transported slaves and auctioned them off, many white male Virginians were very anxious to go to hiring days just to observe the proceedings, and those unable to attend hiring days in person made a point of ascertaining what had transpired. In Princess Anne County, W. V. Montague, who was sick and "confined to [his] bead . . . [and] consequently was not able to attend any of the hirings . . . got [his] neighbor Mr. Twiford to do so" for him. In Lunenberg County in 1859, Robert Allen lamented that he "could not go to [a] negro hireing," but Allen quickly learned what he had missed. "I hear," Allen noted, "they hir[ed] . . . as high as they did last Year & some 10 p[e]r cent hi[gher]." On January 1, 1861, illness kept Allen away, as he wrote that he was "quite sick & consequently did not attend the negro hireing." Yet Allen obtained information concerning the hiring day's happenings; afterward he wrote, "I understand that they hired very high." The following day, Allen finally gratified his desire to go to a slave hiring in person: "Went to a negro hireing at the Court house," Allen boasted in his diary. Slave hirings were the chief destination for white men in local neighborhoods every year, and knowledge of the day's events, if not actual attendance in person, was a high priority for them. White male hiring-day spectators imagined themselves masters of the slaves of others and reminded themselves that, because they were white men, that notion was within the realm of possibility.[18]

Libations often awaited those who attended slave hirings. During the 1790s, for example, Josiah Vick often purchased "brandy for Negro hiring." Since slave hirings commonly took place at courthouses, hiring day represented a variation of a typical eighteenth-century court-day crowd, a "Noisyed Crew . . . 3/4's of them in a state of intoxication." Liquor, one historian notes, was "everywhere in the social world of early nineteenth-century America . . . a taken-for-granted presence," and slave-hiring days were no exception. Since many southern white male farmers included alcohol consumption among their favorite pastimes, hiring-day attendees expected alcohol, and Vick hoped that it would encourage the hiring-day crowd to bid freely.[19]

Virginia's slave-hiring days sometimes were the scenes of considerable violence. Daniel Cobb observed a fight and a murder at two different Southampton County slave hirings in December 1849. On December 27, Cobb saw "a fite at [the] Drewsvill [slave hiring, which involved] Mr. Brantly and Mr. Clemmons." "Brantly shot C[lemmons] 3 times," Cobb observed, "and C[lemmons] stabbed B[rantly] several times." As a result of "there scrape," Cobb noted several days later, "Clements gave Bale of $1500 for his Conduct and Brantly is better." Just a few days after that incident, Cobb witnessed "a negrow man killed [at] Rosses hireing by a negrow man and a White man." Cobb's remarks are unclear as to whether both men ended up "in Southampton Jale."[20]

The scenes Cobb described in his diary reveal far more than alcohol-related violence. As sites of drinking, fighting, and slave trading, slave hirings were the exclusive domain of white males, who utilized them, at least in part, to define themselves publicly among their neighbors. White male Virginians present at hiring days were equal: in contrast to dependent women (white women did not attend slave hirings) or dependent slaves, they were independent men, and their independence was showcased by their hiring-day opportunities: they could auction off slaves, control them in the form of surveillance and transportation to hiring day, and enjoy the day as spectators. Missed opportunities to attend slave hirings in person led white men to ascertain the day's proceedings from others and to assert their independence indirectly in the pages of their diaries. Slave-hiring days in rural Virginia, therefore, were hubs of white manhood that linked neighborhood white men to each other and, in turn, to the slave regime, by the power they, as independent men, wielded publicly over their own slaves or the slaves of others. This web of white male mastery transcended the lines of slave-ownership status, economic class, and occupation.[21]

Virginia white men carried out slave hiring's public, logistical tasks centered around hiring day especially for their slave-owning neighbors who were white women. In Westmoreland County, Walter Bowie's relationship with one of his neighbors, a Miss H. Parker, consisted primarily of the slave-hiring services he performed for her. Bowie recorded his slave-hiring activities in his journal, where he noted that he "hired one of Miss H. Parker's men (Landon) to James Franklin for the year 1861 for $80.00 and on the same day one of Miss H.P.'s men (Jno.) to . . . Murphy." When he was unable to hire out Parker's slaves immediately, Bowie traveled to other neighborhoods to seek hirers for them. "Went up to the Hague to try & hire out Miss H. Parker's negroes," Bowie wrote in his journal. On another occasion, Bowie located a hirer who resided some distance away, and he noted the transaction in his journal: "Hired to Mr. Harris of Northumberland Co[unty] three of Miss H. Parker's men (Joe, Elick & Windsor) at $80.00 each." Three days later, Bowie "went up to Miss H. Parkers to get her negroes off to Northumberland." In return for his services and time on Parker's behalf, Bowie received "her man Jim free of hire in consideration of my attending to the hiring of her negroes & any other business she may call upon me to do." Parker showed her appreciation for Bowie's handling of her slaves by transferring to him control over another of them. White men often presumed to offer white women their slave-hiring services, as when James F. Taliaferro wrote Miss J. M. Waller that she should send her slaves-for-hire "up to Sandridge's Store in the morning and [he] [would] hire them out for [her]." For antebellum white Virginians, slave hiring's logistical activities were white men's business, and white men exhibited their manhood by overseeing the slaves of others. On their part, white women who secured white men to hire out their slaves avoided slave trading in the public sphere and so retained their claims to ladyhood. Such white ladies nevertheless held on to their prerogatives of mastery, which were rooted in their ownership of slaves and which also placed white men at their command when white men hired out the ladies' slaves. Ultimately, both white ladies and white men were masters.[22]

White Virginians' slave-hiring activities reflected their agreement that white women's role in them should be limited. Early in the nineteenth century, Thomas Jefferson wrote John Minor "on the subject of hiring [the] negroes" of a Mrs. Dangerfield, hoping that Minor would "be so good as to forward" his application for the slaves to Dangerfield. Clearly, Jefferson simply assumed that some white man, such as Minor, would act as Dangerfield's slave-hiring agent. Elsewhere, during the early 1850s, Charles Pollard noted in his diary the occasions when he visited, dined, and shopped along with his wife. Revealingly, however, when Pollard went "to Mrs. Miller's to hire hands," his wife did not go with him; those were not activities fit for a white woman. Also, because Mrs. Miller herself was a white woman as well as a master, she received Pollard's application to hire slaves within her home.[23]

White Virginia women's slave-hiring activities were restricted to tasks that fit antebellum white women's expected roles. During a slave-hiring season in 1807, for example, William Macon "paid Joseph Wade's wife for making the Negroes Cloths and her attention to the Negroes in other Respects," and he paid the same woman for similar services on other occasions in 1805 and 1808. As part of their expected role of caregivers to their families, white southern women's benevolence encompassed slaves, too. In Virginia, seeing to hired slaves' needs fulfilled that expectation.[24]

Virginia's slave-owning white women often transferred their slaves-for-hire to a male relative, who would handle the necessary logistical details. Accordingly, in 1859 William Braxton "acted as [his] aunts Agent in hiring out her negroes." In Fauquier County, Mrs. E. M. Marshall directed her nephew John Marshall to say that a Daniel Ward could hire one of her slaves for twenty dollars per month. Ward, who hired slaves for the Fauquier White Sulphur Springs Company, initiated the transaction when he sent a note to Mrs. Marshall, but Marshall's nephew John handled logistical arrangements from there. Also in Fauquier County, John Washington offered his aunt his views of her slaves' behavior, telling her their conduct mandated that she hire some of them out. Yet Washington said that she should decide which slaves to hire out; he encouraged her to "*use* [her] *own discretion*" in that decision. When it came to the actual hiring out of the slaves his aunt selected, however, Washington indicated that his aunt should ask a white man to act as their master, "to look out [for] places for them." Washington respected his aunt's position, as owner of the slaves, to decide which slaves to hire out. Beyond that, Washington's advice to his aunt reflected widespread sentiments among white Virginians. Both white women and white men were masters, but in divergent ways: white women who owned slaves selected which ones to hire out, but they did not actually hire out the slaves thus selected, since that was white men's work. Washington's letter to his aunt shows that slave-hiring activities in antebellum Virginia both acknowledged white mastery regardless of sex and afforded male and female white masters opportunities to showcase their masculinity or femininity.[25]

The same pattern is clear in Charles Montague's letter to his aunt, Frances Hughes, in 1845. Hughes had been considering possible dispositions for troublesome slaves, and Montague offered his views on the matter. Montague named places advantageous for the hiring out of his aunt's slaves and advised her "to place [Phil] in the Coal pits." Montague added that, should his aunt take his advice to hire out Phil in the coal pits, he or another white man would "do the best [they could] for [her] according to [her] directions," and he indicated that he and the other white man "both concur in this advice." In this scenario, master Hughes remained a lady as white men carried out her instructions connected to her slaves, enabling her to remain outside the public realm.[26]

Virginia white men spent much of their time hiring out slaves for their female relatives. This was especially true by the late antebellum period, when quarterly slave-hire payments had become widespread. During 1860 and 1861, Robert Taylor reported quarterly payments he received for the hire of several slaves owned by his grandmother, Elizabeth Temple, and he also hired out slaves for two of his aunts at the same time.[27]

White men of Virginia carried out all the details of slave-hiring arrangements for their female relatives. In 1807 John Hill wrote Thomas Chrystie about Chrystie's application to hire Will, owned by Hill's sister Susanna Dabney. Hill informed Chrystie of Will's price, which Hill believed "full low as [Will] [was] a very good carpenter, & a negro of excellent disposition." Hill sought to convince Chrystie that Will offered good work and little trouble for a low price; that is, he engaged in salesmanship with another white man in public concerning the possible hiring out of a slave owned by a white woman, who had no business in such public affairs. "Should you not want [Will]," Hill then asked Chrystie, "you will be good enough to send him to any person near you, that may want him." White Virginia women's slaves were hired out only as the result of white Virginia men's public machinations.[28]

Frequently, white Virginia women hired out their slaves through white male merchants. During the 1830s, the Daniel and David Higginbotham Company, a general store in Amherst County, included slave-hiring agency among its routine business activities. In 1838 the Higginbothams served as slave-hiring agents for a Mrs. Coleman, on whose behalf they collected hires for Coleman's slaves Tom and Margaret and, on other occasions, purchased hats, shoes, and blankets for Coleman's hired-out slaves. Like other white men who handled slave hiring's logistical activities on behalf of white women, the Higginbothams carried out the most public aspects of the business. These activities rendered the Higginbothams masculine handlers of others' slaves as well as general-store proprietors; their assistance enhanced Coleman's status as a lady who did not hire out slaves on her own.[29]

In Norfolk, Walter H. Taylor and Company, a dry goods mercantile firm, did regular business with Elizabeth Page of Gloucester. Elizabeth's husband had died, so Elizabeth relied upon Walter Taylor to market her produce and to provide her with groceries and other merchandise. In 1845, for example, Page sent down 360 bushels of corn, and Taylor sold it for her and credited it to her account. Taylor then forwarded to Page the flour, sugar, and snuff she ordered, and he charged her account for those items and for their transport to her. At other times, Page ordered molasses, coffee, tea, wine, middling bacon, herrings, lard, apple cheese, raisins, knives and forks, candles, a handkerchief, carpeting, quinine, and morphine.[30]

In addition to making other transactions with Taylor, Page shifted her slaves to Taylor to hire out for her. Consequently, Page's account with Taylor for groceries and other merchandise was credited by money Taylor collected quarterly on Page's behalf for the hiring out of her slaves William and Thomas. In 1845 the slave-hire credits were sufficient to pay Page's account for groceries and merchandise she had ordered from Taylor, and in 1848 Taylor granted Page's request for a cash advance against the hire receipts for her slaves. In its detail of a white man's slave-hiring activities on a white woman's behalf, the relationship between Taylor and Page illuminates gender-role assumptions in antebellum Virginia, which maintained that only white men hired out slaves in the public arena. Those gender assumptions are made clearer still by the fact that Page used her slave-hire earnings to procure food and medicinal and aesthetic items, that is, merchandise for her home, further pointing to her status as a white female household head and slave owner who did not hire out slaves in public.

The Taylor-Page slave-hiring arrangement operated very smoothly. Taylor simply made inquiries concerning Page's preferences regarding her slaves, as when he requested that Page "please express [her] wishes in regard to [her slave] W[illia]m." Taylor informed Page that he would permit William to remain with his current hirers until the beginning of 1846, "or until [she was] heard from," and he asked her, "Please favor with a line at your earliest convenience." Taylor's letters reveal his awareness that he had charge of William in the public realm, until or unless Page exerted her decision-making authority. Taylor's activities on Page's behalf sustained Page's status as a lady, but the fact that she also was a slave owner gave her the power to tell Taylor her desires concerning her slaves. In appreciation for Taylor's dealing with matters connected to her slaves in public, Page sent him gifts of mutton and pats of butter in December 1845, for which Taylor conveyed his "best thanks for so acceptable a present."[31]

When no white male relatives or merchants were available to hire out Virginia women's slaves, any white man would do. Albemarle County resident Joseph Twyman hired slaves regularly during the 1850s, and his records reveal the gendered pattern of slave-hiring activities among whites in antebellum Virginia. Specifically, Twyman dealt with male slave owners directly, but he hired white women's slaves through white men who served as the women's slave-hiring agents, and he made a point to note that fact in his records. In 1857, for example, Twyman wrote that he had "hired of Mrs. Holladay (per Jas. Minor) negro woman Mary Jane & one child James until 25 December 1857 at $50 & gave bond due 25th Dec. 1857." One year later, Twyman hired Jim, owned by a Mrs. C. M. Emmerson, also through James Minor, and at the end of the year, Twyman paid Minor and took in his slave-hiring bond from him. Similarly, in 1860, Twyman "hired of Willis Wood negro girl Clarissa belonging to Mrs. Martha Sellers." In these instances, Twyman's manhood, several slave-owning women's ladyhood, and the mastery of all were underscored, as slaves were moved between three whites: female owner to male agent to male hirer. Sometimes, of course, slave owners who happened to be women could be confusing for some white men. When Beverly Hutchison contacted a Mr. Grigsby "in regard to two negroes [he had] hired of" Grigsby but who were owned by a Mrs. Hooe, Hutchison wondered what, if any, authority Mrs. Hooe possessed over her slaves, since Grigsby had initiated the original transaction with him publicly. Accordingly, Hutchison directed his "proposition" to "Mr Grigsby, or Mrs Hooe if *she* is responsible . . . in the absence of Mr Grigsby" to accept his proposal. For Hutchison, it was not entirely clear whether a white woman had the full authority of a slave owner in all respects in the absence of a white man.[32]

In Middlesex County, Robert Trice worked as a slave-hiring agent regularly on behalf of slave-owning white women. Near the end of the 1843–44 hiring season, Trice told Eliza Chowning that he had notified hirers to pay him as soon as possible, and he assured her that he would forward her the money when he received it. Trice then informed Chowning that he had made clear to hirer Alfred Healy that Chowning "would be glad for him to pay [her] a part of the money for the last year's hires" and later related to Chowning, "[Healy] says he is willing to do so." White women like Chowning were slave owners, but they remained ladies by entrusting the handling of their slaves to white men like Trice, who hired their slaves out, collected on slave-hiring bonds, and tracked down hirers when it became necessary to squeeze money out of them. By 1860, more than fifteen years after his slave-hiring work on Chowning's behalf, Trice continued to work as a slave-hiring agent.[33]

In Virginia, white men of all occupational groups accepted responsibility for others' slaves. In Fauquier County in 1861, Robert Taylor Scott complained to his wife, Fanny, that hiring out others' slaves was "a troublesome and tedious business [which] ought to pay well"; he spent considerable time away from his family doing that for relatively little pay. Scott held assets valued in excess of three thousand dollars, so he did not hire out slaves for others to earn extra cash. Because Scott was twenty-five years old, had an infant child, and was employed as an attorney, he agreed to be away from his family to hire out the slaves of others in order to bolster his budding career as an attorney by ingratiating himself with slave owners who trusted him with their slaves and their money. Young attorney Scott knew that in a slave society, slave owners satisfied with his work pertaining to their hired-out slaves would form the bulk of his future clientele.[34]

An analysis of slave hirers in Fauquier County in 1860 reveals that slave hiring wove many otherwise disparate groups of rural white Virginians into a society-wide web of responsibility for hired-slave control on the eve of the Civil War. The 431 slave hirers in Fauquier County in 1860 included machinists, carriage makers, teachers, tailors, constables, blacksmiths, overseers, cattle drivers, merchants, carpenters, carpenters and builders, milliner tenant women and tenants generally, hotel keepers, elderly female tollgate keepers, ministers, journeyman shoemakers, tanners and couriers, railroad hands, plasterers, coach makers, wheelwrights, laborers, boot and shoe makers, gunsmiths, and elderly female weavers.[35]

Guardians and estate administrators, too, spent much of their time hiring out slaves bequeathed to minor orphans and others. Edward Burke's accounts, kept during the early 1840s, reveal his slave-hiring responsibilities connected to George Buckner's estate. Burke traveled to Richmond and Bowling Green to hire out the estate's slaves, purchased bread and meat for the slaves, paid other white men to hire the slaves out at auction, and made other miscellaneous trips related to the hired slaves. Also, Burke charged the estate for use of a wagon to transport the slaves to the place where they were hired out, for travel expenses to collect the hires, and for his payment to white men to travel to bring the hired-out slaves back at the end of each year. Finally, Burke took out advertisements for the slaves, and he paid other whites to support slave women and children on an annual basis. In many cases, guardianships gave white Virginians an inside track to slave hiring. York County guardian John Smith, for instance, hired a slave and rented sixty acres of land from the estate he had charge of each year from 1807 through 1811. For years at a time, guardians of minor heirs handled matters connected to the heirs' slaves until the heirs reached majority and became full-fledged slave owners in their own right.[36]

Slave hiring in Virginia also was linked to whites' family and household labor requirements. To a considerable extent, households relied upon family members for labor. In 1859, for example, twenty-six-year-old Frank Lewis worked for a local merchant, but in 1860 Frank labored on his mother's farm. The census schedule of free inhabitants of Fauquier County reveals that James and Thomas Lawrence, both in their twenties, assisted their sixty-eight-year-old father on the farm. This pattern of children assisting their parents was common in rural Fauquier County on the eve of the Civil War. Farmer Isaac Beans had the help of his sons Aaron, Osker, Elwood, and William. Nearby, farmhands John and James Cable worked for their father, Alfred, and Alpheus Bray labored for his sixty-year-old single mother, Mary.[37]

Yet many rural white Virginians found that family labor often was not sufficient or, in households where children were mere infants, not available at all. In these circumstances, white laborers were brought in from outside the household. Lewis Lawrence, for example, employed teenager William Harrill to work alongside his sons James and Thomas. Farmers like Mandley Brown, whose children ranged in age from nine down to five, had to look outside the household for all their labor needs. In 1860 Brown employed twenty-three-year-old Joseph Pierson to work on his farm. Tenant Daniel Daugherty had three infant children, so he engaged the help of George Wright and Frank Raines.[38]

These households that employed family or out-of-household white laborers also hired slaves. Consequently, the white laborers present also controlled slaves whom their parents or employers hired to work alongside them. This was the case with Joseph Lyler. On January 2, 1861, Lyler began work as a "laborer and foreman on the farm" of Matthew O'Brien. About one week later, O'Brien sent Lyler to Fenton Fitzhugh's residence to hire a slave, and Lyler returned to O'Brien's place with Fitzhugh's slave Jim. Lyler was a laborer, yet as a white man, Lyler fetched the slave hired by his employer and held that slave in his custody on the way back to his employer's residence, much as other white male Virginians transported hired-out slaves to the hiring grounds and surveilled them along the way. Finally, as his employer's white male "foreman on the farm," Lyler commanded the hired slave at O'Brien's place as though he owned the slave himself.[39]

White laborers' wielding of authority over their employers' hired slaves was common in Virginia. In Charles City County, John Selden employed a Mr. Teuser to build a stable and to make repairs on some of his buildings, but Selden also hired two slaves to assist Teuser with the work. Similarly, when Orange County builder Larkin Stanard contracted to build a house in 1809, he sent to the work site "six hands . . . five negroes and a white man," and the white man functioned as master of the five hired slaves. Mary Dulany wrote in her diary of the assistance she received one harvest season. Dulany had the help of several hired slaves, "and what is more than all," Dulany wrote excitedly, "a white man to take the management" of them. Clearly, slave hiring placed far more whites than owners and hirers alone in positions of racial control, a circumstance that enhanced and enlarged white solidarity behind slavery in Virginia. For hired slaves, this meant that they usually were unable to manipulate owners and hirers to their advantage because many more whites, in addition to owners and hirers, were their masters.[40]

Because slave hiring brought all groups of Virginia whites into contact with slavery, slave hiring is linked to the question of class antagonism in the antebellum South. In Tennessee, another Upper-South state, class resentments centered on slave-ownership status, and they ran highest among non-slave-owners who lived near relatively wealthier slave-owning neighbors. In Virginia, some persons noted a distinct "jealousy . . . between the non-slave holders and slave holders" by the early 1850s, when slave owners' fears of class resentment on the part of non-slave-owning whites brought efforts to "re-open the African slave trade that every white man might have a chance to make himself owner of one or more Negroes." The plan had proposed to "democratize" slave ownership, "to diffuse the slave population as much as possible, and thus secure in the whole community the motives of self-interest for its support." In 1860 several petitioners in Frederick, Jefferson, and Clark counties in Virginia wished to "bring the ownership of 'negro property within the means of the Poor as well as of the Rich'" through measures that would enable "many mechanics and laboring men [to] acquire a slave to wait on their families." Clearly, class resentment and fears of class resentment existed in antebellum Virginia and elsewhere in the South.[41]

Yet, whereas class antagonism in Tennessee was most pronounced in areas where slave ownership was most concentrated, the antagonism was not so prevalent where slave ownership was more widespread. In Virginia, the transfer of slaves to non-slave-owners in the slave-hiring context expanded whites' management of others' slaves and therefore likely served to reduce class antagonism. The slave-hiring patterns in one Virginia County reveal both the pervasiveness of slave hiring in rural Virginia and the way slave hiring facilitated lower-class white Virginians' access to hired slave labor just before secession and war. In Fauquier County in 1860, at least 431 persons hired slaves to work for them, and 40 of the persons who hired the slaves out resided outside Fauquier, primarily in Loudoun, Stafford, and Prince William counties. Of the remaining 391 hirers in Fauquier County, 160 were slave owners, but the remaining 231 Fauquier hirers (the majority) were not slave owners. Non-slave-owning whites who hired slaves became a bit more like their slave-owning counterparts in that they, too, held power over slaves. Slave hiring's diffusion of slaves among other whites in addition to slave owners in antebellum Fauquier County likely served to diminish class resentments there in a manner similar to that noted in antebellum Tennessee.[42]

Slave hiring's significance for white class relations also is shown by the fact that many non-slave-owning slave hirers in Virginia were tenant farmers. In 1860 Fauquier County resident Josiah Leonard was forty-four years old. He worked as a stone fencer, resided on five rented acres, and owned no slaves. Leonard possessed only $195 in personal property, one horse, one cow, and seven hogs; his neighbor Thomas Ambler held more than $90,000 in real and personal property and owned at least thirty-six slaves. These two white men were unequal in wealth, yet they were very much equal in their shared free and independent status as white men who controlled slaves, for, despite his modest holdings, Leonard hired three slaves in 1860. Leonard exemplifies the many whites living on the fringes of antebellum Virginia's economy who owned neither land nor slaves but who rented land and hired slaves. While the agreements by which Virginia's poor whites hired slaves varied, their acquisition of power over the slaves of others often was facilitated in one or more ways. They could hire slave children, relatively cheaper than adults; they could make their hire payments in quarterly installments; and they could accept payment from slave owners to hire pregnant slave women or slave women with young children for one year. For example, in 1860 forty-nine-year-old clerk Alfred Cable was a non-slave-owner with no real property and just $140 in personal property. His sons John and James labored as farmhands while his wife, Mary, cared for their three small children, aged five years, two years, and three months. Cable hired a thirty-five-year-old slave woman that year, along with the woman's children, aged thirteen years, four years, and two years. The slave woman's possession of small children doubtless made the hiring of these slaves more affordable for Cable, who probably reasoned that at least some work could be derived from the slave woman and her oldest daughter.[43]

White journeymen, too, resided on the economic edge of the rural Virginia slave society. Though skilled craftsmen, white journeymen worked for white masters in a society where most persons who worked for white masters were slaves. In 1860 journeyman shoemaker Robert H. Fletcher and his wife, Mary, lived in Warrenton, the Fauquier County seat. The Fletchers had three children who ranged in age from seven years down to nine months. Fletcher labored for a white master in 1860, but he himself also became a master when he hired a seventeen-year-old female slave to work for his family. He was a journeyman, a non-slave-owner, a tenant, and a holder of a mere $70 in personal property, but he migrated from the fringe of rural Virginia slave society to become more like other whites in his community who also commanded slaves. Fletcher's oldest child, the future head of his own household, observed his father's racial authority firsthand as a learning experience.[44]

Fletcher's case highlights many Virginia whites' preference for particular types of slaves, and it reveals *why* many wished to hire slaves to start with. Lower-class whites' hiring of slave women was linked to an idealized notion of the middle-class household, specifically, an effort to relieve white women of household drudgery. The fact that lower-class white male slave hirers' households included infant children to care for suggests that they hired female slaves to assist their wives with child-care duties, in particular. When Robert Fletcher hired a seventeen-year-old slave girl, for example, his household included two infant children: two-year-old Marion and nine-month-old William.[45]

Many other rural white Virginians' circumstances were similar to Fletcher's. In Fauquier County, blacksmith John J. Bowie owned no real property in 1860, and he held $800 in personal property, which probably consisted mainly of his blacksmith tools. Bowie lived with his wife, Ann, and their four sons. Ann's household duties included care of the Bowies' sons William and Carlton, who were six and five years old, respectively, and the one-month-old twins Luther and Arthur. The same year Luther and Arthur were born, John Bowie hired a sixty-five-year-old slave woman to assist his wife with child-care work in the household.[46]

Another rural Fauquier resident of relatively modest means with infant children in 1860 was German immigrant Joseph Seigert. Seigert was a boot and shoe maker, and he worked with Henry Strath, a nineteen-year-old apprentice to that craft. Seigert and his wife, Christine, owned no land in 1860 and held only $650 in personal property. According to the census enumerator, Christine's primary responsibility in 1860 was "housework," including care of the Seigerts' eleven-month-old daughter, Betty. The same year, Joseph Seigert hired a fourteen-year-old slave girl to assist his wife with housework and care of their infant daughter, while he and his apprentice worked with boots and shoes. Of course, apprentice Henry Strath, by virtue of his presence and the fact that he was a white man, also had partial charge of the slave Seigert hired.[47]

Relatively wealthy whites hired slaves to work in their homes as house servants, too. In 1860 Fauquier County resident and Protestant Episcopal minister Thomas Duncan was a bit better off financially than many of his neighbors. Duncan and his wife, Maria, held $2,800 in land and $1,430 in personal property, and the census enumerator identified Maria as a "housekeeper." Probably the bulk of Maria's housekeeping duties revolved around the care of the Duncans' children, two-year-old Murray and nine-month-old William. Cognizant of his wife's child-care and other housekeeping burdens, Duncan hired a mother-child slave unit from Reverend George Norton of Alexandria: a forty-year-old slave woman, along with the woman's eight-year-old and two-month-old daughters. In the same year, 1860, Duncan also had hired an eighteen-year-old male and a seventeen-year-old female, probably to perform field labor on his holdings, but the slave mother he hired likely worked in the house for his wife, while the slave tried to care for her own children at the same time.[48]

Across the class and occupational spectrum, white male Virginians' hiring of slaves for their households enabled them to manifest whiteness, authority, control, success, and masculine independence in a slave society in the midst of the market revolution. White men who hired slave women to help their wives in the home enhanced their wives' femininity even beyond the degree to which it already was sustained by their wives' avoidance of public slave-hiring activities. In particular, white men's hiring of slave women reduced their wives' household drudgery; in this way a man also demonstrated his own manhood, by providing so well for his wife that she did not work inside the home any more than she did outside it—or so it appeared. Because the adoption of middle-class ideals involved the hiring of slaves and transcended class and occupational lines, slave hiring for the purpose of exhibiting middle-class ideals also enhanced white racial solidarity in Virginia. In addition, lower-class white Virginians who hired slaves appeared successful in a society characterized by a growing inequality between themselves and their relatively better-off white neighbors. For lower-class white Virginians, becoming masters meant success precisely because they observed that their most successful white neighbors were masters. Ultimately, lower-class white Virginians' adoption of middle-class ideals through slave hiring strengthened their sense of connection to wealthier whites and helped to gloss over the economic inequalities that increasingly pervaded their society.

These issues are especially significant given that white males' hiring of house servants in Virginia was widespread. In York County, Henry Heth and his associate hired several slaves in 1806, 1807, 1808, and 1809 from the same owner, including a house servant in 1808. Similarly, James Galt of Fluvanna County reported at the end of 1841 that his family had hired Henrietta for seven consecutive years. The hiring transactions went smoothly between these owners and hirers, who therefore repeated their hiring arrangements year after year. In Fauquier County, Thomas Foster attended a slave hiring in December 1839, where he hired a slave "for the dining room." In nearby Loudoun County, a slave was hired as a nurse for Susan Noland's children for 1849. There were many such slave hirers: enough house servants were hired out in rural Virginia for King and Queen County physician B. H. Walker to note slaves' sex and occupation at a slave hiring he attended in 1859. "Cooks [were] hiring for $50 & washerwomen for $40 & upwards," Walker observed.[49]

Not surprisingly, Virginia women and their husbands spent considerable time discussing the subject of hired house servants. Early in 1847, while his wife was away during slave-hiring season, Patrick Catlett wrote her about his decisions related to hiring a house servant. Catlett first apologized to his wife for his failure to hire a particular slave woman. "Negroes are hiring very high this year," Catlett pointed out, "and for that reason I wish to make out with as few as I can conveniently." However, Catlett quickly added, "At the same time I wish to oblige you as far as I *posibly* can I hope you believe that." Catlett ultimately did hire another slave woman as a house servant to cook, and he informed his wife that he was pleased with her apparent obedience, particularly since "having to keep house attend to the farm and attend to workmen is no easy work these short days." Catlett's initial apology to his wife for not hiring a house servant, and his assurance that he would "Explain things," that is, justify to his wife his failure to do so, along with his subsequent hiring of a different house servant, all show that Catlett's wife expected him to hire a house servant to reduce her domestic workload and so enhance her identity as a lady and that Catlett himself was determined to fulfill his wife's wishes. Ultimately, slave hiring promised enhanced manhood for Catlett, enhanced ladyhood for his wife, and mastery for both.[50]

Virginia women attached great significance to having hired slaves in their households. In 1846 merchant John Miller and his wife, Jane, exchanged several letters on the subject of hiring a slave woman as a house servant. The letters reveal that Jane wished to hire a house servant and that she was aware of particular slave women whom she referenced as possible candidates. John, for his part, spent considerable time and effort during September, October, and November of 1846 speaking with other whites about one slave woman or another whom he might hire, pondering the slave's potential living quarters in the house, and conferring with Jane regularly about her sentiments and preferences on all aspects of the matter. Jane wished to hire a house servant, but, in keeping with antebellum white Virginians' gender-role expectations for both men and women, John played the role of a man in public to hire a slave for the house in order that his wife might play the role of a lady in the house with a reduced workload. Elsewhere, while Shenandoah Valley resident Margaret Brooke's husband, Robert, was away in Richmond, Margaret had to run the household on her own. In a letter to her husband, Margaret remarked at length on the extent to which having a newly acquired hired slave promised to reduce the amount of housework she had to do: "I think that my *new* Servant will be a comfort to me. I live in more ease than I have . . . for two years. . . . It makes my family much smaller, that alone reconciles me to the change. I shall not have half the sewing to do—and my new servant will sleep in the house—and is never out of place." Margaret anticipated a home life characterized by comfort, ease, less work, and little trouble. For her, command of a hired-slave house servant also was the stuff of ladyhood.[51]

If hiring slaves *in* gave white women assistance with household chores, hiring slaves *out* provided an income that enabled them to avoid living and working in a manner resembling that of slaves. In Norfolk, Lorrinda McPherson wrote her brother, William Royston, regularly during the 1830s and 1840s about her financial difficulties. "We are yet alive," McPherson once reported to her brother concerning her family. She lamented that she had "to work and provide for [her]self and children" and that she had "no way to suport [her] self and children but by [her] own labour," since the children's father, McPherson's husband, had died. Clearly, McPherson's particular circumstances made it impossible for her to live as a lady, and she was "anxious to get in some place wheare it [was] not thought a disgrace for [her] to have to wo[r]k as hard as" she did. Referring to members of "genteel" society, McPherson bristled at others' perception of her family: "People think that we are poorer than what we really are," she wrote. She was convinced that others looked down upon her family, largely because when a white woman worked, it made the entire family *appear* poor, and it made her seem like anything but a lady.[52]

McPherson viewed slave-hiring income as the remedy to her predicament, and she asked her brother to send "one hundred dollars of their money," that is, money generated from Royston's hiring out of slaves owned by McPherson's daughters. Specifically, McPherson wanted the slave-hire money for her daughters' clothing, because she "want[ed] them to appear like other people does," that is, like little ladies. McPherson also related that she had "been compelled to go and live out on the account of the dull times" and that one of her daughters, too, had "been living out some," working for a woman who "did not treat her well and gave her no clothes to wear." They "work [white girls] night and day besides thay make servants of them and they are exposed to every kind of work," McPherson wrote of white residents who hired white girls as house servants. McPherson likened her daughter's experience to that of a hired-slave house servant when she told her brother that her daughter "was always kept about house and kitchen work and is constantly in the streets going from house to house on errands like the poorest negro in the world." Life in a slave society had instilled in McPherson specific criteria for how to distinguish idealized white women from slaves, and slave-hire income was the way to render the distinction sharp. McPherson asserted that the interest on the hire of one of her daughters' slaves alone "would be quite sufficient to keep them at home and send them to school," particularly given that one of her daughters was "almost grown and scarcely knows any thing." For McPherson, slave-hire income was the means by which she and her daughters could avoid working in the manner of hired slaves and could *appear* in the eyes of others, and to themselves, as the white ladies they were. Ultimately, slave hiring helped to define sharply the boundary between free white women and slaves in a slave society.[53]

Not all white Virginia widows' economic circumstances were as dire as McPherson's, yet the hiring out of slaves by widowed white ladies and white spinsters, as a cohort, was relatively common in Virginia. In Fauquier County alone, there were many slave-owning widows and spinsters with real and personal property who hired out slaves in 1860. Among them was seventy-two-year-old Ann Green, who lived with her three daughters and hired out her forty-year-old male slave to Thomas Wilson. Spinster Cecelia Edmonds, who lived with widow Harriet Murray, hired out a twenty-eight-year-old slave man to James Ferguson, a slave owner who wished to supplement his own force. Elizabeth Ogilvie, who lived with her seven children and no husband, hired out one of her twenty-four slaves to a resident of Fairfax County, and eighty-one-year-old Charity Sinclair, whose occupation was "farming" and who lived by herself, hired out two slave men, eighteen and nineteen years old, to John Meredith in Prince William County. The Fauquier census enumerator also discovered that seventy-three-year-old "Farming (Maiden)" Elizabeth Waller hired out six of the thirty-nine slaves she owned in 1860.[54]

Like other white Virginians who hired out slaves, widows and spinsters did so regularly over extended periods of time. In Loudoun County, Harry S. Cooke's widow hired out several slaves each year from 1829 through 1838 to support herself and her infant children. Likewise, Sarah Rawlings, widow of Stephen Rawlings, hired out slaves annually during the 1830s. In Essex County, Sarah Harriet Apphia Hunter first benefited from slave-hire income when slaves bequeathed to her were hired out by guardians. Shortly after she came of age during the 1840s, Sarah hired out many of her slaves annually as a single woman through the Civil War. Sarah kept some of her slaves on the plantation to continue operations, but she hired out more than a dozen slaves each year from 1845 through 1862.[55]

Slave hiring enabled the interests of these Virginia widows and spinsters to converge with the interests of the slaves they hired out. Hiring out some of their slaves afforded these white women the chance to be slave owners in their own right in the absence of a husband and, in the case of the widows among them, to earn extra income, continue farming operations, or send their children to school. The slaves the women hired out, for their part, escaped sale to the Lower South by virtue of the women's decision to become, or to remain, slave owners and farmers without a husband. Thus the slaves could look forward to seeing their loved ones again at the conclusion of the hiring year. Indeed, slaves like Fannie Berry noted a sharp contrast between being hired out and being sold to a slave trader, as she recollected that her mistress, Miss Sarah Ann, hired out slaves to a railroad contractor. Berry commented, "Miss Sarah Ann ain't never sole none of her niggers but ole man Derby what had hundreds 'ud sell some of his'n any time ole slavetrader come 'round." In some cases, therefore, slave hiring offered the possibility of less disruption in Virginia's slave communities than the sale of slaves following the death of a husband may have entailed. Slave hiring was no less integral to the lives of widows and spinsters than it was to other elements of white Virginia society. Slave hiring's centrality to white Virginia society also is shown in neighbors' hiring out slaves to each other for seasonal work, such as hog butchering. One winter in Southampton County, Jesse Little sent slaves to help his neighbor, Daniel Cobb, butcher hogs, and Cobb noted that his "help was [his] own hands [along with] 4 men from Mr. Littles and 3 women of Mr Littles." Neighborly control of slaves was reciprocal in nature, as when Cobb once "promise[d] 2 hands to help Mr. Little kill hogs."[56]

The summer wheat harvest, too, was important in fostering white Virginians' neighborhood solidarity behind slavery. In Westmoreland County during the summer of 1860, Walter Bowie Jr. moved his slaves between his own farm and several of his neighbors' farms. First, Bowie hired out his slaves Barnett and Nelson to "cut wheat for Doc[tor] Taylor." The next day, Bowie began his own "harvest with twenty Eight hands including seven cradlers," and the day after that Bowie hired out all of his slaves to his mother's place, where by the end of that day the slaves "had the greater part of [her] wheat harvested." Bowie next returned his slaves to his own harvest, completed it, and then hired out "all of [his] hands except one up to help [his neighbor] Laurence in his harvest." The following day, most of Bowie's slaves returned to Laurence's place, "except Barnett," Bowie noted, who had been hired out to cut wheat for yet another of Bowie's neighbors. After about ten days of harvesting wheat around the neighborhood, Bowie's "hands all came home." As with winter hog butchering, white Virginians constructed a neighborly solidarity around a common interest in a successful wheat harvest. For both activities, slave hiring facilitated the successful outcome, which meant that neighborly solidarity was white solidarity.[57]

In rural Virginia, slave owners like Bowie were among the principal lessors of slave labor, linking themselves to many other whites through their extensive, and routine, transfer of slaves to many white hirers. Slave owner Enos Hord, a resident of Fauquier County, was one of those lessors. In 1860 he hired out twenty-one of his sixty-nine slaves to thirteen hirers. Clearly, Virginia's principal lessors of slave labor felt sufficiently comfortable to hire out their slaves to many other white Virginians simultaneously. Like countless other white Virginians who hired out slaves, Hord hired out his slaves to white hirers of various economic classes, occupations, and slave-ownership status. That year, Hord, a fifty-eight-year-old farmer with $28,000 in real property and $71,350 in personal property, hired out slaves to white Virginians with and without real property; to those whose personal property was valued in the tens of thousands of dollars and to those whose personal property was valued in the hundreds of dollars; to farmers, to a wheelwright, and to a merchant; to slave owners and to non-slave-owners. The pattern was plain: white Virginians of varied economic means were alike in that any of them could be a slave's master.[58]

Slave owners hired out slaves to neighbors regularly for a variety of purposes. In 1832 King and Queen County slave owner John Walker "sent [his slaves] Bartlet and Fuller . . . to Ben Griffiths to saw plank . . . for which I make no charge." Other Virginians hired out their slaves to help their neighbors raise tobacco barns and to do general carpentry work. In such contexts of neighborly cooperation, it is little wonder that Virginians like Thomas Randolph took for granted his ability to "let out [slave children] to near neighbours for their food and clothing." Likewise, when Clinton King was away from home and wondered how his wife, Mollie, would "get along about [her] wood and water," he exhibited little doubt that she could "get a little negro Boy [on hire] from [neighbors] John Bell or Mr. Fishburn which [she] might make out with." Whites in rural Virginia neighborhoods knew they could depend on each other for hired slave labor and for getting relatively less productive slave children off their hands for the year.[59]

Slave hiring complemented other interactions of assistance between white neighbors in the Virginia countryside. Many hirers rented land from the same persons who hired slaves to them, for instance. In Loudoun County during the 1830s, James Thomas was paid to keep a slave by the same person who also rented land to Thomas. During the 1850s, Nelson County miller William Faber hired out his slave Ann to John Detter, whom Faber also employed to run his mill. Faber also rented Detter a house and a shop, and he hired out a slave to Detter to work in that shop. In the fall of 1853, Faber provided Detter a "Cart & Steers to haul coalwood 1 Day," and at other times Faber supplied Detter with grain and flour. Similarly, in 1852 Faber hired out his slave Milly to Alexander McClung and also provisioned McClung with clover seed, plaster, a cow, and a calf. In December McClung reciprocated by giving Faber eight hundred pounds of pork. In 1854 Loudoun County slave owner George Rust paid Solemon Everhart seventy-five dollars to work on his stables and carriage house, and Rust also hired out to Everhart one slave for "Board & Cloths" and another for thirty-five dollars, during the same year. Elsewhere, physician William Martin loaned money, rented out his house, rented out his wagon, and hired out his slaves to several of his neighbors. He also spent time "doctoring the Poor" among them. Jake Trail, for example, hired Martin's slave Jim and also rented Martin's wagon, and Trail reciprocated when he brought Martin several bundles of oats in 1855.[60]

White Virginians' provision of hired slaves, loans, employment, carts and wagons, food, livestock, and other agricultural commodities to their neighbors underscored their recognition of those neighbors' membership in the community of white men. That community was a *white* community *before* it was a community of merchants, millers, laborers, and tenants because hired slaves were an integral part of community members' interactions of assistance. Whites involved in slave hiring knew each other because they were neighbors and because of the common activities in which they engaged. Another reason for whites to stand in racial solidarity behind hired slave control, of course, was their shared desire to prevent hired slaves from damaging their interests by running away, stealing, and the like. When hired slave Thornton, owned by George Nelson and hired by Daniel Anderson, was caught stealing, the situation ended in Thornton's being "taken on Friday & put to Jail to be sold for commiting a thief." Anderson's relationship with Nelson remained unaffected by Thornton's actions, since Nelson simply hired Anderson another slave to take Thornton's place. Identification of slave hirers on the 1860 free and slave schedules reveals that many owners and hirers lived near one another and knew one another; thus, they shared many interests, including hired-slave management, in common. For hired slaves, the pervasive nature of whites' authority made it difficult to elude. For white Virginians, mastery itself, and its easy transfer, were inextricable from their daily relationships.[61]

Membership in Virginia's white male communities by virtue of managing and hiring others' slaves was attained and showcased in other ways, too. Throughout the year, non-slave-owning white men sent the slaves they had hired to merchants' country stores, and those white men also went to the stores themselves to purchase items for their hired slaves. These trips were visible to other white men, and they were slave hirers' public expression of racial solidarity with other neighborhood white men who, regardless of wealth, slave-owning status, or occupation, also held slaves. These country-store transactions permitted non-slave-owning hirers to proclaim publicly that they were not journeymen, ditchers, or laborers, but white men and masters, a notion reinforced in the eyes of the larger white neighborhood with every trip they, or the slave they had hired, made to the store.[62]

This scenario could be observed during the last week of December 1860 and into the first week of January 1861, the slave-hiring season, when white male slave hirers streamed into H. A. White's general store in Warrenton, the Fauquier County seat, to purchase hats and blankets for the hired slaves they were about to return to their owners. John N. Grant was one of the slave hirers who showed up at White's store during those days. Grant was a non-slave-owning thirty-seven-year-old machinist who lived with his wife, Lucy, and their eight children, ranging in age from thirteen down to one. Grant's occupation, along with his wife's occupation as housekeeper, the number and ages of his children, and the fact that he produced no crops worthy of note on the agricultural schedule, all indicate that the two female slaves he hired in 1860 worked as house servants. This meant that slave hiring enabled Grant to underscore his own manhood by enhancing his wife's ladyhood while it also conferred mastery upon them both. On December 29, 1860, Grant displayed his white manhood to other white men publicly when he appeared at H. A. White's general store in Warrenton to buy a "serv[an]ts blanket." There were other customers in the store that day, including other hirers who bought hired slaves' hats and blankets. Grant's own purchase of a hired slave's blanket reminded the other whites present in the store that he was not there as a machinist, but as a white man who had hired slaves to assist his wife in the household. Businesses like H. A. White's general store were the arenas where white men like Grant displayed themselves as such annually during each slave-hiring season, and they also reveal the considerable extent to which merchants, too, both profited from slave hiring and helped to sustain it.[63]

Slave hiring helped to unite whites behind slavery and so strengthened slavery considerably by the eve of the Civil War. Yet whites' racial unity connected to slave hiring in Virginia extended beyond their farms and plantations, their neighborhoods and hiring-day activities, and their homes and general stores. It also included Virginia's vibrant industrial and urban sectors. When hired slaves worked there, their experiences were in some ways different from those of hired slaves elsewhere in Virginia and in other ways the same.

CHAPTER 6

SLAVE HIRING, HIRED SLAVES, AND URBAN AND INDUSTRIAL SLAVERY

Because occupations in Virginia's cities and industries differed from those in agricultural and other settings, slave hiring was often different, too. Slave hiring also varied from one urban or industrial occupation to another in a multitude of ways. No one knew these things better than hired slaves themselves, because their labor had sustained Virginia's urban and industrial development since the eighteenth century.

Although it was not a new practice at the time, urban and industrial slave hiring became especially attractive during the Revolution, when Virginia Tidewater firms attached patriotism to planters' desire to rid themselves of excess slaves. In Fredericksburg, cloth manufacturers cried out to "Gentlemen . . . friends of their country" to hire them "a few of their supernumerary little negroes [and thereby] rid themselves of that charge." "Negroes [hired to us] are boarded and clothed clear of expense" and "in a decent manner," the manufacturers assured planters. Elsewhere, revolutionary Virginia hired planters' extra slaves to produce cannon for the war. Some thirty hired slaves labored at the Westham Foundry in 1777, and a 1781 list included thirteen "Negroes hired by Order of the Governor."[1]

Slave hiring for war-related industrial work in Virginia was a precedent for the private employment of hired slaves in industry during the Revolution and afterward. Ironmaster David Ross, for example, had acquired his Oxford Iron Works, located a few miles from Lynchburg, during the Revolution. From the outset, the relatively high cost and the possibility of strikes made Ross disinclined to hire white workers, so he looked to slave labor to fill his initial needs, as well as to serve his plans for the expansion of his operation. In 1777 Ross advertised in the *Virginia Gazette* for "50 or 60 Negro men for one, two, or three Years." Because he anticipated Virginia slave owners' concerns about the welfare of their slave property, Ross assured them, "The situation of [the] Works is very healthy, the Labour of the Slaves moderate, and they shall have a plentiful diet." Ross further offered "an advance Price for Carpenters and Wheelwrights," but he refused to "be concerned with any that are noted Runaways." Clifton Forge and Lucy Selina Furnace employed 90 slaves in 1827, and 70 slaves were working at Bath Iron Works. Meanwhile, smaller iron operations, especially in Botetourt, Page, and Wythe counties, hired slaves regularly. In Rockbridge County, Buffalo Forge had 114 slaves in its employ in 1840, and by 1851, 2,812 slaves were working at iron production in Botetourt County alone, with hundreds more also making iron throughout Appalachian Virginia.[2]

Other Virginia industrialists also were impressed by the usefulness of hired slaves in wartime production. In 1782 the governor of Virginia was informed that slave rope makers, idle since the end of the war and the burning of the state rope walks, "could be hired out to advantage . . . [because] the proprietors of the private rope-walks near Richmond [were] very anxious to hire these negroes and [would] give high wages for them." Virginia lead mine owners had similar thoughts, and the governor declared his readiness "to receive proposals from the proprietors of the lead mines for . . . hiring the public negroes" who previously had worked in Virginia's mines.[3]

Hired slaves worked in a variety of industries throughout the antebellum period. Between 1829 and 1860, hired slaves labored as gold miners in several Virginia counties, and in 1850 the gold mines in Eastern Orange County alone hired approximately one hundred slaves. Ultimately, hired slaves extracted several million dollars' worth of gold from Virginia mines, much of which the U.S. Mint used to coin gold dollars, along with double eagles, eagles, half eagles, quarter eagles, and other denominations that circulated across the United States during the antebellum period and beyond. Additionally, some gold extracted from Virginia with hired slave labor was sent to Europe for the production of jewelry.[4]

Virginia's coal industry hired slaves, too. Coal had been mined in eastern Virginia in the vicinity of Richmond and Petersburg since the middle of the eighteenth century, and it rapidly grew in importance as one of the chief products shipped to cities and to the coast. Shortly after the Revolution, a coal mine owner in Goochland County hired slaves to mine coal and to serve as boatmen to float it down to Richmond. Henry Heth, owner of the Black Heath Pits in Chesterfield County, hired slaves to supplement those he owned. In 1810 Heth advertised to hire "30 or 40 able bodied Negro Men, for whom a liberal price [would] be given." Virginia coal mines varied in size from an average of 50 or 60 slaves to more than 150 slaves, and the number of coal mines in Virginia increased from about a dozen early in the nineteenth century to over two dozen by the 1830s. The eastern Virginia coalfields became one of Virginia's largest coal production centers and also one of the principal hirers of Virginia planters' superfluous slaves. Just before the Civil War, one Richmond-area operation alone wished "to hire for the year 1859, thirty or forty able-bodied Negro Men, for surface and underground operations, at Carbon Hill Mines in Henrico County"; Virginia coal operators as a whole employed a total of nearly two thousand slaves.[5]

In western Virginia, slave-mined coal sustained slave-mined salt. In 1836, 995 slaves were employed specifically to mine coal to fire salt companies' saline kilns. Salt production itself had been under way in Virginia since the late eighteenth century, especially in the Kanawha Valley and other Appalachian regions. Like other industrial enterprises that utilized hired slave labor, salt companies sent agents out to hire slaves for their works. Consequently, the slave population of Kanawha County rose from 352 in 1810 to 1,073 in 1820 and reached 1,717 by 1830. In 1850, 3,140 slaves were found in Kanawha County, more than half of whom were in the possession of salt companies. That year Dickinson & Shrewsbury, Kanawha County's largest employer of hired slaves in salt, held 232 slaves in its employ. Whites in salt enterprises preferred slave labor to fill their needs because of its relative cheapness and tractability and because a reliable supply of free labor was largely unavailable in any event. The majority of slaves who worked at Kanawha salt operations were hired slaves, because of the lower cost and the flexibility for annual labor needs relative to owned slaves. This was true even though hired slaves in salt commanded prices 25 to 30 percent higher than slaves hired in other Upper South concerns owing to the risk of accidents and escape to Ohio and the fact that salt manufacturers paid still higher rates for skilled and experienced hired slaves. Salt production in the Kanawha region totaled 3 million bushels per year by 1846, and a historian of antebellum Kanawha County salt production concludes that "the salt enterprise could not have expanded or flourished as it did without slave labor and the hire system." In short, slave hiring in the antebellum Virginia salt industry was extraordinarily effective and "suggests what might have occurred in southern Appalachian extractive industries had slavery continued to exist."[6]

From the 1830s through the Civil War, urban tobacco manufacturing was an important market for hired slaves, too, and many white Virginians hired out their slaves to process tobacco in tobacco factories in Richmond, Petersburg, Lynchburg, and Danville, among other places. Just before the Civil War, Richmond alone was home to forty-nine tobacco factories, employing some thirty-four hundred laborers, the vast majority of whom were slaves. Richmond tobacco manufacturers hired about half of the slaves who worked in their factories in 1850, and they hired some two-thirds of their slave-labor force in 1860. The scale of hired-slave employment in tobacco factories was such that hired slaves made up one-eleventh of Richmond's total population and one-seventh of the populations of Petersburg and Lynchburg. These figures do not include slaves hired by tobacco factories in Danville and other towns.[7]

Slave hiring was central to Virginia's urban development generally. Hired slaves in grain production, for example, enabled Richmond to become one of the largest flour- and grist-milling centers in the United States by the early nineteenth century, and the considerable shipping tonnage that wheat required also hastened the expansion of port facilities. These developments increased the demand for hired slaves to process, handle, and ship increasing quantities of grain in Virginia's eastern cities. Additionally, the urban white Virginians who exported grain and other agricultural products hired slaves to construct and repair their ships. In 1802 an Alexandria resident advertised his wish "to Purchase or Hire, For one or more years, or taken as Apprentice to the Sail Making Business, A young Negro Boy." Similarly, Portsmouth merchant and plantation owner Richard Blow hired slaves to work as caulkers on his vessels. Blow's copious records show that he hired slaves as vessel hands regularly from numerous slave owners during the 1780s. In the spring of 1785, for example, Blow paid Isaac Murray "two pounds five shillings in full for hire of negro George Caulking seven & half Days on [Blow's] ship." During the summer of 1786, Blow paid another slave owner "one pound nineteen shillings in full for 6 ½ days work caulking of [the slave owner's] fellow."[8]

Other whites in Virginia's growing cities, including carpenters, tailors, wagoners, and stone masons, hired slaves to assist them. In 1792 John Hall of the Norfolk-Portsmouth area "wanted on hire, by the year, a negro man, who perfectly understands the whole process of making bricks." "Good wages will be given for one that can be well recommended," Hall assured slave owners in his advertisement. Demand for skilled hired slaves in Virginia's cities enticed many slave owners to hire out their extra slaves as apprentices to acquire skills. Slave owner Henry Harrison, for example, wished to have his slave Bob instructed "in the art of shoe and boot making." Accordingly, Harrison hired out Bob, a boy, as an apprentice to Etheldread Evans for three years. In York County, William Macon hired out "Godfrey a Boy [to work] with Matthew Anderson of Richmond to learn the blacksmith trade." Both Macon and Anderson were satisfied, as the following year, Godfrey remained with Anderson "in Richmond on the same terms as the last year." Godfrey's sentiments are unknown. White Virginians found hired-slave apprenticeship mutually beneficial. White tradespeople acquired assistance and the opportunity to hold a slave, and slave owners who hired out surplus slaves as apprentices benefited at a later date when they hired out newly skilled slaves who commanded higher prices than unskilled hands.[9]

Transportation construction projects paralleled Virginia's urban development, and they absorbed whites' surplus slaves, too. Early in the nineteenth century, white Virginians pressed the state legislature for transportation infrastructure improvements to facilitate their grain shipments to Virginia's cities. In 1805 grain producers in Orange and Spotsylvania counties petitioned the legislature that they "Labor under many inconveniences and difficulties in travelling with their waggons and other carriages of burthen to their market Town [Fredericksburg]," a circumstance that they claimed was caused by "the badness of the roads, occasioned by the great number of Carriages which pass[ed]" upon them. Petitioners claimed that the lack of adequate transport facilities cost them one-third of their produce on the way to market.[10]

The petitioners' complaints were heard. Between 1802 and 1819, thirteen turnpike companies were incorporated to link rural Virginia farmers to markets in Fredericksburg, Alexandria, and Washington, and many of them hired farmers' slaves for construction and maintenance work. The Southwestern Turnpike Company, for example, hired all the slaves in its charge. The Swift Run Gap Turnpike Company, too, hired slaves from 1823 through 1833 to work on its road, which connected farmers in the hinterland town of Orange to the market town of Fredericksburg. The Swift Run Gap Turnpike Company normally spent several hundred dollars each year to hire slaves; it never owned any slaves outright. In Fairfax County, the Middle Turnpike Company, which gave farmers access to markets in Alexandria, also hired slaves in considerable numbers, and in 1832 "there were forty or fifty hands" at work on the company's sixteen-and-a-half-mile road. Many turnpike companies preferred to hire, rather than own, slaves because they repaired roads on a seasonal basis. Meanwhile, the Upper Appomattox Company worked to improve the Appomattox River. Like turnpike construction and maintenance, river-improvement projects became a market for Virginia farmers' surplus slaves. The Upper Appomattox Company owned several dozen slaves during the 1790s, but it also hired many slaves regularly beginning in 1797.[11]

River-improvement firms were the precursors of Virginia's nineteenth-century canal companies, which hired slaves for their operations, too. In January 1849 Cornelia Quarles of Halifax County hired out five slaves "to the Canal Company at one hundred dollars a piece." Quarles's slaves probably toiled on the James River and Kanawha Canal, which linked western Virginians to eastern Bay markets. Even after the main period of canal construction in Virginia ended, the James River and Kanawha Canal continued to hire slaves for its ongoing operations. James Harris, one of the James River and Kanawha Canal Company's agents in charge of hiring slaves for the company, reported in 1859 that the company offered $150 for "young able bodied men" and $120 for "old men as cooks."[12]

By the late antebellum period, railroad construction had become the most important of Virginia's transportation construction projects. Like turnpike and canal companies, Virginia's railroad companies hired slaves for construction, maintenance, and general operations. One white Virginian observed that work on the Richmond and York River Railroad would benefit from the proposed line's proximity to "Plenty [of] Corn & *Negroes*," and he boasted of his acquaintance "with nearly all the principal owners of negroes in [the] section of [the] county" where the railroad would be constructed. The Virginia and Tennessee Railroad, begun in January 1850, was one of Virginia's largest railroad-construction projects. Over a seven-year period, hundreds of hired slaves from farms and plantations across Virginia shoveled earth, built 233 bridges and 19 depots, blasted five tunnels, and laid 213 miles of track through the southwestern Virginia mountains. The hired slaves labored in contingents under white contractors in charge of particular sections of the line. An 1851 order for shoes and clothing reveals that contractor John Buford had charge of thirty hired slaves in his sector alone. During the 1850s, the railroad hired slaves year after year. At the end of 1854, slave owner David Clark assured Buford that "all the hands [he] ha[d] on the V[irgini]a & Tennessee RailRoad w[ould] again be for hire [at his] hiring" at Pittsylvania Courthouse for 1855. The railroad company approached slave owners, too, as when it offered one slave owner $150 for the hire of his slave Absalom, "to drive a team distributing ties on the Va & Tenn RR" in 1855. Many Virginians, in fact, hired out their slaves to the Virginia and Tennessee Railroad, as 435 labored on the line in 1856 alone.[13]

Hired slaves who labored in Virginia's industrial sectors found a wide range of living and working conditions. Many of the on-site shelters in which Virginia's rural industrial hired slaves were forced to live were of poor quality, as slave-hiring agent Hezekiah Ford noted in January 1852. "There is a great difference between hard work, through cold & hot wet & dry & living under a shantee," Ford observed, "and being provided with good lodging & kep'd in the house in bad wether." Ford's remarks underscore that hired slaves' material circumstances varied in accordance not only with hirers' whims and the depth of their pockets, but also with the nature of certain occupations. The temporary nature of internal improvements construction projects meant that hired slaves who constructed Virginia's railroad lines and turnpikes were afforded rudimentary shelter at best. A series of letters written by whites associated with railroad construction reveals that hired slaves along the lines had only shanties to protect them from the rain and other elements. "We have got all of our shanties done and nothing to do now but to go to work," T. W. Leftwich reported in 1854. Elsewhere, R. M. Burke noted shanties on his work site for hired slaves that stood between the railroad line and a hillside. Turnpike construction involved similar shelter conditions, so that a white agent employed at the site where the Middle Turnpike was constructed in Fairfax County reported about the slaves who worked there, "Several . . . were very ill, & some died, of the hands employed on . . . [the] road." Hired slaves who labored on public works projects had little choice but to accept the housing that was provided for them, sometimes at the risk of their health or their lives.[14]

In relative terms, hired slaves' living conditions in rural industries more permanent in nature were better than those on public works projects. The cabins for the more than one hundred laborers at an Orange County gold mine, for example, were described as "all in good order and new," and those at the Culpeper Gold Mine were "framed substantially, and clapboarded." Similarly, ironmaster William Weaver lodged his hired slaves in houses constructed of stone; hired slaves who worked in Virginia's coal mines, too, usually had housing of better quality than the temporary shanties in which hired slaves on public works projects were forced to reside.[15]

Yet even relatively adequate housing did not shield Virginia's hired slaves from the physical dangers inherent in industrial occupations. Virginia's fishing and water-transport businesses endangered hired slaves' lives by placing them near and on the water, where drowning was a danger. In 1853 William James hired out his slave Frank to Adam Keeling. The hiring agreement limited Frank's employment to "carting fish in & from the . . . county of Princess Anne from the beach the fishing grounds therein to the City of Norfolk," and hirer Keeling was not to employ Frank "in taking or hauling fish out of the water to wit in fishing." Nonetheless, Keeling "direct[ed] [Frank] to go on board [a] boat . . . upon the waters . . . during [a] severe . . . storm," whereby Frank "lost his life." Regardless of stipulations in the slave-hiring agreement, Frank was serving at the whim of a hirer who, having management of a slave, simply did as he pleased. Being a slave, Frank had little choice but to submit to the hirer and board the boat. The fact that many slave owners sought to assure that hirers would not employ their slaves at occupations that increased the likelihood of their drowning suggests that other hired slaves met with a similar fate. One slave owner's "Terms of Hiring" included the stipulation that his hired slaves be "restricted or prohibited from being worked . . . as Boatmen in the River," yet Frank's experience underscores that written prohibitions did not guarantee that a hirer would not employ slaves as boatmen. Similarly, when John Benthall hired out a slave in 1849, he reminded the hirer that the "negro is not to go by water"; this, too, however, was no guarantee of the hired slave's safety. Ultimately, hired slaves' deaths did not deter slave owners from hiring out their slaves in the vicinity of potential danger, and hirers, too, risked hired slaves' lives by placing them in dangerous occupations, owners' stipulations notwithstanding.[16]

Hired slaves worked at numerous other dangerous industrial occupations, too. In the salt-manufacturing sector, only slave coopers who constructed salt barrels escaped jobs that threatened their physical safety. For other hired slaves working in salt production, severe injury and death often resulted from coal-mine cave-ins, roof collapses, falling into machinery and heated brine, boiler explosions, and epidemics of Asiatic cholera brought to the Kanawha salt region by steamboat. Additionally, hired slaves tempted to flee to Ohio sometimes drowned in the Kanawha River. The wood-cutting business placed hired slaves in the vicinity of falling trees. In 1854 Jinnie Buford remarked that hirer "John Crenshaw has had bad luck—last Wednesday they were felling some trees & a tree fell on a [hired] boy named Washington & killed him instantly he belonged to *Mrs Boyd*." "Crenshaw came very near being killed himself," Buford added. Buford's emphasis upon a hirer's lost labor time as the consequence of a hired slave's death reveals that many whites valued hired slaves' lives solely in monetary terms.[17]

Hired-slave life insurance was a manifestation of the same view. The availability of life insurance for industrial hired slaves in Virginia testifies to the dangerous nature of their work, and it also reveals slave owners' willingness to hire out their slaves to hirers who would place them in dangerous situations or otherwise neglect and abuse them. Owners of slaves hired out to work on internal improvements projects, in particular, had the option of purchasing life insurance for their slaves for the duration of the year they were hired out. Railroad contractors who employed hired slaves, for example, used blasting powder to lay track through mountainous regions. In 1854 railroad contractor John Buford, who relied on hired-slave labor on a regular basis, was informed "that the Richmond [Fire Association] ... [would] insure negro fellows (rail Road hands) from 18 to 40 years of age to the amount of $600." Southampton County slave owner Samuel Drewry purchased such a policy for his slave Colonel, who was killed on the line of the Virginia and Tennessee Railroad in 1854, where Buford operated. Revealingly, a representative of the Richmond Fire Association later briefed

Buford on "what has been the practice of [his] office in the settlement of nearly 60 losses." Because of the demand for them, the Richmond Fire Association kept on hand a supply of preprinted life insurance policies for slaves, and other firms, including Knowles & Walford in Richmond, also advertised for sale "INSURANCE ON YOUR LIFE, Or the lives of your SERVANTS." Slave life insurance enabled Virginia slave owners to escape financial risk, which made them willing to risk the lives of the slaves they hired out.[18]

In 1853 a slave-hiring agent for a railroad contractor revealed that many Virginia slave owners were willing to hire out their slaves to work at dangerous occupations if they knew they would not incur monetary loss in the event that their slaves were killed. "[The slave owners] are unwilling, they say to put their hands on any Publick work unless there is a Guarantee for the value of the slave in case he should come to his death by being on such work." Even though slave owners saw "instances sufficient before them . . . [of] deaths by accidents &c," they felt it was acceptable to place their slaves in danger—so long as the slave owners themselves were not in financial danger. "[I]t is true," the same slave-hiring agent admitted, that "there has been several valuable servants killed on the Publick work . . . which h[as] brought about [slave owners'] state of feeling" the need for slave life insurance. On the one hand, slave owners were anxious about their slaves' welfare on internal improvements projects. "For the last two years . . . [at] the hireings," the agent observed, "the first thing done is to make [a] proclamation [that] no hand will be permitted to go on any Publick work," and he was "determined to do every thing in [his] power to do away [with] the prejudice now existing against hands being put on publick works." On the other hand, life insurance policies tempered slave owners' anxieties about sending their slaves to work on the internal improvements construction projects that proliferated across the Virginia landscape by the 1850s.[19]

Hired slaves who worked in coal mines, too, suffered injuries and death from the rock falls, flooding, fires, and explosions that occurred in the mines on a regular basis. Yet as with hired slaves in other industrial settings, slave owners simply sought to insure the lives of the slaves they hired out to the coal mines. Revealingly, however, insurance companies were reluctant to issue life insurance for slaves hired out to coal mines, which indicated just how dangerous the work was. Hired slaves themselves often tried to refuse to work in coal mines for precisely that reason (a circumstance not unlike that which David Ross encountered when slaves refused to enter an iron ore vein following the death of three other slaves in it from a rock fall). For slaves hired out to the coal mines against their wishes, escape remained one of the only viable alternatives; hired slaves ran away from the Black Heath Pits, for example, as well as from other Virginia coal mines, on a regular basis, a fact reflected routinely in newspapers. Yet despite reluctance of slave owners to hire out their slaves to coal mines, of the slaves themselves to go to the pits, and of insurance companies to insure hired slaves' lives, hired slaves remained the primary labor force in the coal mines of antebellum Virginia.[20]

Industrial hired slaves also faced danger in the form of work-site overseers, who, motivated by fear of lost time and money, worked hired slaves beyond their levels of endurance. One railroad contractor grew frustrated at not being permitted to work hired slaves as hard as he would have preferred, and he lodged his complaints to his associate in the fall of 1854. "I have Don every thing in my Power to forward the Work But all to no use," the contractor wrote, because a doctor, "Mr Leftwich Dont want me to Push the hands nor even make them Doo what every Industrious man would make them Doo." The contractor related his views about how hard the hired slaves should work, and he expressed his frustration with the idea that Dr. Leftwich's satisfaction with the hired slaves' work meant that he should be happy with it as well. "I have been rail Roding for some time," the contractor complained, and he insisted that his was "the Damdis managed Piece of work [he] ever was on or heard of any whare in all [his] life time." The contractor believed his hands were tied by Dr. Leftwich, who would not permit the hired slaves to "doo what [he told] them to Doo and what thay would Doo If [Leftwich] would let them aloan." "[T]he Doctor is a Disadvantage to the Work & spoils all the negroes," the contractor insisted to his associate, and he concluded that "if you had been hear In the Doctors Place we would [have] made some money But . . . I think that you all will be 4000 Dollars Behind." For many white supervisors of hired slaves, money brought white authority and power to the fore, and these together were harmful to hired slaves' welfare.[21]

Such was the experience of Stephen, who was hired out by John Reid to work on the Middle Turnpike Road in Fairfax County. Isaac Davis, an agent who worked on the road in close proximity to the slaves, was "constantly with" Stephen on the turnpike, and Davis once witnessed a confrontation between Stephen and one of the overseers. According to Davis, Stephen was "very insulting to Thompson Wright one of the overseers." As a result, Stephen was "moderately chastised with [illegible], Chesnut & maple switches." Davis quickly added that "Neither a Cowhide nor a hickory was used." He then admitted that both "Corbin Darnes & Gunnell Darnes [also] saw [Stephen] whipped," but Davis himself concluded that Stephen "was not whipped half enough I thought for such an offence." Davis's view is significant, particularly given another person's description of Stephen's condition following the whipping: "[Stephen's] whole back was intirely skin'd [from] his shoulders to his hips, and in a high state of inflamation, and his body in bandage from his shoulders to his hips," the witness observed, "and Dr Milles who was then in attendance on Step[h]en, gave it as his oppinion that one or two or more of his ribs was broken, which caused the bandage to be applyed." Like other hired slaves under the control of several different whites, including owners, hirers, agents, urban factory overseers and other nearby whites, Stephen worked under the eyes of white agents, overseers, and other whites who were present, some of whom whipped Stephen while the others observed white punishment of a hired slave in action.[22]

Virginia whites' drive for profits often fueled their desire to whip industrial hired slaves, and as a result many suffered injury or death in hirers' employ. Because hirers and their agents lacked long-term interest in slaves' welfare, they focused solely on profits during the period when hired slaves worked at their sites. For such whites, profit or loss was determined by the amount of labor they could derive from a hired slave within the space of time they hired that slave, and the amount of labor they could extract was determined by the degree of power they asserted over hired slaves in their charge. In the end, white hirers' compulsion of hired slaves was necessary to make money, illuminated the meaning and prerogatives of whiteness in a slave society, and underscored whites' expectation of hired slaves' complete obedience. The fact that the slaves were industrial hired slaves, as opposed to agricultural hired slaves or nonhired slaves, did not eliminate those expectations.

Many southern industrialists, however, emphasized positive incentives over force (although the threat of it remained) to compel hired slaves to work and to control them generally. This was especially important for industrialists, who, being hirers of slaves, were unable to use the threat of sale as a means of coercion. The most widely used incentive was the task system and overwork payments, whereby industrialists paid hired slaves in their employ for work done beyond a specified quota, or task. Overwork payments made to industrial hired slaves were in the form of cash, credit for merchandise, or time off, and the practice was utilized by southern industrialists beginning in the eighteenth century. Both task and overwork payment rates varied from one industrialist to another. Tobacco factory hands who worked beyond a daily task of forty-five pounds of tobacco earned overwork payments ranging from a few dollars per week to considerably more; enslaved coopers in the salt industry received ten cents for each salt barrel they made beyond a forty-two-barrel weekly task; coal-pit hands near Richmond made from twelve to fourteen dollars' overwork income per year; and hired slaves in the iron industry earned overwork payments of hundreds of dollars per year. Very often, hired slaves' overwork earnings were comparable to pay earned by free laborers engaged in the same occupation. Some slaves hired out to industrial operations even supplemented overwork money from their employer if they happened to have been hired out to an industry located in the vicinity of local whites who wished to hire them for special tasks. In eastern Orange County, for example, slaves hired out to gold mines also were hired by area whites to dig ditches.[23]

The task system was central to the success of Kanawha County's salt manufacturers. Both owned and hired slaves in the salt industry were given overwork incentives for labor performed on Sundays, a practice that became customary; they were also paid for work done in the evening and during the Christmas period. Thomas Friend, for example, paid between $1,200 and $1,482 in overwork to between thirty-five and forty slaves each year for five years. As in other industries, overwork payments made to slaves in the salt sector assumed the form of cash or store credit for goods. The fact that some salt firms sometimes ran twenty-four hours per day and seven days per week made overwork payments to slaves essential to ongoing operations. Like other industrial concerns that hired slaves, the salt industry's task system and overwork payments made slavery there different from slavery in other settings, but they also made the salt firms very successful precisely because incentives were a part of "the effective functioning of a hire system."[24]

In the Valley of Virginia, ironmaker William Weaver relied heavily on the task system and overwork payments as a labor incentive for the slaves he hired, too. Like other southern industrialists, Weaver hoped overwork payments would make the slaves less inclined to run away or engage in acts of sabotage and more inclined to return to work for him the following hiring year. Such a hired-slave labor force, Weaver reasoned, would assure an amount and quality of work that would facilitate successful competition with other ironmasters and return a handsome profit, without reliance on the whip as a means of control.

The slaves employed at Weaver's operation earned overwork payments by laboring beyond their minimum task, often on Sundays and in evenings, and spent the payments as they chose. Many of Weaver's hired slaves put their overwork credit toward coffee, tobacco, sugar, molasses, and flour, as well as cloth, boots, linen, and other apparel. Others took their overwork in cash or used some of it to purchase time off, in addition to their food and clothing purchases.

In some cases, the slaves at Weaver's place supplemented their overwork receipts by selling livestock and crops they raised themselves. The results were impressive. Slave refiner Phill Easton and his assistants divided up among themselves eight dollars' overwork per ton of iron, the same rate received by white workers; he made additional cash by selling calves and placed still more money to his credit in Weaver's books by declining Weaver's clothing allotment. Ultimately, Easton earned between twenty and thirty dollars in overwork credit each year during the 1830s, with which he purchased coffee, sugar, clothing, and things for his home. He also took cash in order to shop in local stores with his wife, Betsy, at Christmastime. Easton was one of Weaver's own slaves, yet the hired slaves who worked for Weaver took advantage of the opportunity to earn overwork payments, too. Absolom, Jim Derest, Jack Holmes, and Major Watson, all hired slaves who worked for Weaver, earned overwork through the performance of a variety of chores and Sunday work, supplemented it by raising and selling crops and livestock, and took it in the form of clothing and cash. Weaver paid hired slaves what was due them before they departed at the close of the hiring year, which meant that they, like Weaver's own slaves who remained behind, had cash to spend on themselves and their families at Christmastime.

The significance of overwork payments cannot be overemphasized. For some hired slaves, the opportunity to enjoy things like coffee and tobacco made their extra labor worthwhile. For others, the chance to buy particular items of food and clothing that suited their tastes and preferences seemed like rewards for their hard work. Also, overwork money enabled hired slaves to buy things for their families, such as gifts during the Christmas season, when hired slaves returned to their families for a brief period at the end of the hiring year. Most significantly, overwork payments enabled hired slaves to retain some human dignity, pride, independence, manhood, and self-esteem within the context of their enslavement. These purely human characteristics derived, for example, from the personal discretion inherent in hired slaves' purchases of luxuries for themselves and from being able to buy the clothes in which they were married. Also, for enslaved husbands and fathers within a system in which slave owners provided food, clothing, and, perhaps, occasional gifts, overwork payments offered the opportunity to be the providers of those things for their families and so feel more like men in their own homes than slaves. The same sense doubtless emerged from hired slaves' very decision to perform overwork to begin with, a decision entirely theirs concerning the use of time also entirely theirs. Finally, it could not have been lost on hired slaves that their own work done on their own time was compensated at the same rate as white men's work at similar tasks and that the white men who hired them often owed them money.[25]

Overwork payments were made to industrial hired slaves in Virginia's cities, too. There, however, the characteristics of certain industries combined with peculiarities of urban slavery itself to create an environment in which hired slaves had opportunities to employ overwork payments to assert their humanity in a wider variety of ways. Because Virginia's tobacco-processing industry, for example, was located in cities like Richmond, among others, it lacked space on its premises to house the hired slaves in its employ. Consequently, in addition to overwork payments they made to hired slaves, tobacco factories gave them board money with which to find their own food and lodging elsewhere in the city. This meant that, unlike hired slaves who worked in rural industries, who experienced greater white scrutiny and no discretion as to accommodations, industrial hired slaves in Virginia's cities lived out apart from both owner and hirer once their work was done for the day; they traveled to their own place of lodging somewhere else in the city and returned to work the next morning.[26]

Hired slaves like Ezekiel sometimes used the opportunity offered by urban Virginia's living-out system to roam about Richmond before going to their rooms to retire for the evening. After the "manufactory of tobacco" where Ezekiel worked closed for the day, he wandered about for several hours during the evening, probably shopping or socializing with family and friends. Ezekiel was seen at ten o'clock one evening "at the corner of main & 21st street, crossing the street," a spot several blocks from the place where he slept. Presumably, Ezekiel returned eventually to where he "live[d] at W[illia]m Freeman's on Franklin [Street] between 17th & 18th Streets, [as he] never sle[pt] at the factory, but had a monthly pass to go to Mr. Freeman's house." Ezekiel and other hired slaves also frequented the shops that sprang up to cater to their wants and needs. Significantly, some of those shops were operated by other hired slaves. In 1853, for instance, "Jack, a negro, the property of William Lumpkin, and hired to T. C. Baptist . . . [kept] a cook-shop on Cary street, contrary to law." Many hired slaves must have taken meals and shared conversations at Jack's place, since "the evidence showed Jack had been for years engaged at his unlawful business." Some hired slaves with cash spent it on drinking and gambling, too. Other hired slaves who worked in urban industries used their off time and cash to purchase a wide array of personal items in shops about the city. Hired slave Ryland, for instance, spent a Saturday evening off from the tobacco factory where he worked to go to the shop of Moses Pike, where he inquired about "some cheap suspenders."[27]

Opportunities to wander about, visit, and go shopping doubtless made Ezekiel, Jack, and Ryland feel more like men than slaves. The enhanced sense of human dignity that hired slaves derived from overwork payments in industries everywhere in Virginia may have been greatest among tobacco-factory workers in the cities. Those hired slaves' capacity to move about in the evening gave them a greater degree of discretion in items purchased, lodging and meals selected, and places frequented. Such hired slaves who were able to walk about the city, especially, were accustomed to doing as they pleased with the money they had earned through their own labor and so became inclined to do as they pleased generally. Indeed,

Richmond City court records reveal that many hired slaves who worked in Virginia's tobacco factories manifested a considerable amount of independence in their actions and interactions with whites on the job, not just on city streets in the evenings. Overwork payments and other "various indulgencies augmented the problem of discipline," as Joseph Robert put it several decades ago, that is, they instilled in the hired slaves of the tobacco factories a sense of self-importance and independence that whites deemed intolerable. Consequently, hired-slave self-esteem often met with white factory overseers' threats and violence.[28]

In Richmond, hired slave William was too proud to carry out every order of white men in the factory where he worked, but he discovered that white men would not put up with independent attitudes on the part of slaves. William's trouble began when his "habit of getting drunk and neglecting his work" in a Richmond factory captured the attention of his overseer. One day in 1852, the overseer scolded William "and ordered him to go to his work." William went to his assigned place, "but instead of doing his work, he laid down the work and went away from the shop." When the next day the overseer demanded to know why William had not done the work he had been ordered to do, William "replied, that he did not feel like it," whereupon the overseer told William that "he would make him feel like it." William asked the overseer what he intended to do about the matter, and the overseer replied "that he meant to whip him." William refused to allow the overseer to whip him, and he "took up a poker" in his defense. The owner of the place then appeared, who, together with the overseer, took the poker from William. William then picked up a knife and began to stab the overseer with it. At length, the men overpowered William, threw him to the ground, and tied him up until a police officer appeared and took him into custody. In October William was "Tried, convicted, & sentenced to be sold & transported beyond [the] U[nited] States." As a hired slave in a tobacco factory, William earned overwork money to spend, and he had the opportunity to move about and spend it as he pleased. The overwork payments, board money, and mobility led him to think highly enough of himself to decide when he would and would not work, even to refuse to suffer a whipping. But when urban industrial hired slaves like William refused to do what whites told them to do and instead assaulted them, they were punished for doing so, much as agricultural hired slaves and nonhired slaves were punished for similar infractions.[29]

In another situation also in Richmond, hired slave Benjamin chose to report to work at a factory "after eight oclock, which was an hour later than usual." Indignant at Benjamin's tardiness, a factory overseer ordered Benjamin to set to work, but Benjamin "refused and complained of being sick." Benjamin ignored the overseer's order to procure medicine, refused to begin his work, and "spoke very insolently" to the overseer, who threatened to beat Benjamin with a poker if he did not get about his business. The overseer swung the poker at Benjamin, who blunted the blow with his hand "and instantly struck [the overseer] on the head with [a] stone" about four inches in diameter. The overseer then retreated from the room, and another overseer appeared in response to the commotion. Benjamin struck the second overseer twice with his stone and then made his escape by jumping from the second story of the factory. Here, too, an urban, industrial hired slave with overwork and board money had developed sufficient self-assurance to show up for work when he pleased and to ignore whites' orders. Ultimately, however, Benjamin discovered that whites refused to tolerate slaves of his sort, who did not behave as they believed slaves ought to behave.[30]

William, another industrial hired slave in Richmond, also illustrates the tension between hired-slave self-esteem and white authority, and the violence that often resulted. Owned by James Gentry of Hanover County, William was hired out to work in a Richmond factory. Although the factory's rules prohibited slaves from leaving the factory without permission, William walked out without leave one Saturday in 1847. When he returned, Eliasa Cox, one of the whites in charge of the factory, told William "that if he went out again without leave, he would whip him." William remained undeterred, for two days afterward, he again left the factory without permission. Fifteen minutes later, William returned and was confronted by Cox, who "asked [William] who told him to go out," to which William replied, "No one." Cox then asked William why he went out, and William "replied that he would go out when he *damned* pleased." Cox then slapped William, who "took up a knife" in response. In the struggle that ensued, William lost the knife, and Cox reiterated to William "that if he ever went out again without leave, he would give him a whipping." But that did not end the confrontation, because William responded "that no one in that house should whip him." Cox then "took [William] by the collar," and William again grabbed the knife. William wielded his knife several times at Cox, who then chased William downstairs and out into the street. Outside, William "wheeled round and struck at [Cox] again with the knife." Cox then stepped back, William ran ahead, and Cox resumed the chase. William took one final swing at Cox before he ran away, after which Cox quit his pursuit. William's positive view of himself, along with his actions reflecting it, were rooted in his receipt of overwork payments and board money and in his being accustomed to moving about during his off hours. Specifically, William's determination to come and go as he pleased, along with his refusal to be whipped, were manifestations of his own sentiment that he was a human being, no less so than persons who believed they had the right to whip him solely because they happened to be white. Indeed, William's feelings were not unlike those of a hired slave elsewhere hired out to Moses McKenny. When McKenny threatened to whip the hired slave for "behave[ing] himself in a very impudent and refractory manner," the hired slave declared that "no man should whip him that he was as good a man as another and wou[l]d suffer no correction from [McKenny]." For some Virginia whites, including tobacco factory overseers and McKenny, hired slaves' sense of human dignity represented the greatest challenge to their attempts to control them.[31]

Although many urban Virginia hired slave men who worked in tobacco factories had chances to acquire self-esteem by moving about and spending their cash at their discretion, their status as slaves still imposed strict boundaries on their actions and behaviors, boundaries drawn and maintained by the power of all whites. As the court papers themselves indicate, the significant factor in William's case was that he was a slave who physically assaulted a white person. "William, a Slave," the papers show, was "convicted of criminal assault on a white person, & sentenced to 39 lashes" by the Richmond City Hustings Court. The fact that William happened to have been a *hired* slave meant nothing. As Joseph Robert has shown, hired-slave altercations with white tobacco factory overseers were a relatively common occurrence, and they typically resulted in court-ordered whippings of the slaves in question. Additionally, even though they were permitted to move about either for occupational responsibilities or to go home in the evening, the tobacco factories' hired slaves (and other urban hired slaves) still had to have a pass to do so, much as nonhired slaves required a pass to travel about. Also like nonhired slaves everywhere, urban hired slaves who ventured about without permission or who were otherwise "insolent" or shirked their work risked severe punishment at the hands of whites in factories and at the public whipping post.[32]

The employment of hired slaves in cities raises a question about slave hiring that has been long debated among historians. That question is whether slavery was viable in urban settings, given slave hiring's pervasiveness and hired slaves' manifestations of independence in cities. More specifically, did facets of urban slave hiring such as self-hire, freedom of movement, and living out represent slavery's adaptability to a city environment, or did they signal slavery's disarray and imminent collapse in urban centers? Did slave hiring strengthen urban slavery or weaken it? Among historians who contend that slavery was incompatible with cities is Richard C. Wade. In his study of slavery in southern urban centers, Wade maintains that urban slavery had undergone a general decline by the close of the antebellum period, not from a lack of work for slaves but because of whites' fear of large numbers of hired slaves wandering about the streets after work. Urban white Virginians' fear of slaves roaming in their midst was reflected in legislation passed to limit hired slaves' autonomous activities, especially their self-hiring, their assembly with other slaves, and their operation of shops. Yet to argue that urban whites' fear of slaves was a manifestation of slavery's disintegration in cities, one also must argue that slavery was decaying everywhere across the South and always had been decaying everywhere across the South, because whites always had feared their slaves. The argument that slavery was dying during the course of its entire existence, is, of course, untenable.[33]

Historian Claudia Goldin concludes that any apparent decline of slavery in cities owed not to whites' fear, as Wade argues, but primarily to an elasticity of demand for slave labor in cities. Competition for hired slaves among urban and rural sectors during the antebellum period drove slave-hire rates upward, inducing some urban employers to switch to cheaper white labor. This view squares with the fact that the decline in numbers of slaves, which Wade emphasizes was *relative* to the white population, was not a decline in *absolute* numbers of slaves.[34]

By all indications, slavery in antebellum Richmond was not declining at all. On the one hand, increased employment of white northern and foreign-born workers relative to slave labor in some aspects of the iron industry during the 1850s reflected rising slave prices and concern about white workers' animosity at the use of slave labor in any event. On the other hand, however, Richmond's elite groups as a whole "believed deeply in slavery," writes a historian of Richmond, and in 1850 more than 80 percent of them owned slaves. Additionally, Richmond's tobacco factories hired thousands of slaves each year from the adjacent countryside. Specifically, like other Virginia cities, Richmond was linked to hinterlands tied to slavery, and its factories employed rural hired slaves to process the products that slave labor produced in surrounding rural areas. Use of slave labor in households, too, was widespread, and Richmond also was a major center of the domestic slave trade. Ultimately, Richmond slavery "was never more profitable than in the economy of the 1850s," and for all these reasons, Richmond occupied a "critical position as a nexus of slavery." Fully aware of slavery's importance to their city, white Richmond residents, both native-born and foreign-born, professed the superiority of slave labor over free labor and, like their rural counterparts, were sensitive to criticisms of the institution. Perhaps the clearest indication that slavery meshed very well with Richmond is that the city witnessed a constant increase in its slave population throughout the forty-year period 1820–60.[35]

Slavery flourished in antebellum Richmond and other Virginia cities also because legislation designed to curtail hired slaves' activities, especially their moving about the city, was ignored widely. The hired slaves themselves ignored such laws, of course. Significantly, however, the legislation also was scarcely observed by whites, whose operations benefited economically from widespread slave hiring, including the tobacco factories, which employed hired slaves in large numbers. Those whites' economic interests squared off against other whites' fear of hired slaves when Richmond tobacco manufacturers united in opposition to the outlawing of the board system, whereby tobacco factories' hired slaves found food and lodging on their own. Richmond authorities tried to require the tobacco factories to provide lodging for the hired slaves in their employ, to prevent slaves from wandering about the city, but the tobacco factories refused to do so on the grounds that such a requirement would cut into their profits. Although a law mandating hired-slave lodging eventually was passed over the resistance of tobacco factories when they were weakened by the Panic of 1857, it, like other laws designed to control hired slaves in the city, was ignored. In the end, some urban whites' drive for hired-slave-based profit won out over other urban whites' fears of hired slaves. A historian of slavery in Richmond summarizes the situation: "City authorities' efforts to regulate slaves both on and off the job often were unpopular with owners and employers, whose ability to conduct slave transactions was threatened. As a result, Richmond authorities found themselves in the awkward position of trying to preserve slave discipline in ways that conflicted with the economic interests of local residents and businesses who owned or hired slaves."[36]

Furthermore, tobacco factories do not encompass the whole story of hired slaves in Virginia cities. Specifically, gender is almost entirely absent from most studies of slave hiring's impact on the viability of slavery in cities. Historians have debated the question of slave hiring and slavery in cities in terms of wandering hired slaves and in terms of slavery as an institution related to urbanization and industrialization as abstract processes of growth and development. These two arguments rest implicitly and exclusively on *male* hired slaves, for it was they, for the most part, who moved about the streets and elicited white urbanites' fears, and it was they, for the most part, who labored in the industrial sector.

Claudia Goldin's consideration of all urban slaves, rather than only males, makes her argument about urban slavery the most plausible. Goldin rejects "push factors" (forces that might have pushed slaves out of cities), such as urban whites' fears, to explain the relative decline of slavery in some cities, because of the apparent selectivity of urban slavery's supposed decline. Specifically, Goldin shows that the slaves who remained in cities were primarily skilled men and women, precisely the slaves in high demand there. Her observation refers to what is largely absent from other historians' arguments: the presence of literally thousands of hired female house servants in cities. These women were hired slaves in cities, yet they are scarcely considered in the scholarly debate about slave hiring's impact on the viability of slavery in cities. The terms of the debate about slave hiring and urban slavery's viability, then, have been imprecise, because they have excluded a significant proportion of the hired slaves—almost half, in the case of Richmond in 1860. The slavery-in-cities debate must encompass all demand for urban slave labor, that is, demand for hired female house servants who labored in urban whites' private homes as well as for the men who worked in tobacco factories. The demand for female hired-slave house servants was not seasonal. Rather, urban white Virginia residents' desire for hired female house servants was prompted by a rise in per-capita income among white residents of southern urban centers during the antebellum period, white residents who made a conscious choice to hire female slave house servants. Consideration of these slave women illuminates another way in which slavery in Richmond and other Virginia cities was strengthened by slave hiring, not weakened because of it.[37]

Outside the cities, industrial slave hiring strengthened antebellum Virginia slavery, too. The Virginia and Tennessee Railroad, for example, continued to hire Virginia farmers' surplus slaves for regular operations and maintenance following its construction in the 1850s. Just before Virginia seceded from the Union, an agent for the Virginia and Tennessee Railroad informed a slave owner about the railroad's ongoing slave-hiring activities. "This Company hires about 400 hands annually," the Virginia and Tennessee official wrote in December 1860, "and will not get through hiring before the 5th of [January]" 1861. "We do not want old hands as the service requires active young men," he went on, and he noted that the railroad had "been paying for *depot hands* from 120 to 135 dollars, for hands for road repairs from 130 to 145 dollars, and for wood train hand[s] from 140 to 150 dollars." The Virginia Central Railroad hired almost three hundred slaves for work on its line. The hired slaves performed manual labor, and they also worked as firemen, brakemen, and boilermakers and in other capacities.[38]

The Virginia and Tennessee Railroad's significance for antebellum Virginia slavery cannot be overemphasized. In addition to its creation of a tremendous demand for hired slaves from across Virginia, the Virginia and Tennessee Railroad connected southwestern Virginians with distant urban markets, which furthered the development of slave-based agriculture in the southwestern mountains. This is seen clearly in increases in tobacco production over the ten-year period before secession and the Civil War. From an output of 107,720 pounds of tobacco in 1850, southwest Virginia's production of the leaf soared to 2,284,167 pounds by 1860. Ultimately, in many of Virginia's southwestern counties, numbers of both slaveholders and slaves increased between 1850 and 1860. On his way back up the mountains from Tennessee, Frederick Olmsted noticed the changes. "There are more slaves here than I have seen before for several weeks," Olmsted noted near the southwest Virginia town of Abington. Olmsted was right. Hired slaves built the railroad, which then led more white Virginians in the railroad's vicinity to want slave labor. The construction and ongoing operation of the Virginia and Tennessee Railroad alone, therefore, coupled with increased demands for slave labor in its vicinity following its completion, allowed Virginia slave owners to hire out several hundred slaves each year within Virginia rather than sell them to the Lower South.[39]

The Virginia and Tennessee Railroad's fortification of slavery in southwest Virginia occurred precisely when east-west sectionalism in Virginia politics reached a peak. Intrastate sectionalism in Virginia swirled around the issue of legislative apportionment. During the early nineteenth century, legislative apportionment was tipped in favor of eastern elites, who held more slaves and other property than did people in the western portions of Virginia. The westerners demanded representation along the lines of, as one historian puts it, "one-white-man, one vote," in sharp contrast to traditional eighteenth-century republicanism (favored by easterners), wherein the propertied, and hence virtuous, ruled over the nonpropertied, and hence selfish and nonvirtuous, among them. Sustained by eighteenth-century republicanism, some (eastern Virginia) whites' power over some other (western Virginia) whites, as well as over all blacks, characterized Virginia politics for much of the antebellum period. This circumstance fostered resentment among white westerners, which in turn led to uneasiness among white easterners, who worried whether white westerners would always support slavery.

In 1851 resentments and uneasiness were tempered when a constitutional convention established universal white male suffrage and one-white-man, one vote apportionment in the lower house of the Virginia legislature. Significantly, however, white easterners retained control of the upper house and so remained in a position to thwart their greatest fear: any future white western attempts at abolitionism in the form of legislation crafted to tax white easterners' slaves out from under them. But the Virginia and Tennessee Railroad also helped to ease east-west tension because it brought more slaves to the west, increased tobacco production in the west, and connected westerners commercially to easterners with new access to eastern markets like Richmond. By the 1850s, western white Virginians resembled eastern white Virginians in that all white males among them had a vote and in that their lives centered increasingly around slavery. Ultimately, the hired-slave-built Virginia and Tennessee Railroad and the increase in tobacco and slaves that the railroad brought to southwest Virginia linked southwest Virginia to disunionist elements by the end of the 1850s. As one historian writes, it was "just in time for secession and war."[40]

Hired slaves' construction of railroads elsewhere in Virginia also enhanced slavery's importance in areas near the lines. Completion of the Richmond and Danville Railroad increased the slave population in the southwest piedmont and near Richmond, where the line ran, and the Virginia Central Railroad led to a 10 percent increase in the slave populations of four counties in the Shenandoah Valley. Completion of the Northwestern Railroad, too, resulted in slave population increases in several counties along its line.[41]

White Virginians recognized that railroads benefited agriculture and slavery in their neighborhoods. In Fauquier County, Edward Turner, a stout supporter of the Manassas Gap Railroad, gave a speech in support of the railroad in 1850, telling his neighbors "of all the advantages which must accrue from a liberal system of publick works":

> You who have more property than you know what to do with, and who have vainly sought for years to sell . . . your lands will come instantly into market and will be sold at high prices to the hoards of settlers who will scatter themselves along the line asking only a few acres upon which to build their fortunes. . . . the road . . . will enable you to turn to some account the corn & oats . . . which now lie mouldering in your barns a shelter . . . for rats & all manner of vermin. [As to] the transportation of heavy articles particularly, to and from market—I will only remind you of the difference between 16 & 75 cents of carriage for forty miles on a barrel of flour . . . and between 5 & 17 cts on a bushel of wheat. Go home and make for yourselves the calculations.

Although he did not use the specific words, Turner and those who heard him knew that the railroad meant hired slaves and slavery generally, the foundation of their new prosperity. Turner continued:

Nor are you required to wait for the completion of the road before you begin to reap the fruits of the enterprise, but as soon as the work begins thousands of men & horses will be brought into the country to carry it on, which, men and horses must be fed & you will become their feeders. All your surplus corn and oats and hay & potatoes & every thing else, which, has hitherto been comparatively useless will find a cash market in your midst, and as hundreds of dollars will be daily spent among you, you will be better off than ever you were before in your lives. . . . give us the road, and the plow will start again an increasing demand for labour will spring up, and in proportion to the demand must be the rise in price. . . . give us a market for the various kinds of produce with which our country abounds, and there would be no more croaking about hard times.

Elsewhere, a Virginian acquainted with plans for work on another railroad pointed out more succinctly a railroad's impact on markets for agricultural products and hired-slave labor. Specifically, the Virginian noted the proposed railroad's proximity to "Plenty [of] *Corn & Negroes*," and he boasted of his acquaintance "with nearly all the principal owners of negroes in [the] section of [the] county" where the railroad would be constructed. It seemed the wave of the future: hired slaves would build the railroads that would connect farmers to distant markets and bring them prosperity. Ultimately, Turner felt proud of his effective railroad boostering by the end of 1850, as he once made a point to note in his diary that he saw "hands engaged in excavating the rail road (Manasseh's)." By 1860 Virginia had nearly eighteen hundred miles of railroads in operation, more than any other southern state and over three hundred miles more than second-ranked Georgia.[42]

Turner's predictions about railroads' benefits were correct. By the 1850s the completion of several rail lines in Virginia coincided with a dramatic surge in the prices of tobacco, wheat, and corn. The railroads so reduced transport costs that Virginia farmers shipped more of their products, more cheaply, to Virginia's growing urban centers. And although the prices of Virginia's agricultural products fluctuated during the 1850s, the trend was upward. With increased production and higher prices, farm income soared. Daniel Cobb noted in 1857, "Farmers produce all high at this time," and in December he observed the general trends in his area: "Grate many sales and property sells high with 6 or 9 months Credit . . . land negrows & other property." Cobb felt so assured of future prosperity that he went "to Sussex

Corte to a negrow sale," where he bought himself a slave for nine hundred dollars. Several years earlier, in economic hard times, Cobb had not been confident enough to hire a slave.[43]

Good fortune came to Edward Turner, too. His confidence, like Cobb's, was manifested by slave purchases in 1850, and Turner did not fail to recognize the sharp contrast between his circumstances in 1850 and those of several years earlier: "Kerby gets home with the servants—Jack a man 35 years of age, for whom I pay $605 seems to be an excellent hand & bears a good character—Eliza is 21 years old, very likely & *efficient* & of good character—I pay for her $630—We had long needed such servants but have never before been in a situation to purchase."[44]

Earlier in the antebellum period, Cobb and Turner had weathered economic depression with slave hiring's help. Specifically, slave hiring enabled Cobb to reduce the size of his slave labor force, and slave hiring allowed Turner to avoid having to purchase a slave outright. In short, slave hiring offered white Virginians like Cobb and Turner annual flexibility in the size of their labor force to cope with economic fluctuations. Consequently, slave hiring assured that Cobb, Turner, and slavery survived in Virginia. In the 1850s, prosperity replaced the dismal economic prospects that had plagued Cobb, Turner, and other white Virginians. This prosperity, too, arrived with, and was sustained by, slave hiring's assistance, since hired slaves had built the railroads upon which the economic good times were based. Virginians then produced more crops because they could ship them more cheaply on those railroads to distant markets where they sold them for higher prices. And in those urban markets other hired slaves processed those products. White Virginians thereby made more money, with which to acquire more slaves, to produce more crops, whose prices increased during the 1850s, and so on. By the 1850s, then, white Virginians like Cobb and Turner cherished expectations of a bright future built upon slave hiring and slavery generally. White Virginians' optimism also was fueled by the Virginia economy's tremendous demand for hired-slave labor. The agricultural, industrial, and urban sectors of Virginia's economy competed fiercely for the slaves white Virginians wished to hire out. Ultimately, this competition contributed to a surge in slave-hire rates before the Civil War, and that increase encouraged many white Virginians to hire out their slaves in Virginia rather than sell them to the Lower South.

There was less competition for slave labor within Delaware and Maryland, Virginia's Upper-South neighbors, than in Virginia. This owed primarily to geographical factors that precluded the scale of transportation infrastructure construction that had helped to create and sustain competition for hired slave labor in Virginia. Delaware's relatively small size, coupled with its encirclement by water on one side, Pennsylvania on another side, and Maryland on two other sides, meant that internal improvements construction of the magnitude carried out in Virginia was not possible there. As for canals and river improvements, Delaware built only the Chesapeake and Delaware, a project just over twelve miles in length. As for railroads, Delaware constructed only 39.19 miles from 1850 through 1853. Thereafter, Delaware added only a few miles per year each year through 1860, when it recorded a total of only 136.69 miles of railroads in operation, the lowest mileage of all the Middle Atlantic states.

Maryland outpaced Delaware to some extent, yet its internal improvements record as a whole also paled alongside that of Virginia. Although Maryland had more mileage than Virginia in river improvements and canals (229.5 miles as compared with 196.98 miles), Maryland's railroad construction lagged far behind Virginia's. The gap became especially pronounced during the 1850s, when railroad construction overshadowed other forms of internal improvements construction. In 1851 Maryland had a total of 274.26 miles of railroad in operation, as compared with Virginia's 652.44 the same year. By 1856, while Maryland's railroad's mileage stood at 326.80 miles, white Virginians' hired slaves had placed 1,531.17 miles of operating rail throughout the countryside. The trend continued through the eve of secession, as Maryland's construction totaled only 380.30 miles of track by 1860. Virginia, by contrast, had a total of 1,771.16 miles of railroad in operation in 1860, more than four times the mileage of Maryland.[45]

Whereas geography prevented considerable internal improvements construction in Delaware and Maryland, it was precisely the factor that permitted Virginia to undertake an enormous internal improvements program. Virginia had hundreds of miles of territory to the west, territory in which to build canals and railroads, such as the James River and Kanawha Canal and the Virginia and Tennessee Railroad. These industrial projects demanded hired-slave labor for construction and ongoing operations, and they created competition for hired-slave labor among all economic sectors.

Delaware and Maryland, which did not have such a large amount of internal improvements construction, were not characterized by the level of demand and competition for hired-slave labor that developed in Virginia, a circumstance that increased slave-hire rates and so persuaded Virginia slave owners to hire out their surplus slaves within Virginia rather than sell them to the Lower South.

The often distinctive nature of urban and industrial slave hiring sometimes presented hired slaves with opportunities to enlarge their autonomy, discretion, and self-esteem, and it sometimes subjected them to hirers' profit-motivated exploitation. As in other settings, then, hired slaves' experiences in cities and industries were no less varied and changing than was Virginia's economy itself, marked at once by industries, cities, and agriculture; it was an economy that slaves' labor was central to developing. In short, slave hiring was everywhere in Virginia, and it placed both Virginia whites and Virginia slavery on a steady course toward the future.

CHAPTER 7

SLAVE HIRING AND SLAVERY

Slave hiring's strengthening of, and inherency to, Virginia slavery was evident throughout the antebellum period. In the years leading up to secession and war, Virginia whites used slave hiring to derive maximum returns from their slaves within the contexts of economic diversification and a rapidly increasing slave population prevalent across Virginia. In 1846 one slave owner asked a prospective slave hirer whether he would hire a slave woman as a house servant, since the slave owner "had too many about the house and . . . must hire some of them out." In 1854 southeast Virginia slave owner Samuel Drewry informed a railroad contractor of "the surplus of labour we have here." Fanny Ewing told the hirer of her slave Mary, "It is impossible for [Mary] to live at home as we are already overrun with servants." Alexander Findlay implored William Gray to find something to keep one of his slaves occupied: "If you can find anything for Maria to do at your house I would prefer you should take her home & employ her at it." "Place [Maria] some where that she can be doing something," Findlay continued, "as I do not wish her to be running about doing nothing." Many antebellum Virginia whites, like their eighteenth-century predecessors, had too many slaves, but slave hiring enabled them to bring benefits to themselves and to Virginia slavery itself.[1]

Economic factors persuaded some Virginia slave owners to hire out their surplus slaves, particularly in view of slaves' natural increase. At William Jerdone's farms, the problem was so great that Jerdone refused to receive additional slaves as payment for a debt. "My negro property has increased so fast that in addition to what I Hire Out up the Country I am obliged to dispose of some in the same way from my Farm in Ch[arle]s City [County] as I have more than I can profitably Employ there," Jerdone complained to his cousin in 1845. "Under these circumstances," Jerdone confessed, "I should dislike to become the Owner of any more" slaves. Jerdone hired out his superfluous slaves as soon as they were old enough to work and bring a return against the costs of their rearing. For Virginia slave owners like Jerdone, slave hiring turned possession of superfluous slaves from a financial disadvantage into a profitable remedy. Slave owners recognized their slaves' natural increase, and they utilized slave hiring as a way to benefit from it.[2]

For other Virginia slave owners, control, not money, was the issue when it came to extra slaves. Many antebellum white Virginians believed that possession of too many slaves led to frequent loafing, and so they hired out their extra slaves to solve the problem. "I am sorry to hear the House servants are so much laid up and consequent calls for the Doctor, who I fear will have a long bill for a healthy country," John Washington wrote his aunt. "If you think this laying up is caused by having a superfluity of them (as is sometimes the case)," Washington went on, "select such as you think can be best spared—and . . . look out [for] places for them—if only for their support." Washington did not believe that a sudden transfer to the fields would alter the house servants' attitude. "*It is useless to put them out on the farm at home,*" Washington insisted. "*They will then lay up altogether.*" "They will be better off at good homes with something to do," he advised. "*Use your own discretion,* retaining those who will really attend & render you most comfortable—sending off such (whatever thier former reputation) as wont or dont attend to thier work." Washington's suggestion that his aunt hire out slaves for their support only, if necessary, revealed his belief that hiring out otherwise idle slaves was a way to enhance control over them by compelling them to work for another white elsewhere.[3]

Other Virginia slave owners' comments about surplus slaves were manifestations of their diminished sense of power over their slaves, or of their disinclination to be bothered by their slaves. Many white Virginians agreed with merchant Benjamin Brand, who insisted, "Ones happiness in a great measure depend[s] on the good character and disposition of his slaves." Slaves whom whites deemed troublesome could be hired out, as when Jane Edmunds "proposed . . . to hire out Simon, James, and William, [as] they were giving [her] great trouble." Elsewhere, slave owner John Whitehead held similar sentiments. Whitehead wanted his slave Joshua, who already was hired out, to remain hired out, as Whitehead did "not wish to be troubled with him any more untill Christmas."[4]

The nature of Virginia whites' professed troubles with their slaves varied, but many hired out their slaves to others in order to render them more tractable in the future. One slave owner, for example, wished to hire out a teenage slave to the coal pits. The slave was "a very active, smart boy," the slave owner conceded, "but my wife cannot controul him, & I think the pits w[oul]d suit him exactly." In Portsmouth in 1806, Richard Blow reported that Henry was hired out to him specifically because Henry "appear[ed] to have been brought up tenderly, & never used to hard work [and consequently] his master wishe[d] him to be taught how to work." In 1849 a Leesburg slave owner explained that her slave Margaret was hired out to the same person who had hired Margaret the previous year. Margaret, whom the slave owner observed when Margaret returned during the Christmas holidays, was "improved but [was] still too slow for [the slave owner] to be willing to take her back yet." "I am in hopes," the slave owner continued, that "another year [hired out] will be a great improvement to [Margaret]." William Cabaniss complained about some of his slaves' laziness being his only "objection" to them. "It is not because [I had] no work to do that [I] want[ed] to hire them Out for [I] ha[d] as much as they [could] do the year," Cabaniss insisted. "*It is* because [I cannot] attend to them and make them work." The issue for Cabaniss was not financial in nature but rather his authority over the slaves, and Cabaniss responded to his sense of diminished authority over his slaves by hiring them out to someone else. Insofar as whites hired out slaves simply to remove them from their immediate vicinity or to enhance control over them in the future, slave hiring was indicative not of a weakening of Virginia slavery's institutional constraints but of slave owners' enhanced power over their slaves, even if that was attained by hiring them out to another person.[5]

Throughout Virginia, numerous whites were extremely anxious to acquire the slaves so many others wanted to hire out. In Fauquier County, Edward Turner's difficulties in locating slaves to hire manifested the extent to which agricultural, internal improvements, and other sectors of antebellum Virginia's diversified economy competed fiercely for hired slaves. In 1839 Turner anticipated a general scarcity of hired-slave labor in his vicinity, which prompted him to begin his search for hired slaves early in the slave-hiring season. On December 4, 1839, Turner ate breakfast and went to his uncle's place to see about hiring some slaves from him. After an all-day ride, Turner was dismayed to discover that his uncle had no slaves available to suit his needs. "I have had my ride for nothing," Turner grumbled in his diary. Turner spent that night at his uncle's place, and he rode home the following day.

One week later, on December 12, Turner renewed his efforts. That evening, he noted that he planned to "go down the Thoroughfare . . . to see Tho[ma]s Foster about hireing negroes for next year," but he quickly added, "There is some doubt about my being able to obtain them from him." Turner did not succeed, since he made no mention of hiring any slaves from Foster, and four days later, he began to worry. "I am much afraid of trouble about hireing negroes next year," Turner wrote in his diary, his anxiety fueled also by his discovery that John, a slave Turner then held on hire, would be taken back by his owner for the following year.

But Turner did not give up. On December 28 he resumed his search for hired slaves in earnest. "I start to day in search of Negroes," Turner wrote confidently in his diary. Whatever hope he may have held, however, he shortly lost, and he recorded the day's fruitless efforts in his diary. "I go to John Brown whom I understand has negroes to hire," Turner wrote, "but he informs me that his are all disposed of." Many other prospective slave hirers wanted slaves as badly as Turner did, and they had beaten him to them.

On Monday morning, December 30, Turner got back on his horse. He rode for a neighborhood where he was informed there were "many negroes to hire," but, "in consequence of the bad roads which [were] altogether impassable," Turner never reached his destination. He had no choice but to return to the place where he had slept the previous evening. The following day, Turner decided to try his luck at a public hiring, but he fared no better there. "In consequence of the high prices of negroes I do not get any," Turner noted in his diary. Competition for hired slaves rendered them scarce and, when they were available, extremely costly.

After the public hiring, Turner knew he had little time left. On January 1, 1840, he sent his overseer to Warrenton, the Fauquier County seat, to search for slaves for hire. The following day, the overseer returned and informed Turner of "his in a bility" to hire any slaves in Warrenton, and

Turner noted that he was "as yet without hirelings." On January 4, Turner made a final comment on his efforts to hire slaves for 1840. "I have not succeeded as yet in getting Negroes & had as well despair of ever doing so" Turner lamented. "I trust in God however," Turner continued, "that I shall never have occasion throughout the year to regret the disappointment more than I do at present."[6]

Farmers like Turner competed against the railroad men, who also found it difficult to secure hired slaves to construct their lines. Competition for hired slaves compelled one railroad contractor's agent to initiate a precise plan of action to obtain some. "You must come down to my house as soon as you can," the agent implored his boss, "and let us come to some understanding as to the best plans to be pursued in hiring." The agent advocated a plan to comb several counties with several other agents in search of slaves to hire. "I think it important we should send some efficient man or men to points we cannot attend," the agent remarked, suggesting that "Albemarle [County] would . . . be a good point—and perhaps Nelson and Louisa" counties as well. "In Bedford [County]," the agent went on, "I think we can get some hands."[7]

The relative prosperity Virginia farmers enjoyed by 1850 fueled the competition for hired slaves in Virginia. In Southampton County, Samuel Drewry recognized that high prices in the agricultural sector persuaded many planters to keep their slaves in their own fields, rather than hire them out elsewhere. "I am rather inclined to think there will not be as many hands offered [for hire] this season as last," Drewry warned his friend in December 1854. "Owing to the high price of produce more hands will be kept on farms." The upward trend in Virginia agricultural prices during the 1850s made slave labor scarce in other sectors of the economy, increasing the overall demand for, and cost of, hired slaves in Virginia.[8]

White Virginians recognized that the great demand for hired slaves in several sectors of antebellum Virginia's economy was the principal cause of rising slave-hire rates. In Spotsylvania County, Jonathan McCalley informed a correspondent, "Public work[s] & the Iron mines &c, have raised the hire of negroes more than 20 per cent in this country this year." Campbell County resident Mark Anthony noted a price of $120 to hire slave men in December 1849, but Anthony supposed, "They will be higher before the first of January" 1850 because the "Rail road . . . will make hands hire very high." In 1852 one Virginian noted simply, "Negroes are hiring quite high." In 1854 a slave owner informed a railroad contractor that "hires ha[d] advanced very much" in Southampton County, and he observed, "They are offering on the saw mill & lumber business equally as high as you offer. one company . . . now offer[s] $160 & Insures their lives." In 1855 a slave-hiring agent informed his boss, "[Since] hands hired . . . from . . . 150 to 160 to work in the field . . . it is imposible for you to get hands at the prises you naim." One year later, the same agent reported that prices had climbed still higher. "Negros are hireing from $180 to 200 no 1," the agent observed, and he said, "[I] refused to pay the prises beleving $150 is as much as we ort to pay." "I had a lot of fine fellows offered to me on yesterday," the agent told his boss, but he "refused to take them at the above prises." Elsewhere, another slave-hiring agent confirmed the high rates. "You couldaint to have got them at any price," the agent told his boss of a group of slaves he had tried to hire. "I run Anderson to $200 but did no good." "I know of no other negroes to Hire," the agent confessed. "I am sorry to see them so high." At Halifax Courthouse, an observer noted somberly: "I no of no negroes for hire in this county [as] there in grate demand." In 1857 another Virginian noted, "Hands are high and hard to get." Following a slave-hiring day held during the 1850s, James Taliaferro reported, "Negroes hired very high today plantation hands men from $150 to $200 young women from $70 to $80 Girls 13 to 14 years old $65." Taliaferro's observation reveals that the strong demand for hired-slave labor within Virginia encompassed even slave girls. By the 1850s, several sectors of Virginia's diversified economy had developed a seemingly insatiable demand for hired slaves, a demand that caused hire rates to soar just before secession and the Civil War.[9]

Rapidly advancing slave-hire rates encouraged Virginia slave owners to make calculated decisions to hire out their slaves within Virginia rather than sell them to the Lower South. In Spotsylvania County, one white Virginian reached such a conclusion with respect to his slave George: "It is best to hire him [out] as he will bring 80 or 90 dollars per annum & would not sell for more than $450 if that sum," the slave owner observed. Significantly, slaves' value on the slave-*hiring* market in Virginia remained stable despite occasional decreases in their *sale* value. As early as 1823, Wilson Cary informed Virginia Cary, "Negroes I am told continue to hire very well, notwithstanding their low prices." Therefore, Wilson continued,

"I think, [after] another year, we might be able to spare a good number for hire from the plantation, without materially reducing the chance of crops." In Richmond in 1846, P. M. Tabb & Son assured Robert Carter, "There will be no difficulty in disposing of" one of Carter's slaves in that city, and they informed Carter that the slave "would doubtless hire for more in proportion to his value than could be obtained for him were he offered for sale" in Richmond, so that it would be more financially advantageous for Carter to hire out, rather than sell, his slave. Also in Richmond a few years later, Robert Baylor Lyne informed a slave owner that he would not "have any difficulty in hiring [the slave owner's slave] out as a house servant and [that] perhaps [he] could hire him to some of the upholster[er]s." Lyne told the slave owner that his confidence was based on the fact that he had "hired out several house servants [that] year [1859], [at] prices ranging from $150 to $175." Lyne felt compelled to request that the slave owner waste no time on the matter. "A good price can be obtained," Lyne wrote, "and think you had better send him over immediately," as he "had applications all ready" for hired slaves. Also in 1859, John Winfree remarked to his brother that since his slave Peter was "bring[ing] very good hire [he] reckon[ed] [he] had better keep him a while, at least." Winfree's remark about Peter reflected many Virginia slave owners' conscious decision to retain ownership of their slaves, not sell them into the domestic slave trade, but rather hire them out within Virginia. Even white Virginians with no immediate plans to sell or hire out large numbers of their slaves thought about the numbers. In Loudoun County, slave owner George Rust outlined his various types of property, which included slaves, land, livestock, draft animals, horses, and implements, and their value. In a separate section of this sheet of paper, Rust noted anticipated amounts for land rent and "Hire of Negroes," and he referred to these amounts of money as "what would be my income in a certain contingency." Rust valued his slaves alone at $30,000 and recorded $3,000, or 10 percent of their value, as the expected amount of hire they would bring, should Rust need cash in a hurry. Merely the potential for slave hire inclined George Rust to hang onto his slaves. White Virginians' views regarding their slaves differed little from those of white North Carolinians. An observer at a slave sale in North Carolina in 1847 noted that, while numerous slaves were sold at the sale, most slave owners "hold onto their slaves to the last . . . [as] this is always a cash article."[10]

Ownership of skilled slaves, generally more valuable economically than unskilled slaves, reinforced many Virginia slave owners' inclination to keep their slaves and hire them out in Virginia rather than sell them to the Lower South. From Charlottesville, Robert Rives wrote his brother that good blacksmiths could not be hired cheaply, particularly because "the demand for Hirelings [generally], ha[d] been unprecedently great [that] season." Usually, neighborhood whites were familiar with particular skilled slaves whose labor services were in great demand. During the 1850s, Henry Carrington of Charlotte County hired out his slaves Lewis and Davy to make bricks and to build chimneys. Lewis and Davy possessed skills that Carrington's neighbors deemed valuable, and they went from one residence to another to work for Carrington's neighbors, keeping their own work records. Hiring out Lewis and Davy to his neighbors went smoothly for Carrington, who reaped considerable financial returns and therefore was not likely to sell Lewis and Davy to the Lower South at any time in the foreseeable future. The same was true for Elijah Fletcher, an Amherst County resident who in 1857 received a letter from M. M. Hastook seeking to hire Fletcher's "boy Preston," a blacksmith. "I will give you one hundred and seventy five dollars for one year for him," Hastook wrote. Fletcher, however, believed Preston commanded $190. Similarly, Gloucester County resident William Smith "collected $135.43 cash in full for hire Philip," a carpenter, in 1860. Fletcher and Smith, like Carrington and countless other owners of skilled slaves, did not sell those slaves to the Lower South but rather retained them and hired them out in Virginia, where considerable demand for them brought handsome annual hire returns.[11]

White Virginians kept their slaves and hired them out because they were optimistic about the future. Specifically, slave-hire rate increases during the 1850s led many Virginians to regard slave-hire income as superior to the value of other assets over an extended period of time. This point was illustrated in Princess Anne County in 1857, when court litigants debated the most advantageous disposition of land and slaves bequeathed to the orphaned children of Robert Benthall. The weight of opinion recorded in the court papers fell on the side of sale of the land to pay off Benthall's debts but retention of the slaves. One deponent stated that the slaves should be kept "because the negroes are worth so much more than the land." In a direct reference to slave hiring as an excellent income source for the orphans, one of the orphans' slaves, Jasper, was described as "a very valuable slave yielding annually some ninety or a hundred Dollars and the others are growing in value and in a short time will also yield if no misfortune occurs a handsome yearly income." The land, by contrast, "does not yield so good an income," the complaint charged, and a deponent concurred, saying, "[Whereas] a majority of the negroes are growing in value . . . the land and improvements must necessarily decrease in value by cultivation & natural decay." These white Virginians' references to steady increases in slaves' annual value show that slave children, and their future value in the slave-hiring market, were the objects of consideration in the case. This means that even though Virginia slaves were reproducing at a rapid rate, white Virginians saw sufficient economic advantage in retaining them and hiring them out in Virginia, rather than selling them to the Lower South, and they expected this circumstance to carry them forward into the future.[12]

In Nansemond County early in the eighteenth century, slave owner John Yeats, too, linked slave hiring to thoughts of the future. Yeats had established two schools, and he wished to provide for teachers and textbooks for the schools' future. Yeats believed that revenue from slave hire would be the best means of assuring the continued operation of his schools. In September 1731, Yeats drew up his will, in which he left "the rents of his lands and the hire of his negroes for the perpetual support and endowment of his schools, and incidentally the Church of which he was a member." Yates was correct in his conviction that slave hiring would provide ample funds for the future. By 1804 nineteen Yeats slaves were being hired out, and by 1860 eighty-five slaves brought a hire of $3,672.75 that year alone. Ultimately, the Yeats "schools continued to flourish until the year 1861, when the War Between the States caused them to lose a portion of their revenue, by the freeing of the slaves, and thus causing changes to be made in their management." Before the Civil War, the income raised by hiring out the Yeats slaves was sufficient to support John Yeats's schools for more than a century.[13]

Because they were certain of slave hiring as the basis of a stable future, many white Virginians hired slaves out on an ongoing basis for a steady income. Slave-hire income had sustained orphans since the colonial period, and it continued to do so throughout the antebellum years. Yet other white Virginians, too, hired out slaves to provide them with an income. In the 1820s, William Cary wrote his wife, Virginia, that his "desponding mood about [their] prospects for an income" at one point led him to conclude that "it would be prudent to hire out all that could be spared." In Culpeper County, Isabella McNeale put slave-hire receipts toward her expenses throughout the 1840s. In Alexandria, a slave owner begged the Reverend John Hargrave to "collect George's hire," because the slave owner would "greatly need it." The slave owner also asserted that he could not retain another of his slaves, Ben, at his place "longer than the spring [since he could not] do without his hire as [the slave owner's] income [that] year [was] two or three hundred dollars less than it ha[d] ever been." The slave owner further added that he was "in a constant state of anxiety about [his] pecuniary affairs & if [he] knew [hire receipts were] forth comming it would be a *great relief* to [his] mind."[14]

Throughout the 1850s, slave-hire income enabled Norfolk resident William Carrick to pay his bills and avoid going broke for want of employment as a coach maker. Carrick relied on his uncle, William Royston, to hire out his slaves for him in Caroline County, where Royston lived. Carrick's anxious letters to his uncle referred continually to high prices and scarcity of money and employment in Norfolk, as well as to Carrick's dependence upon slave-hire income to save him from ruin. In 1853 Carrick told his uncle, "All provisions of every description are very high"; "meal is a dollar a bushel and [I have] to get two bushels every three weeks." Carrick added, "It takes all that I can make to buy some thing to eat."

Carrick's anxiety did not dissipate as the decade progressed. From Norfolk in 1854, Carrick reported, "Times down here are very hard everything is so very high that I can scarcely make a living and my family is so large and increasing that I am compelled to look out for some where else where I can live cheaper." Carrick was still in Norfolk in January 1855 when he related to his uncle that he was "sadly disapointed . . . nearly broke [and] sorry that [Royston had] not collected the hire" for his slaves. Carrick added that he was "out of money and work [and had been] out of work for two months past" and that "it cost a fortune to live" in Norfolk. Near the end of the year, Carrick wrote, "Provisions are very high I am in hopes that times will be better after awhile," but the following month he conceded that his "situation [was] now very bad."

In Carrick's view, income from the hiring out of his slaves was all that stood between him and ruin. By 1858 Carrick confessed that the absence of slave-hire income would "cause [him] to make a great sacrifice as [it was] all pretty much that [he had] to depend upon to pay [his] expences doctors Bills and so on" and that his uncle's failure to collect slave hires then due would "put [him] a long way behind." Over the next three weeks, Carrick's anxiety mounted, and he again raised the issue of slave-hire money with his uncle, whom he begged to "send it as soon as possible [as he] was very much in want of it." He confessed that his failure to receive it would "break [him] up." Carrick's predicament was that he relied upon slave-hire income to be able to afford living in Norfolk, where he found it difficult to secure work, but he was unable to travel in search of work elsewhere without the assistance of slave-hire income. By 1861 Royston's failure to collect slave-hire money from 1859 again filled Carrick with anxiety, demonstrating the significance of slave-hire income for Carrick. "It would go very hard with me if I were to lose" the slave-hire money, Carrick wrote his uncle. "In fact," Carrick insisted, it would "all most Break me up." Carrick, thirty years old with a wife and three children, one of whom was "quite sick," then indicated that he had been working only half time for the previous three months, because his employer lacked the money to pay him for full-time work. Under the circumstances, Carrick's receipt of $257 in slave-hire money from his uncle for 1860 slave hires proved very beneficial, and his dependence upon such income made him, and other white Virginians like him, extremely disinclined to sell their slaves to the Lower South.[15]

The widespread reliance upon hiring out slaves for a perpetual income in antebellum Virginia was reflected in efforts to enhance slave hiring's reliability and security for owners of slaves hired out for that purpose. In 1850 a legislative petition drafted by several persons who "had much, and long experience in the Negro hiring business" sought to change the law that rendered slave owners responsible for expenses incurred in the apprehension of runaway hired slaves. The petitioners insisted, "Many persons depend upon the income derived from this kind of property for their living, and it is necessary that such persons should know what they will have to meet their expenses, &c." By the late antebellum period, the pervasive utilization of slave hiring for the sole purpose of generating a steady income meant that slave hiring was an integral facet of Virginia slavery, and it reflected white Virginians' confidence in the future of slavery itself.[16]

Because hiring out slaves within Virginia promised economic benefits well into the future, Hanover County resident Bickerton Lyle Winston purchased slaves solely to hire them out. With competition between several sectors of Virginia's diversified economy driving slave-hire rates upward, Winston bought several slaves and began to hire them out immediately. Winston also periodically purchased additional slaves to hire out, using the income brought by the slaves he had hired out earlier; he hired out some thirty slaves on a regular basis.

Winston's records for individual slaves illustrate the attractive returns slave hiring offered white Virginians in the last few years before secession and war. In January 1846 Winston purchased Randal for $425, and he immediately hired out Randal the same year for $97. Winston continued to hire out Randal each year thereafter, and by 1850 Randal's hire receipts had added up to the amount Winston had spent to purchase Randal. By the time of Randal's death in April 1853, he had earned Winston a total of $779.64 in hire.

Another slave, Garland, brought Winston impressive hiring-out returns, too. Winston paid $265 for Garland in 1846 and began to hire Garland out the same year. Within two years, Garland's hire receipts equaled, and then surpassed, the amount Winston had paid for him, and by June 1851 Winston had collected a total of $595.48 in hire from Garland's labor. Garland brought no more hire after that. On June 30, 1851, Winston noted in his account book, "Garland came to his end this day by an explosion in the black Heath Pits, he being the only person of Colour in the pits in attendance on a furnace." Ironically, Garland was killed at a job that was a part of the economic diversification that had increased slave-hire rates in Virginia, which development had enticed Winston to buy slaves like Garland in order to hire them out for a profit in the first place. Yet because Winston's primary goal was to make money by hiring out slaves, Winston had purchased slave life insurance in order to sustain himself financially in events such as Garland's death. By the mid-1850s, insurance, medical, and other costs aside, Winston's total slave-hire receipts exceeded two thousand dollars in just one year.[17]

Many antebellum Virginia farms and plantations hired slaves in or out (or both) as an integral part of operations at their inception, and they continued to do so afterward to increase production and enhance their income by supplementing their slave-labor forces with hired slaves. On land that became Roslin Plantation near Petersburg, slaves had been hired during the second decade of the nineteenth century to drain and clear land and to construct buildings. By the early 1830s, Roslin was a well-established plantation of eleven hundred acres. There were twenty-nine owned slaves working on it, yet the plantation continued to hire several slaves each year to facilitate its ongoing operations, and the plantation manager recorded expenses for attendance at slave hirings for that purpose on a regular basis. In Fauquier County, farmer Richard Cunningham hired slaves annually to supplement his own force at least from 1835 through 1842. Machinist John Grant was hiring slaves in the mid-1840s, and he continued to hire slaves in 1860. As of 1858, Lancaster County resident Richard Douglass had been hiring slaves for fifteen years. The 1860 slave schedules, too, show that many slave hirers were slave owners who supplemented their own slave forces as a regular part of their endeavors. These examples reflect positive relations between owners and hirers in Virginia and slave owners' comfort with hiring out their slaves regularly over periods of many years, as well as optimism for a slave-based future. During the 1840s, for example, Fauquier County brick-maker Daniel Anderson hired out slaves to whites for plastering, laying hearths, building chimneys, and mixing mortar. Slave hiring was a routine aspect of Anderson's activity and was central to his livelihood, gained by doing brick-related work for other whites. In the Shenandoah Valley, the owner of Folly Farm Plantation hired out between one dozen and two dozen slaves each year throughout the 1850s. Other Virginians collected money from slave owners who paid them to support their slaves. In Fluvanna County, David Baker supplemented the income of Byrd Plantation in 1860 by collecting a total of one hundred dollars for "boarding & clothing & taxes" for the slaves Rhody, Watsey and her children, and Sarah and her children. This money, in conjunction with income earned from the sale of wheat, oats, Irish potatoes, butter, and eggs, enabled Baker to pay for an overseer, ditch work, painting, and blacksmith work. Clearly, slave hiring was a fundamental facet of slavery everywhere in Virginia.[18]

Available figures for slave hires within Virginia and Virginia's slave sales to the Lower South show both the considerable extent of slave hiring in antebellum Virginia and, consequently, the tremendous degree to which slave hiring served to bolster slavery in a slave-exporting state by keeping significant numbers of slaves within Virginia and out of the domestic slave trade. Certainly, the number of slaves Virginians sold to the Lower South was considerable. Whereas Michael Tadman estimates that number at a bit under a half million sold between 1810 and 1859, Ira Berlin posits more than 1 million during the period 1810–61 in what he terms the Second Middle Passage. The significance of slave hiring in Virginia in connection to the interstate slave trade is that, had white Virginians not hired out large numbers of slaves within Virginia, the volume of the interstate slave trade would have been far greater. In 1860, for example, at least 1,040 slaves were hired out in Fauquier County alone. In Loudoun County during just that one year, the large scale of slave hiring was nearly identical: 1,037 slaves were hired out to 516 people in Loudoun, which represented 34 percent of Loudoun's adult slaves. Still more impressive are 1860 figures for Virginia's Appalachian counties, where 40,783 slaves were hired out. The figure for the Appalachian counties encompasses only slaves aged fifteen to fifty-nine. But considerable numbers of slave children and elderly slaves were also hired out, placing the number of slaves hired out in Virginia's Appalachian counties even higher. Taken together, these figures mean that, although large numbers of slaves were sold out of Virginia, large numbers of slaves also were hired out within Virginia. These statistics reveal that many, not just a few, white slave owners in Virginia perceived economic advantages to slave hiring over slave sale, and they acted upon them. Slave hiring, therefore, strengthened Virginia slavery because many Virginia slave owners with surplus slaves hired out those slaves within Virginia and did not place them in the domestic slave trade for sale to the Lower South. Also, slave hiring assured that economic diversification and a rapidly growing slave population created the context not for Virginia slavery's disarray, but for its adaptability and strengthening in a changing economy whose labor markets competed for large numbers of hired slaves. Slave hiring was everywhere as a routine part of white Virginians' endeavors, it helped to make Virginia slavery unique, and it fortified Virginia slavery in the years before secession and Civil War.[19]

CONCLUSION

Slave hiring in Virginia involved all types of slaves in all settings, became a pervasive and routine practice that offered slaves to all groups of whites, and strengthened Virginia slavery during the years just before the Civil War.

Slave hiring emerged in Virginia during the eighteenth century as a consequence of economic diversification and significant growth in the slave population, and by the turn of the nineteenth century, hired slaves were everywhere slavery was in Virginia: in industry, aboard ships, on transportation construction projects, in fields, in houses, and in cities. Slave hiring continued to flourish because white Virginians perceived numerous benefits in hiring slaves in and out on a routine basis. Many white Virginians relied upon hired slaves to establish plantations and considered them indispensible to their ongoing operations. For others, slave hiring offered the opportunity to adjust the size of their labor force, to assist neighbors with common seasonal chores, to generate an income, to mortgage property, to pay debts in local barter economies, and to avoid expenses associated with pregnant slave women and other slaves considered unproductive. For these reasons, slave hiring became a central part of slavery in Virginia. It was a regular topic in whites' living-room conversations, letters, bonds, account books, and business cards, as well as at the numerous crossroads and taverns across the Virginia landscape.

Slave hiring reveals much about slave women's experiences and about slave families. In Virginia, slave women were hired out at least as often as slave men. Hired slave women endured challenges drastically different from those faced by hired slave men. In particular, their challenges included childbirth and child-rearing while hired out and, with the exception of hired-slave midwives, far more white scrutiny and far fewer opportunities for mobility than slave men had. These unique experiences shaped hired slave women's patterns of resistance, which included attempts to poison hirers and set fire to hirers' residences. Both slave women and slave men, however, contended with being hired out away from family and friends. Given that white Virginians regularly hired out slave children alone once they were old enough to work, such separations were routine in nature.

Slave hiring's centrality to Virginia slavery was a source of institutional strength because it entailed the transfer of control over slaves from owners to countless white Virginians society-wide in the years before the Civil War. Specifically, ever-larger numbers of otherwise disparate groups of Virginia whites assumed power over slaves by hiring slaves and in the form of engagement in slave hiring's logistical activities, such as conveyance and surveillance of hired-out slaves from one point to another, auction of slaves at slave-hiring days, and work as slave-hiring agents. In fact, large numbers of white men *had* to exercise authority over hired slaves in their performance of slave hiring's logistical activities in order for slave hiring itself to function at all, let alone on the grand scale by which it did. This Virginia-wide white slave control also meant that the proliferation of slave hiring culminated not in Virginia slavery's institutional weakness or in whites' diminished control over hired slaves, but in whites' *enhanced* control over the hired-slave population because so many whites in addition to owners and hirers held power over hired slaves. Other examples of whites' smooth and successful transfer of authority over hired slaves between them included whites' apprehension of runaway hired slaves, white owners' encouraging white hirers to whip their slaves and to return runaway hired slaves to them, whites' work alongside hired slaves at their parents' and employers' residences, and white owners' and white hirers' enjoyment of positive relationships that lasted for many years. Additionally, whites who hired slaves included non-slave-owning journeymen. Journeymen worked for white masters in a society where most people who worked for white masters were slaves, but white journeymen became masters themselves when they hired slaves. Other white slave hirers included merchants, farmers who wished to supplement their own slave-labor force, laborers, clerks, and a host of others. Ultimately, therefore, although some hired slaves succeeded in manipulating owners and hirers against each other for their own benefit, white racial unity often precluded their doing so.

Because the logistical activities of slave hiring were public in nature and as such were white male activities exclusively, white male Virginians who performed them also underscored their own masculinity publicly, just as they did when they hired house servants to assist their wives in the home. The consequent reduction of white women's household drudgery made white women ladies (and created the appearance of middle-class homes), as did white women's securing of white men to hire out their slaves for them in the white public sphere of hiring day. Those white ladies, however, remained masters nonetheless by virtue of their ownership of the slaves white men hired out on their behalf. This gave ladies decision-making power concerning their hired-out slaves, whereby they told white men who hired out their slaves what to do, and it further reinforced their identities as ladies by enabling them to utilize slave-hire income to avoid working for other whites in the manner of hired slaves.

In the years before the Civil War, hired slaves worked in all of Virginia's economic sectors. Hired slaves built and maintained turnpikes, canals, and railroads that linked Virginia whites economically, and they worked in factories, on farms, and as house servants. Broad demand for hired slaves pushed slave-hire rates upward, which led white Virginians to hire out their slaves in Virginia rather than sell them to the Lower South, and slave hiring became a routine, ongoing facet of white Virginians' endeavors. Consequently, slave hiring retained in Virginia large numbers of slaves who otherwise would have ended up in the interstate slave trade, and it therefore strengthened Virginia slavery on the eve of the Civil War.

NOTES

ABBREVIATIONS

DU	Rare Book, Manuscript, and Special Collections Library, William Perkins Library, Duke University
EA	Estate Accounts
FCCA	Fairfax Circuit Court Archives, Fairfax County Judicial Center, Fairfax, VA
GA	Guardian Accounts
LCPSCV	Loose Court Papers of Sussex County, VA, Sussex Courthouse, Sussex, VA
LDS	Church of Jesus Christ of Latter-Day Saints, Salt Lake City, UT
LVA	Library of Virginia, Richmond, VA
OA	Orphan Accounts
SHC	Southern Historical Collection, Wilson Library, Library of the University of North Carolina at Chapel Hill
UVA	Albert and Shirley Small Special Collections Library, University of Virginia
VHS	Virginia Historical Society, Richmond, VA
WM	Earl Gregg Swem Library, The College of William and Mary in Virginia, Williamsburg, VA

INTRODUCTION

1. Deposition of Joseph L. Potts, March 21, 1842, George Gunnell v. Samuel Coleman, 1841, CFF 36N (1 of 4), FCCA. Articles on slave hiring that have appeared since the 1960s include the following: Sarah S. Hughes, "Slaves for Hire: The Allocation of Black Labor in Elizabeth City County, Virginia, 1782 to 1810," *William and Mary Quarterly* 35 (April 1978): 260–86; Randolph B. Campbell, "Research Note: Slave Hiring in Texas," *American Historical Review* 92 (February 1988): 107–14; William A. Byrne, "The Hiring of Woodson, Slave Carpenter of Savannah," *Georgia Historical Quarterly* 77 (Summer 1993): 245–63; Keith C. Barton, "'Good Cooks and Washers': Slave Hiring, Domestic Labor, and the Market in Bourbon County, Kentucky," *Journal of American History* 84 (September 1997): 436–60; John J. Zaborney, "Slave

Hiring and Slave Family and Friendship Ties in Rural Nineteenth-Century Virginia," in *Afro-Virginian History and Culture*, ed. John Saillant (New York: Garland, 1999), 85–107. Book-length works on slave hiring are John J. Zaborney, "Slaves for Rent: Slave Hiring in Virginia" (Ph.D. diss., University of Maine, 1997); and Jonathan D. Martin, *Divided Mastery: Slave Hiring in the American South* (Cambridge, MA: Harvard University Press, 2004).

2. Clement Eaton, "Slave Hiring in the Upper South: A Step toward Freedom," *Mississippi Valley Historical Review* 46 (March 1960): 663–78; Richard C. Wade, *Slavery in the Cities: The South, 1820–1860* (New York: Oxford University Press, 1964). The contrary view, that hired slaves fared ill in hirers' possession and secured few if any advantages, was posited by Kenneth Stampp, who maintained that hired slaves were subject to "ruthless exploitation" and "stood the greatest chance of subjection to cruel punishments as well as to overwork." Stampp further believed that "hired slaves doubtless suffered most from lack of medical care." Kenneth M. Stampp, *The Peculiar Institution: Slavery in the Ante-Bellum South* (New York: Vintage, 1956), 84, 185, 318. This view of slave hiring was sustained by Robert S. Starobin, *Industrial Slavery in the Old South* (New York: Oxford University Press, 1970), 133–35.

3. Lynda J. Morgan, *Emancipation in Virginia's Tobacco Belt, 1850–1870* (Athens: University of Georgia Press, 1992), 57; Deborah Gray White, *Ar'n't I a Woman? Female Slaves in the Plantation South* (New York: W. W. Norton, 1985), 76; Jacqueline Jones, "'My Mother Was Much of a Woman': Black Women, Work, and the Family under Slavery," in *Our American Sisters: Women in American Life and Thought*, ed. Jean E. Friedman, William G. Shade, and Mary Jane Capozzoli (Lexington, MA: D. C. Heath, 1987), 176.

4. Midori Takagi, *"Rearing Wolves to Our Own Destruction": Slavery in Richmond, Virginia, 1782–1865* (Charlottesville: University Press of Virginia, 1999); William A. Link, *Roots of Secession: Slavery and Politics in Antebellum Virginia* (Chapel Hill: University of North Carolina Press, 2003); Martin, *Divided Mastery*.

5. For the conclusion that slave hiring rendered conflict between owners and hirers "nearly inevitable," see Martin, *Divided Mastery*, 190.

6. Mason Family Papers, Mss 1 M3816c, 4754–4812, sec. 74, VHS.

7. Martin, *Divided Mastery*, 190 and passim.

8. Peter Kolchin, *American Slavery: 1619–1877* (New York: Hill and Wang, 1993), 242.

CHAPTER 1. THE ORIGINS AND PROLIFERATION OF SLAVE HIRING IN VIRGINIA

1. Curtis P. Nettels, *The Emergence of a National Economy, 1775–1815* (New York: Harper & Row, 1969), 194–95.

2. Timothy H. Breen and Stephen Innes, *"Myne Owne Ground": Race and Freedom on Virginia's Eastern Shore, 1640–1676* (New York: Oxford University Press, 1980), 39; Stuart Bruchey, *Enterprise: The Dynamic Economy of a Free People* (Cambridge, MA: Harvard University Press, 1990), 64.

3. Joyce Appleby, "Commercial Farming and the 'Agrarian Myth' in the Early Republic," *Journal of American History* 68 (March 1982): 838–39.

4. Patience Essah, *A House Divided: Slavery and Emancipation in Delaware, 1638–1865* (Charlottesville: University Press of Virginia, 1996), 29, 70; Barbara Jeanne Fields, *Slavery and Freedom on the Middle Ground: Maryland during the Nineteenth Century* (New Haven, CT: Yale University Press, 1985), 4–5; Christine Daniels, "Gresham's Laws: Labor Management on an Early-Eighteenth-Century Chesapeake Plantation," *Journal of Southern History* 62 (May 1996), 215–18.

5. Bruchey, *Enterprise*, 84.

6. David Klingaman, "The Significance of Grain in the Development of the Tobacco Colonies," *Journal of Economic History* 29 (1969): 268–78.

7. Ronald P. Dufour, *Colonial America* (St. Paul, MN: West, 1994), 193; Allan Kulikoff, "The Origins of Afro-American Society in Tidewater Maryland and Virginia, 1700 to 1790," *William and Mary Quarterly* 35 (1978): 230; Peter Kolchin, *American Slavery*, 11; John B. Boles, *Black Southerners, 1619–1869* (Lexington: University Press of Kentucky, 1984), 38–39; Allan Kulikoff, *Tobacco and Slaves: The Development of Southern Cultures in the Chesapeake, 1680–1800* (Chapel Hill: University of North Carolina Press, 1986), 340, 342; Brenda L. Stevenson, "'All My Cherished Ones': Marriage and Family in Antebellum Virginia" (Ph.D. diss., Yale University, 1990), 332; Kolchin, *American Slavery*, 242; Nettels, *National Economy*, 195.

8. Clement Eaton, *The Growth of Southern Civilization, 1790–1860* (New York: Harper & Row, 1963), 183; T. H. Breen, *Tobacco Culture: The Mentality of the Great Tidewater Planters on the Eve of the Revolution* (Princeton, NJ: Princeton University Press, 1985), 45; Winthrop D. Jordan, *White Over Black: American Attitudes toward the Negro, 1550–1812* (New York: W. W. Norton, 1977), 319; W[illia]m Fleet to James Webb, March 25, 1798, William Fleet Letter, Mss 2F6247a1, VHS; Albert E. Cowdrey, *This Land, This South: An Environmental History*, rev. ed. (Lexington: University Press of Kentucky, 1996), 58; Ira Berlin, "The Revolution in Black Life," in *The American Revolution: Explorations in the History of American Radicalism*, ed. Alfred F. Young (DeKalb: Northern Illinois University Press, 1976), 357; Kulikoff, *Tobacco and Slaves*, 405.

9. Berlin, "Revolution in Black Life," 357–60; Stevenson, "'All My Cherished Ones,'" 331; William W. Freehling, *The Road to Disunion: Secessionists at Bay, 1776–1854* (New York: Oxford University Press, 1990), 1:24.

10. Urban and industrial slave hiring in Virginia is examined in chapter 6. Sylvia R. Frey, *Water from the Rock: Black Resistance in a Revolutionary Age* (Princeton, NJ: Princeton University Press, 1991), 222; Sarah Shaver Hughes, "Elizabeth City County, Virginia, 1782–1810: The Economic and Social Structure of a Tidewater County in the Early National Years" (Ph.D. diss., College of William and Mary, 1975), 140, 142, 158, 160, 163, quotation on 158.

11. Letter Book of William McKean, overseer for James Dunlop, 1809–18, James and John Dunlop Records, 1809–41, acc. 23873, Business Records Collection, LVA.

12. Account Book of J. W. Twyman, ca. 1840–ca. 1850, December 24, 26, 1849, Twyman Family Papers, acc. 7808, UVA; [?] Rogers to [?], December 23, 1848, Buford Family Papers, acc. 9782, microfilm no. M-2188, Correspondence, 1844–49, UVA.

13. Slave-hiring bond, John Fitzgerald and Sam Scott to Patrick H. Foster, December 31, 1855, John Fitzgerald Papers (photocopies), VHS; slave-hiring bond, Isaac Fletcher and John E.

Fletcher to Henry G. Dulany, December 11, 1858, sec. 8; slave-hiring bond, Isaac Fletcher and John E. Fletcher to William L. Childs, December 29, 1859, sec. 10, John E. Fletcher Papers, Mss 1F6353c, VHS; Elizabeth Feutress Deposition, in Sykes and Wife v. Griggs' Executors etc., 1854-08, Princess Anne County Circuit Court Chancery Papers, box 1, LVA.

14. Hughes, "Elizabeth City County," 181–89, quotation on 184.

15. GA, York County, VA, 1823–46, 1, 2, 19, 45, 56, 78, 94, microfilm, LDS; Bacon, Coleman, & Company, Memo[random] Book, 1836–37, 1842–49, Business Records Collection, acc. 33081, LVA; Conley L. Edwards III, Gwendolyn D. Clark, and Jennifer D. McDaid, comps., *A Guide to Business Records in the Virginia State Library and Archives* (Richmond: Virginia State Library and Archives, 1994), 158.

16. Stafford County, VA, EA, 1827–34, 154, LDS; Suzanne Smith Ray, Lyndon H. Hart, and J. Christian Kolbe, "Guardian," in *A Preliminary Guide to Pre-1904 County Records in the Virginia State Library and Archives,* comp. Suzanne Smith Ray, Lyndon H. Hart, and J. Christian Kolbe (Richmond: Virginia State Library and Archives, 1994), xviii; GA, Essex County, VA, 1857–67, 48, LDS; GA, Sussex County, VA, 1839–50, 202–5, LDS.

17. Peter Hitt Account Book, 1758–1824, Personal Papers Collection, acc. 25119, LVA; slave-hiring bond, Edmond Stacy and William Gilliam to James Holloway, Administrator of Samuel Jones, Deceased, December 28, 1797, in Jones' Administrator v. Stacy and Gilliam, 1803-66, LCPSCV; Levi Gilliam Complaint, in Gilliam v. Moore, 1800-63, LCPSCV.

18. Hughes, "Slaves for Hire"; slave-hiring bond, Wyatt Bailet and Thomas Hartley to William Allen, executor of Colonel William Allen, deceased, January 1794, in Allen for Selden v. Bailey, 1802-2, LCPSCV.

19. Tho[ma]s C. Read to Henry Carrington, April [?] 1852; January 16, 1853, Carrington Family Papers, 1817–95, Mss 1C2358g, sec. 1, VHS; Sarah Harriet Apphia Hunter Accounts, 1837–42 (folder 2 of 5), Hunter Family Papers, Mss 1H9196a FA2, box 26, VHS; GA, York County, VA, 1780–1823, 159–60, 224, 257, LDS (for entries by Macon and Burt); "Bond of William L [Coughlin] [and] James [G.] Maynard to Mary H. (Byrd) Claiborne (concerning a negro slave)," in Jones Family Papers, 1808–42, Mss 1J735b, sec. 6, VHS.

20. "Terms of Hiring," in Burwell Family Papers, 1813–1928, Mss 1B9585b, sec. 1, VHS; Lewis Hill to W[illia]m Gray, March 22, 1843, William Gray Papers, 1819–75, Mss 1G7952a FA2, VHS; slave-hiring bond, Owens & Miles agents to Paul Hull, January 8, 1864; slave-hiring bond, John Swyney to John L. Tate, February 3, 1853, both in George Family Papers, 1733–1820, Local Government Records Collection, acc. 24642, box 4, folder 24, LVA.

21. Slave-hiring bond, John H. Thomas, Wyatt Cardwell, and H. Carrington to Benj[amin] B[.] Jackson, December 28, 1853, Carrington Family Papers, 1832–84, Mss 1C2358e, sec. 2, VHS; Thomas Chrystie to Philip Croxton, May 19, 1811, Thomas Chrystie Papers, 1783–1818, Mss 1C4695a, sec. 1, VHS.

22. Hughes, "Elizabeth City County," 172, 219n92; "Transcription of the will of Bolling Starke as recorded in Henrico County Will Book 2 at page 39 by Gary M. Williams [Clerk of the Circuit Court, Sussex, VA]," LCPSCV.

23. Nathaniel Green Bill of Complaint and Court Decree, Green v. Maclin, LCPSCV.

24. Levi Gilliam Bill of Complaint and Deposition, Gilliam v. Moore, 1796-52, LCPSCV.

25. Joseph J. Lewis to his brother, May 26, June 28, 1818; August 19, 1819; June 16, July 23, 1820; March 24, May 22, October 3, 19, 1822, Papers of the Lewis Family, 1768–1824, acc. 2345, UVA.

26. Edward Carter Turner Diary, September 16, October 18, November 8, 1839, Turner Family Papers, Mss 1T8596a, VHS.

27. Daniel William Cobb Diary, August 24, September 1, 1842, Mss 5:1C6334:1-25, VHS; Emmett B. Fields, "The Agricultural Population of Virginia, 1850–1860" (Ph.D. diss., Vanderbilt University, 1953), 161.

28. Daniel William Cobb Diary, May 14–16, June 21, December 29, 30, 1846.

29. B[enjamin] F[ranklin] Nalle to Anne Nalle, December 14, 1839; February 3, 1841, Nalle Family Papers, Mss 1N1495a, VHS.

30. E[benezer] Cooley to Thomas J[efferson] Cooley, December 21, 1829, John G. Devereux Papers, subseries 1.1, 1791–1848, 2149, SHC.

31. Anna C. Hoge to Susan C. Noland, December 24, 1849, Susan C. Noland Papers, 1847–62, DU; W[illia]m Day to Mrs. Ann Nalle, n.d., Nalle Family Papers, Mss 1N1495a, sec. 5, VHS; John W. Nash to William Howard, January 4, 1832, Nash Family Papers, Mss 1N1786a, VHS; Tom Ford to [William] Gray, January 30, 1848, William Gray Papers, Mss 1G7952aFA2, VHS; Robert J. Cole to Cynthia Beverley (Tucker) Washington Coleman, December 18, 1858, Coleman Family Papers, Mss 1C6773a, sec. 8, VHS; William Boone to William Drewry, December 31, 1862, William Boone Letter, Mss 2B64472a, VHS; Robert Henderson Allen Diary (microfilm reel B1), December 25, 1858; January [?] 1860, Allen Family Papers, Mss 1AL546a, VHS.

32. John H. Martin Account Book No. 1, February 9, 10, 12, 13, 14, 15, 16, 17, 20, 1849; July 17, 1850, Account Book No. 2, July 12, 1852; July 21, 1856, Papers of John H. Martin, acc. 4224 and 4224-a, UVA; Sarah Waller to David G. Waller, April 29, 1852; [?] to David G. Waller, October 31, 1851, David Garland Waller Papers, 1842–61, DU.

33. Daniel William Cobb Diary, January 5, 1857; January 5, 9, 10, 1859; January 16, 1858, VHS. Data on hogs are found in Fields, "Agricultural Population of Virginia, 1815–1860," 176.

34. B[enjamin] F[ranklin] Nalle to Mrs. Ann Nalle, August 15, 1860, Nalle Family Papers, Mss 1N1495a, sec. 5, VHS.

35. GA, Elizabeth City County, VA, 1827–43, LDS; "Memorandum Book of Hirelings 1846," in "Slave Documents 1815–1846" folder, Chichester Family Papers, acc. 11047, UVA. Leannah was but one of several slaves who were "hired by the year & by the month," according to the book. Thomas Calvert to James D. Massenburg, December 31, 1829, Harrison v. Calvert, 1830-52, Southampton County Chancery Papers, box 34, LVA.

36. GA, Orange County, VA, 1827–52, December 1, 1822, LDS; agreement, August 25, 1809, between Walker R. Carter and Larkin Stanard, and deposition of Bruce Chisholm, June 1, 1819, in Carter v. Stanard, 1818-02, Caroline County Chancery Causes, box 3, LVA.

37. Kenneth Stampp observed that slave hirings usually took place "at southern crossroad stores, on the steps of county courthouses, and in every village and city." Stampp, *Peculiar Institution*, 67. For the reference to the ordinary as the site of a hiring, see papers pertaining to the hiring out of slaves belonging to the estate of Thomas Walton in Eggleston Family Papers, Mss 1Eg396b, sec. 1, VHS; Daniel William Cobb Diary, December 31, 1842; December 26, 1847;

December 27, 31, 1849; December 28, 1857, VHS; B. H. Walker Diary (photocopy), January 1, 1858; January 1, 1859, Personal Papers Collection, LVA.

38. Wyche's Administratrix v. Parker, 1773-86, LCPSCV; Bilbro, Guardian v. Jordan, 1785-18, LCPSCV; Clements' Executors v. Partin, 1786-48, LCPSCV.

39. Dunn's Administrator v. Mitchell and Beddingfield, 1793-42; Hawthorne v. Wilkerson and Mitchell, 1801-54; Jones' Executor v. Newsum, 1797-83; Mason's Executrix, Assignee v. Pettway, 1797-97; Burton's Guardian v. Lightfoot and Ammons, 1809-49; Smith's Administrator for Nance v. Harrison and Thompson, 1798-118; Chappell v. Wallis, 1804-50; Parham v. Wilkerson, 1807-161; Bailey, Assignee v. Mitchell and Rainey, 1802-9; Magee v. Magee, 1825; Bailey, Assignee v. Williams' Administrator, 1843, all in LCPSCV; slave-hiring bond, John Letcher to Elizabeth McDowell, due December 25, 1851, John Letcher Papers, 1770–1970, series 1, folder 71, Mss 1 L5684 a FA2 series 1, VHS; John Fitzgerald Papers (photocopies), Mss 1F5764c, VHS; slave-hiring bond, G. W. Reintzer to John Letcher, due December 25, 1860, John Letcher Papers; Marables' Guardian v. Weathers and Edwards, 1843, LCPSCV; slave-hiring bond, James Miller and John F. Singleton to Mary S. Miller, 1849, Miller Family Papers, 1821–65, acc. 28957, Personal Papers Collection, LVA; Ida Dulany to John E. Fletcher, n.d., John E. Fletcher Papers, 1858–84, Personal Papers Collection, acc. 31718, folder 1, LVA.

40. Merchant Records, 1796–1801, Unidentified, Ledger F (1800–1801), LVA; William & Benjamin Horner Account Books, 1789–1841 & 1838–41, UVA; Scott, Skipwith, and Cardozo Daybook, 1854–55, 173–75, LVA; Manuscript Volumes, Diaries, December 23, 1843, Ms V D9, WM; GA, York County, VA, 1780–1823, 371.

41. Slave-hiring bond, John Swyney to John L. Tate, February 3, 1853; slave-hiring bond, Owens & Miles agents to Paul Hull, January 8, 1862, both in George Family Papers, box 4, folder 24, LVA.

42. Lucien Lewis slave-hiring business card and 1860 letter, Beale Family Papers, Mss 1B3658a, sec. 4, VHS; Auction Sales Record Book, 1847–54 (Thos. Branch & Bro., etc.), Branch & Co., Richmond Va., Records, 1837–1976, Mss 3B7327aFA1, VHS.

CHAPTER 2. HIRED SLAVE WOMEN

1. Slave-hiring bond, John Wrenn and Rich[ar]d B. G[r]igg to Nath[anie]l Rives, Decem[be]r 27, 1809, Eppes' Guardian v. Wrenn, 1811-120, LCPSCV.

2. GA, Essex County, VA, 1838–44, 308–9, LDS; Samuel H. Bell Ledger, 1844–67, Business Records Collection, acc. 25459, LVA; *Leesburg Democratic Mirror*, December 22, 1858; Bureau of the Census, Eighth Census of the United States, 1860, Original Returns of the Assistant Marshals, microfilm, Schedule II, "An Enumeration of Slave Population, Loudoun County, Virginia" (hereafter Slave Schedule for _____).

3. Jones, "'My Mother Was Much of a Woman,'" 182; "Transcription of the will of Bolling Starke," LCPSCV; G[eorge] R. Waddey Complaint, July 14, 1853, Commonwealth v. Louisa, Lancaster County, VA, County Court Judgments, Commonwealth Causes, 1853, LVA.

4. Reeses' Guardian v. Reese et al., 1855-34, Southampton County, VA, Chancery Papers, 1855, box 63, LVA.

5. Slave-hiring bond, James Phillips to Elizabeth Skinker, January 1, 1826, Quesenberry Family Papers, Mss 1Q375a, sec. 4, VHS; GA, Lancaster County, VA, 104, LDS; GA, York County, VA, 1823–46, 100, LDS.

6. Fauquier County, VA, Register of Births, 1853, 19–20; 1854, 13–14[?]; 1858, 4[?], LDS.

7. Loudoun County, VA, Register of Births, 1856, 79, 81; 1857, 91, LDS.

8. Accomack County, VA, OA, 1836–49, 105–6, LDS; Bacon, Coleman, & Company Memo[randum] Book, 1836–37, 1842–49, Nat Nelson's account, second sec., 17, Business Records Collection, acc. 33081, LVA.

9. Jordon Taylor to Dr. I[verson] L. Twyman, July 29, 1859; Taylor to [?], December 4, 1859, Austin-Twyman Papers, 1765–1865, folder 47, Letters to Iverson L. Twyman, 1859–60, both in Kenneth M. Stampp, gen. ed., *Records of Ante-Bellum Southern Plantations from the Revolution through the Civil War,* microfilm, Series L: Selections from the Earl Gregg Swem Library, College of William and Mary in Virginia. According to Taylor's July letter, he had hired Lavinia from a "Miss Austin," although the December letter, apparently directed to Lavinia's owner, is among Taylor's correspondence.

10. Bill of Indictment in Commonwealth v. Douglass, Lancaster County, VA, Commonwealth Causes, 1855, Court Judgments, 1850–61, LVA.

11. White, *Ar'n't I a Woman?* 83–84, 111–12.

12. Ibid., 110–12, 119–41; Daniel William Cobb Diary, December 2, 1857, VHS.

13. G. S. Crittenden to John D. McGill, July 25, 1839, Joseph Lyon Miller (Collector) Papers, Mss 1M6154a, sec. 5, VHS; John H. Martin Account Book, Papers of John H. Martin, 1842–70, acc. 4224, 4224-a, UVA.

14. GA, York County, VA, 1780–1823, 137, 393; 1823–46, 41, LDS; Tho[ma]s W Banks in a/c w/Jno W C Catlett his g[uar]d[ia]n, Manuscript Volumes–Account Books, Farms and Farming, Ms V Af14, WM; William Perrin's account with James Thomas, and Thomas's receipt to Perrin, May 15, 1855, "Papers relating to the hiring out and management of slaves by William K. Perrin, 1800–1855 & n.d.," William K. Perrin Papers, acc. 95 P42, folder 3, WM; GA, Orange County, VA, 1827–52, 139, LDS.

15. Charles B. Dew, *Bond of Iron: Master and Slave at Buffalo Forge* (New York: W. W. Norton, 1994), 321, 325; Charles L. Perdue Jr., Thomas E. Barden, and Robert K. Phillips, comps. and eds., *Weevils in the Wheat. Interviews with Virginia Ex-Slaves* (Charlottesville: University Press of Virginia, 1976), 120; Joan Rezner Gundersen, "The Double Bonds of Race and Sex: Black and White Women in a Colonial Virginia Parish," *Journal of Southern History* 52 (August 1986): 366–68.

16. Stafford County, VA, EA, 1852–59, 22, LDS; Patrick Catlett to Elizabeth Catlett, January 4, 1847, Papers of John Catlett, acc. 9398-j, UVA.

17. *American Beacon and Norfolk and Portsmouth Daily Advertiser,* January 2, December 23, 1839; *Leesburg Democratic Mirror,* December 15, 1858; January 5, 1859; Charles A. Washington to George F. Washington, January 6, 1847, Charles A[ugustine?] Washington Papers, 1847, DU.

18. White, *Ar'n't I a Woman?* 101; Thadius Forester Complaint, in Walker's Guardian v. Walker, 1853, Lancaster County, VA, Chancery Papers, 1853, LVA; OA, Accomack County, VA, 1836–49, 644, LDS; Polley Fletcher Deposition and other papers in Daniel and Wife v. Doles Executor, 1832-07, Southampton County, VA, Chancery Papers, 1832, box 36, LVA.

19. "Louisa Griggs orphan of Thomas Griggs dec[ease]d in accounte with Charles Griggs Ex[ecuto]r of the estate of Charles Griggs sen[io]r dec[eas]ed who is acting as Guardian," in Sykes and Wife v. Griggs' Executors etc., 1854-08, Princess Anne County, VA, Circuit Court Chancery Papers, 1852–54, box 1, LVA.

20. S[amuel] Cooper to Sarah Maria (Mason) Cooper, October 3, 1864, Samuel Cooper Letter, Mss 2C7876a1, VHS; Receipt, T. S. Stubbs to John Perrin, April 5, 1802, William K. Perrin Papers, folder 3, WM; Robert N. Trice to Miss Eliza B. Chowning, January 3, 1844, Harrison Family Papers, Mss 1H2485a, sec. 32, folder 4 of 4, VHS; Daniel William Cobb Diary, December 29, 1846, VHS.

21. Jno J. Alston to Asa Dupuy, December 17, 1827, Dupuy Family Papers, Correspondence of Asa Dupuy, sec. 1, VHS; James O. Carr to Dabney S. Carr, June 11, 1819, Carr-Cary Family Papers, acc. 1231, box 2, UVA; Patrick Catlett to Elizabeth Catlett, January 4, 1827, Papers of John Catlett, acc. 9398-j, UVA.

22. Sam[ue]l Hannah to A. F. Biggers, June 20, 1827, Barksdale-Hannah Family Papers, 1811–70, Collection No. 331, DU; William McGuire to Judith B. Alexander, July 1, 1858, Alexander Family Papers, acc. 4800, UVA; Edw. Lucas Jr. note, "To The Conductor of the B & O Railroad," January 2, 1857, James Markell Correspondence, 1826–72, n.d., box 4, Shepherdstown, Virginia Papers ca. 1808–1945, UVA.

23. GA, Essex County, VA, 1844–51, 101–33, LDS.

24. Ibid., 101–7.

25. GA, York County, VA, 1780–1823, 291, 359, 360, 390, 406, LDS.

26. Ibid., 415, 417; Thomas W. Banks account with John W. C. Catlett, his guardian, in Manuscript Volumes–Account Books, Farms and Farming, WM.

27. EA, Stafford County, VA, 1827–34, 151, LDS; Taliaferro Family Papers, 1820–1920, Mss 1T1438a, sec. 2, VHS.

28. "List of Negroes hired out at Gloucester Town December 23:1801," "List of Negroes hired out at Gloucester Town Dec[embe]r 23 1802," John W. Perrin to Thomas Crue, December 27, 1803, "Papers relating to the hiring out and management of slaves by William K. Perrin, 1800–1855 & n. d.," folder 3, William K. Perrin Papers, WM; Maria Rebecca Roane (Barnes) Gooch Slave Lists, 1839–52, Gooch Family Papers, 1812–1961, Mss 1G5906a, sec. 8, VHS; Robertson Coons Account Book, acc. 4323, UVA; Minnie Buerbaum Morgan Books, 1496-z, vol. 1, SHC.

29. E[lizabeth] L. C[arter] to Robert W. Carter, February 4, 1834, Robert W. Carter, folder 25, Carter Papers, 1667–1862, in Stampp, *Records of Ante-Bellum Southern Plantations*, Series L.

30. Mitchell's Guardian v. Mitchell, Lancaster County, VA, Chancery Papers, 1857, LVA; Eugene D. Genovese, *Roll, Jordan, Roll: The World the Slaves Made* (New York: Vintage, 1974), 496; White, *Ar'n't I a Woman?* 112–14.

31. John A. Rutter v. Henry S. Kane, Scott County, VA, Circuit Court Chancery Causes, 1859-01/cc, LVA.

32. Legislative Petition, December 5, 1817, Nancy Conn (Washington County), box 250, folder 16, microfilm reel no. 198, acc. 36121, LVA.

33. Midori Takagi, "Slavery in Richmond, Virginia, 1782–1865" (Ph.D. diss., Columbia University, 1994), 48–49; *American Beacon and Norfolk and Portsmouth Daily Advertiser*, Decem-

ber 23, 1839; Commonwealth v. Maria, a Slave, Richmond City Hustings Court Ended Causes, February 1848, box 180, LVA; *Alexandria Expositor and Columbian Advertiser*, December 14, 1803; January 19, 1804; *American Beacon and Norfolk and Portsmouth Daily Advertiser*, January 2, December 23, 1839; Takagi, "Slavery in Richmond," 144; Wade, *Slavery in the Cities*, 28–30; Richmond City Slave Schedule, First and Second Wards, 1860.

34. Takagi, "Slavery in Richmond," 220.

35. Commonwealth v. Fanny, a slave, Richmond City Hustings Court, Ended Causes, February 1849, box 183, LVA. Fanny actually belonged to a John W. Morris, so Hill had rehired her to Seaman.

36. Commonwealth v. Frances, a slave, Richmond City Hustings Court, Ended Causes, March 1854, box 194, LVA.

37. Commonwealth v. Mary, a slave, Richmond City Hustings Court, Ended Causes, October 1850 (misfiled in August term), box 186, LVA.

38. Commonwealth v. Maria, a slave, Richmond City Hustings Court, Ended Causes, February 1848, box 180, LVA; Commonwealth v. Nancy, a slave, Richmond City Hustings Court, Ended Causes, July 1849, box 184, LVA.

39. Commonwealth v. Lucy, a slave, Richmond City Hustings Court, Ended Causes, July 1852, box 190, LVA; Genovese, *Roll, Jordan, Roll*, 361.

CHAPTER 3. SLAVE HIRING AND HIRED SLAVES' FAMILY AND FRIENDSHIP TIES IN RURAL AREAS

1. GA, York County, VA, 1780–1823, 239, LDS.

2. This slave family and the ages of its members were reconstructed from "A List of negroes belonging to Briery Congregation Dec[embe]r 1841," Treasurer's Book, 1840–47 (photocopy), Board of Briery Presbyterian Church Records, Church Records Collection, acc. 23834, LVA. The hiring-out experience of these slaves was reconstructed from the hiring-out lists contained in the Treasurer's Book.

3. Slave Schedule for York County, 1860, 5; Stampp, *Peculiar Institution*, 57. See also Wilma King, *Stolen Childhood: Slave Youth in Nineteenth-Century America* (Bloomington: Indiana University Press, 1995), 21–23.

4. William McKean to James Dunlop, January 25, 1816, Letterbook of William McKean, Overseer for James Dunlop, 1809–1818 (photocopy), 62, Roslin Plantation Records [near Petersburg], Business Records Collection, acc. 23873, LVA. For Zek's separation from his wife, see Nancy Sorrells, "Francis McFarland and the Black Community: A Case Study of the Hiring Practices within the Upper Shenandoah Valley," 16, Special Collections, Carrier Library, James Madison University, Harrisonburg, VA.

5. GA, Orange County, VA, 1827–42, 169–71, LDS; GA, Middlesex County, VA, 1825–42, 201, LDS. According to his accounts, Madison hired out a slave woman and her child ("Lydia & child") as a unit in 1840, and they have been counted as one slave in order to illustrate the manner in which individuals in a group of hired-out slaves were scattered in several different directions.

6. "The Session Book of Briery Church, Volume I. Containing the records of 80 years, namely, from 1760 to 1840 inclusive," 9–12, LDS.

7. Ibid., 120–22.

8. Slave families and their ages were reconstructed from "A List of negroes belonging to Briery Congregation Dec[embe]r 1841," "A List of hires of the negroes belonging to the Briery Congregation for the year 1840," "Hires of negroes for the year 1841," "A List of negroes belonging to Briery Congregation Dec[embe]r 1841," "Hires of negroes for the year 1841" all in Briery Treasurer's Book, LVA. The fact that Charles Anderson was Jincy's son is clear in "Hires of negroes Dec[ember] 1841 for [the] year 1842," and his birth is recorded in "A List of negroes belonging to Briery Congregation Dec[embe]r 1841," Briery Treasurer's Book.

9. Briery Treasurer's Book.

10. "Hires of Negroes belonging to Congregation for the year 1843," Briery Treasurer's Book.

11. "A list of hires of negroes belonging to Briery Congregation made 26th Dec[ember] 1843"; "A List of negroes belonging to Briery Congregation Dec[embe]r 1841," Briery Treasurer's Book.

12. "A List of hires of negroes belonging to Briery Congregation 26th Dec[ember] 1844"; "A List of negroes belonging to Briery Congregation Dec[ember] 1841," Briery Treasurer's Book.

13. "A List of Hires for the year 1846"; "A List of negroes belonging to Briery Congregation Dec[ember] 1841," Briery Treasurer's Book.

14. "A List of the Hires for the year 1847," Briery Treasurer's Book.

15. "A List of negroes belonging to Briery Congregation Dec[embe]r 1841," Briery Treasurer's Book. The relationship between Frank and Vilet was determined by comparing the hiring out lists for different years. For example, the list for 1840 names "Frank & wife & 3 children," and Vilet does not appear anywhere else on the list. In 1841 Vilet is named and begins to appear together with Frank in the entry "Frank Vilet & 4 children." Approximate ages for Spencer, Brister, and Catherine for December 1839 were determined through the use of ages given for them by the church as of December 1841.

16. "A List of hires of the negroes belonging to the Briery Congregation for the year 1840"; "Hires of negroes for the year 1841." Amy was listed as two years of age in December 1841. As Spencer, Brister, and Catherine were about seven, five, and four, respectively, at that time and do not appear apart from their parents on the hiring list, they must have been the "3 children" referred to in the hiring-out list of 1840. Therefore, Amy was not yet born as of hiring season 1839–40, so in order for her to have been two years old in December 1841, she must have been born sometime during 1840. "Hires of negroes Dec[ember] 27th 1841 for year 1842." Frank's birth is recorded in "A List of negroes belonging to Briery Congregation Dec[embe]r 1841." "Hires of Negroes belonging to Congregation for the year 1843." Spencer's age in December 1843 was determined by adding two years to the estimation made of his age by the church in "A List of negroes belonging to Briery Congregation Dec[embe]r 1841." For the 1844 hiring-out agreements, see "A list of hires of negroes belonging to Briery Congregation made 26th Dec[ember] 1843." All documents in Briery Treasurer's Book.

17. "A List of hires of negroes belonging to Briery Congregation 26th Dec[ember] 1844," Briery Treasurer's Book.

18. The downward trend in hire received by the congregation for Frank, Vilet, and their children can be traced through the hiring-out lists in "A List of hires of the negroes belonging to the Briery Congregation for the year 1840," "Hires of negroes for the year 1841," "Hires of negroes Dec[ember] 27th 1841 for year 1842," "Hires of Negroes belonging to Congregation for the year 1843," and "A list of hires of negroes belonging to Briery Congregation made 26th Dec[ember] 1843," Briery Treasurer's Book.

19. "A List of hires for the year 1846," Briery Treasurer's Book.

20. "A List of the Hires for the year 1847"; "A List of negroes belonging to Briery Congregation Dec[embe]r 1841," Briery Treasurer's Book.

21. Jennifer Oast, "'The Worst Kind of Slavery': Slave-Owning Presbyterian Churches in Prince Edward County, Virginia," *Journal of Southern History* 76 (November 2010): 879.

22. Ibid., 867–68, 879–82, 894–900.

23. Loudoun County, VA, Register of Births, No. 1, 1853–59, 27, 25, 21, LDS. If the births were the result of contact with a partner the women already knew but who resided at a place other than that to which the women were hired, it is likely that the men came to visit them from elsewhere, since slave men normally traveled to a spouse in an abroad marriage. For this point, see Genovese, *Roll, Jordan, Roll*, 472; and Kolchin, *American Slavery*, 141.

24. Deposition of James Coleman, in George Gunnell v. Samuel Coleman, 1841, CFF 36N (2 of 4), FCCA; William McKean to James Dunlop, February 23, 1816, Letterbook of William McKean, 64, Overseer for James Dunlop, 1809–1818 (photocopy), 64, Roslin Plantation Records [near Petersburg], Business Records Collection, acc. 23873, LVA.

25. Bowers v. White, etc., 1814-054, Southampton County, VA, Chancery Papers, 1814, box 18, LVA; John C. Willis, "From the Dictates of Pride to the Paths of Righteousness: Slave Honor and Christianity in Antebellum Virginia," in *The Edge of the South: Life in Nineteenth-Century Virginia*, ed. Edward L. Ayers and John C. Willis (Charlottesville: University Press of Virginia, 1991), 41.

26. William McKean to James Dunlop, February 23, 1816, Letterbook of William McKean. The hiring-out material pertaining to Mary Hall's slaves is in Bacon, Coleman, & Company, Memo[randum] Book, 1836–37, 1842–49 [second sec.], Business Records Collection, acc. 33081, LVA.

27. The persons who hired Charles and Reason each year from 1840 through 1847 are found in the hiring-out lists for those years contained in Briery Treasurer's Book, LVA.

28. William McKean to James Dunlop, December 11, 1816, Letterbook of William McKean; deposition of Richard Douglass, December 20, 1858, in Perciful's Guardian v. Perciful, 1858, Lancaster County, VA, Chancery Papers, 1858, LVA.

29. "Minority report to Bri[e]ry Congregation May 15th 1846," in "Presbyterian Churches" folder, Eggleston Family Papers, Mss 1Eg396b, sec. 30, box 54, VHS.

30. Bacon, Coleman, & Company Memo[randum] Book [second sec.], 43, 17.

31. Alex[ander] Findlay to W[illiam] Gray, September 15, 1850, William Gray Papers, Mss 1G7952aFA2, VHS; GA, Essex County, VA, 1851–57, 197, LDS; Estate Book B, Northumberland County, VA, 1849–51, 156, LDS; Herbert Gutman maintained that a slave hired out away from loved ones "could also form new kin ties that supplemented the older ones," but findings pre-

sented here show that hired slaves' new ties, much like their older ones, could be severed at any time. Herbert G. Gutman, *The Black Family in Slavery and Freedom, 1750–1925* (New York: Vintage, 1976), 138.

32. John W. Perrin to Thomas Crue, December 27, 1803, folder 3, "Papers relating to the hiring out and management of slaves by William K. Perrin, 1800–1855 & n.d.," William K. Perrin Papers, WM.

33. Perdue, Barden, and Phillips, *Weevils in the Wheat*, 318 (for Nancy); Fisk University, *Unwritten History of Slavery*, in *The American Slave: A Composite Autobiography*, ed. George P. Rawick (Westport, CT: Greenwood, 1972), ser. 2, 18:162 (for Kelly).

34. Joseph Jackson Halsey to Andrew Glassell Grinnan, December 22, 1854, Grinnan Family Papers, Mss 1G8855c, sec. 21, VHS.

35. Slave Schedule for Fauquier County, 1860, 65, 51 (first sec.), 9 (second sec.) for Colbert and 19, 24 (second sec.) for Payne; Slave Schedule for Loudoun County, 1860, 9, 11, 19, 31, 42 for Mead and 12, 22, 23, 24 for Chamblin. Herbert Gutman speculated that "individual slaves hired out and thereby cut off from an immediate family might have found kin to sustain them while 'hired out.'" Gutman, *The Black Family*, 599n35. The material presented here suggests that for many hired slaves this may not have been the case.

36. Perdue, Barden, and Phillips, *Weevils in the Wheat*, 215.

37. For a discussion of abroad-marriage visiting, see Genovese, *Roll, Jordan, Roll*, 472–73; Slave Schedule for Loudoun County, 1860, 22. Paxson's (and therefore also the hired slave's) approximate location is indicated by Paxson's ownership of 85.25 acres of land eight miles northwest of Leesburg. Since Williams owned land about ten miles northwest of Leesburg, he and Paxson must have resided fairly near each other, which meant that Williams's slave was certainly much closer to home than were some of the slaves hired to Buford's railroad. See Auditor of Public Accounts, Land Book, Loudoun County, VA, 1860, District of George K. Fox, 41 (for Paxson), 58 (for Williams), LVA. For Higs's hiring of the slave to Sexton, see Slave Schedule for Loudoun County, 1860, 3. According to a letter of Sam[ue]l Drewry to John Buford, February 10, 1854, Drewry acted as Buford's agent to procure slaves from Southampton County and vicinity, and Drewry mentioned that some of the slaves he had secured for Buford came from owners in Sussex County, as well. The letter is in John Buford Papers, 1804–98, in Kenneth M. Stampp, gen. ed., *Records of Ante-Bellum Southern Plantations from the Revolution through the Civil War*, microfilm, Series F: Selections from the Manuscript Department, Duke University Library.

38. B. H. Walker Diary (photocopy), January 1, 1859, Personal Papers Collection, acc. 20800, LVA. Concerning weekend and other leisure time, Genovese observed that "field hands had one big advantage over house servants: firmer control over assigned periods of leisure time. The field hands had Sundays, certain prescribed holidays, and the late evening of each day to relax as best they could [while] [h]ouse servants had to remain on call." Genovese, *Roll, Jordan, Roll*, 337. The ex-slave's recollections are taken from Fisk University, *God Struck Me Dead*, in Rawick, *American Slave*, ser. 2, vol. 19, 185.

39. Slave-hiring bond, Gabriel H. Wren and James Wren Jr. to Eleanor Cooksey, February, 1839, Loudoun County Free Negro and Slave Records (Slave Hires), Melvin Steadman Collec-

tion, box 8, folder 7, Personal Papers Collection, acc. 34683, LVA; slave-hiring bond, Ch[arles] Ja[me]s Faulkner to Mary Timberlake, December 14, 183[?], "Slaves" folder, Faulkner Family Papers, Mss 1F2735aFA2, box 44, VHS.

40. Slave-hiring bond, Richmond and Danville Railroad to Benjamin B. Jackson, December 28, 1853, Carrington Family Papers, Mss 1C2358e, sec. 2, VHS; Gutman, *The Black Family*, 285.

41. Fisk University, *Unwritten History of Slavery*, in Rawick, *American Slave*, ser. 2, 18:162–63.

42. Joseph Jackson Halsey to Andrew Glassell Grinnan, December 22, 1854, Grinnan Family Papers.

43. See copy of the will of William Deneale in Hunter v. Deneale, CFF 42u (2 of 2), FCCA. See also the notation contained in a letter of John Hopkins to J[ames] C. Deneale, April 17, 1818, in Hunter v. Deneale (1 of 2): "Peter's father (Tom) by W[illia]m Deneale's Will remained on the plantation where J[ames] C. Deneale lived."

44. Hopkins to Deneal[e], April 7, 1818, Hunter v. Deneale (2 of 2); Hopkins to Deneale, April 17, 1818, Hunter v. Deneale (1 of 2).

45. Hopkins to Deneale, April 17, 1818, Hunter v. Deneale (1 of 2). For Hopkins's dissatisfaction with Peter, and his view that Peter deserved punishment, see Hopkins to Deneal[e], April 7, 1818, Hunter v. Deneale (2 of 2).

46. GA, York County, VA, 1780–1823, 241, LDS; GA, Lancaster County, VA, 1835–42, 38, 41, 43, 45, 47, 49, LDS.

47. GA, Lancaster County, VA, 1835–42, 35, LDS; *Nebraska Narratives*, in Rawick, *American Slave*, supp., ser. 2, 1:319.

48. Whether Willis ran away in 1826 or in 1827 is unclear. Willis's separation from loved ones is shown by the fact that his manager hired out several other slaves who belonged to the same person in both 1826 and 1827. For Willis's experience as a hired slave, see EA, Stafford County, VA, 1827–34, 149–50, 152, LDS.

CHAPTER 4. HIRED SLAVES, WHITES, AND SLAVERY

1. Will[ia]m D. Cabell to Iverson L. Twyman, December 25, 1858, Letters to Iverson L. Twyman, 1856–58, folder 46, Austin-Twyman Papers, in Stampp, *Records of Ante-Bellum Southern Plantations*, Series L.

2. Wade, *Slavery in the Cities*, 49.

3. John Gault to Sam[ue]l Gault, December 31, 1853, John Gault Letter, Mss 2G2365a1, VHS; Wade, *Slavery in the Cities*, 48; Commonwealth v. William Bonner, Richmond City Hustings Court, Ended Causes, December 1851, box 189, LVA; Nick to his mistress, Dec[embe]r 20, 1845, James D. Blackwell Papers, 1839–1929, Mss 39.1 B57, WM.

4. Marcus to Geo[rge] W Nelson, January 10, 1860, George William Nelson Papers, 1850–1900, Mss 2N331b, VHS.

5. Ephraim's experience is drawn from letters contained in Carrington Family Papers, 1817–95, Mss 1C2358g, sec. 1, VHS. For specific items, see note 6.

6. Thomas C. Read to Henry Carrington, October 22, 1847; February 9, May 15, 1849; September 5, 1851; April [?] 1852, Carrington Family Papers, 1817–95, Mss 1C2358g, sec. 1,

VHS; W[illia]m Watts to H[enry] Carrington, March 6, 1855, Carrington Family Papers, sec. 1, VHS.

7. Fanny's experience is reconstructed from letters in Barker-Cooke Papers, 1809–89, Mss 65 B24, series 1, subseries 1: Plantation Letters, 1848–53, folder 2, WM. Particular items cited in note 8.

8. Hez[ekiah] Ford to James E. Cooke, December 23, 1850; March 18, December 24, 1851; January 20, 1852, Barker-Cooke Papers, 1809–89.

9. Journal (Roslin, VA; w/inventory of property, inc. slaves) 1829–31, Papers of the McGill-Mahone Families, acc. 1627, UVA.

10. Richard M. Cunningham, Farm Diary, 1835–69 (item e), folder 2, Cunningham-Downman Family Papers, 1790–1875, acc. 28093, Personal Papers Collection, LVA.

11. Richard B. Buckner Diary, 1829–38, January 14, July 6, 18, August 5, 1836, WM.

12. Garland's experience was reconstructed from letters in Socrates Maupin Papers, 1790–1921, acc. 2769-a, UVA. Specific items cited in note 13.

13. Socrates Maupin to Addison Maupin, December 9, 24, 1836; September 23, December 21, 30, 1843; December 21, 1847; December 12, 21, 1848; January 1, May 31, December 2, 23, 24, 28, 1849; January 3, 1851, Socrates Maupin Papers.

14. Hez[ekiah] Ford to James E. Cooke, November 29, 1849, Barker-Cooke Papers, folder 2; Blackford Arthur & Co. to Jesse Nalle, December 12, 1819, Nalle Family Papers, 1800–1862, Mss 1N1495a, sec. 4, VHS; GA, Essex County, VA, 1844–51, 127, LDS. Moss's tenant status is revealed in account entries near the statement with respect to the slaves' clothes.

15. Keeling v. Ewell, Princess Anne County, VA, Court Judgments, 1840, box 38, folder 3, LVA; George Gunnell v. Samuel Coleman, 1841, CFF 36N (1 of 4), FCCA.

16. Chappell's Executors v. Wilcox and Watson, 1793-31, LCPSCV.

17. James M. Harris to Iverson L. Twyman, April 23, 1856, Letters to Iverson L. Twyman, 1856–58, folder 46, Austin-Twyman Papers, in Stampp, *Records of Ante-Bellum Southern Plantations*, Series L.

18. William Taliaferro account with Philip M. Tabb & Son, 1859, Taliaferro Family Papers, Mss 1T1438a, sec. 2, VHS; slave-hiring bond (photocopy), John Fitzgerald and Sam Scott to Patrick H. Foster, December 31, 1855, John Fitzgerald Papers, Mss 1F5764c, VHS.

19. "Inquisition Taken on the Body of Henry J. Harrison's Julius," LCPSCV, 1840–59.

20. Heath's Guardian v. Mason and Smith, 1790-81, LCPSCV.

21. Coleman Smith to Robert W. Carter, October 19, 1857; Elias Harroll to unknown slave on Coleman Smith's plantation, n.d.; Coleman Smith to Robert W. Carter, October 31, 1857; Carter Papers, folder 44, in Stampp, *Records of Ante-Bellum Southern Plantations*, Series L.

22. Conflicts rooted in claims of exclusive mastery over hired slaves, made by both owners and hirers alike, are explored in Martin, *Divided Mastery*.

23. Thomas Chrystie to Philip Croxton, May 19, 1811, Thomas Chrystie Papers, Mss 1C4695a, VHS; Gray and Farr Depositions, Johnson v. Coleman, 1857, CFF 52X, FCCA.

24. John Hopkins to James C. Deneale, April 7, 1818, Hunter v. Deneale, 1835, CFF 42u (2 of 2), FCCA; Hopkins to Deneale, April 17, 1818, Hunter v. Deneale, 1835, CFF 42u (1 of 2), FCCA.

25. Dew, *Bond of Iron*, 69.
26. Ibid., 151.
27. Ronald L. Lewis, *Coal, Iron, and Slaves: Industrial Slavery in Maryland and Virginia, 1715–1865* (Westport, CT: Greenwood Press, 1979), 97–100; John W. Tomlin to Benjamin Brand, January 6, 1809, Benjamin Brand Papers, Mss 1B7332b, Microfilm Reels C515–C517, VHS; I. L. Twyman to Thomas Austin, January 2, 1851, folder 26, Austin-Twyman Papers, in Stampp, *Records of Ante-Bellum Southern Plantations*, Series L; Charles B. Dew, "Disciplining Slave Ironworkers in the Antebellum South: Coercion, Conciliation, and Accommodation," *American Historical Review* 79 (1974): 404.
28. Dew, *Bond of Iron*, 161–62. The significance of overwork payments is considered in greater detail in chapter 6.
29. Perdue, Barden, and Phillips, *Weevils in the Wheat*, 58–59.

CHAPTER 5. WHITE LADIES, WHITE MEN, MASTERS ALL

1. Martin Webb to Messrs. Scott & Buford, June 12, 1857, Buford Family Papers, 1844–64, acc. 9782, UVA.
2. William Mathews to John Dundore, April [?] 16, 1856, Mathews Family Correspondence, 1856, acc. 10274, UVA.
3. Samuel Drewry to John Buford, December 30, 1854; R. P. Clements to John Buford, January 1, 1855, John Buford Papers, in Stampp, *Records of Ante-Bellum Southern Plantations*, Series F.
4. Drewry to Buford, January 16, 1855, John Buford Papers.
5. Ibid.
6. Ibid.; Dunaway's Adm'r v. Dunaway et al., Lancaster County, VA, Chancery Papers, 1852, LVA.
7. Sullivan's Guardian v. Sullivan, Lancaster County, VA, Chancery Papers, 1852, LVA.
8. Chilton's Guardian v. Chilton et al., Lancaster County, VA, Chancery Papers, 1852, LVA.
9. Edward Carter Turner Diary, April 4, 14, 1850, Turner Family Papers, Mss 1T8596a, VHS.
10. Ibid., April 25, 1850; Elizabeth Noland to Ella (Noland) MacKenzie, December 29, 1856, Ella Noland MacKenzie Papers, 3667, SHC.
11. Charles B. Dew, "Black Ironworkers and the Slave Insurrection Panic of 1856," *Journal of Southern History* 41 (August 1975): 322, 328, 333–38.
12. James Harrison Deposition, August 18, 1836, in Hunter v. Deneale, 1835, CFF 42u, FCCA; GA, York County, VA, 1780–1823, 138; Journal (Roslin, VA; w/inventory of property, inc. slaves), 1829–31, Papers of the McGill-Mahone Families, 1771–1919, acc. 1627, UVA; GA, Essex County, VA, 1857–67, 175–76, 178–80, 264.
13. Bureau of the Census, Eighth Census of the United States, 1860, Original Returns of the Assistant Marshalls (microfilm), Schedule I, "An Enumeration of Free Inhabitants," Fauquier County, VA, 52–53, 78 (hereafter Free Schedule for _____); Slave Schedule for Fauquier County, VA, 1860, 18, 35.

14. Elkanah Talley to Benjamin Brand, September 10, 1809, Benjamin Brand Papers, Mss 1B7332b, sec. 4, VHS; Joseph Hiden to Frances Todd (Johnson) Barbour, November 11, 1863, Barbour Family Papers, Mss 1B2346b, sec. 6, microfilm reel C4, VHS; Nelson Hicks to John Letcher, June 6, 1850, John Letcher Papers, 1770–1970, series 2, folder 194, Mss 1 L5684 a FA2 series 2, VHS.

15. George Twyman to Mrs. Lucy Twyman, 1804, Papers of George Twyman, 1750–1911, acc. 1261, UVA.

16. Shepherd Family Papers, 1732–1907, sec. 9, Mss 1Sh485a, VHS; Henry Parker to Henry Blunt, December 20, 1806, in Turner's Administrator v. Parker, 1813-102, LCPSCV; GA, Essex County, VA, 1838–44, 77, 79, 146, 243, LDS; GA, Essex County, VA, 1844–51, 39, 171, 229, 231, 272, 311, 348, 350, LDS; Slave Schedule for Fauquier County, 1860; Slave Schedule for Loudoun County, 1860; GA, Middlesex County, VA, 1825–42, 34, 35, 36, 56, 96, 97, LDS; lists of slaves hired out in Folly Farm Papers, acc. 9380, UVA; William Wirt to Sam Washington, December 12, 1850, "A list of the servants hired last year 1850 and for hire the coming year 1851," Lawrence Washington Papers, Mss 2 W2776b, VHS.

17. GA, York County, VA, 1780–1823, 137–40, 159–61, 163–64, 179–82, 192, 194–96, 207, 209–11, 213–14, 216–21, 223–24, 413; GA, Loudoun County, VA, 1838–52, LDS. Beale made entries for January 1 in each year from 1829 through 1837; GA, Middlesex County, VA, 1842–57, 13, LDS; Thomas W. Banks Account with John W. C. Catlett, His Guardian, entry for March 8, 1845, in Manuscript Volumes–Account Books, Farms and Farming, Ms VAf14, WM; GA, Sussex County, VA, 1839–50, 321–22; Fairfax County, VA, Will Book Z, No. 1, 31–43, FCCA; Isham Newsum Affidavit, in Crichlow v. Gurley, etc., 1821-19, Southampton County, VA, Chancery Papers, 1821, box 25, LVA; GA, Lancaster County, VA, 1835–42, 92, LDS; GA, Essex County, VA, 1857–67, 55, LDS; Weldin B. Parks receipt, January 25, 1849, John Letcher Papers, 1770–1970, series 2, folder 194, Mss 1 L5684 a FA2 series 2, VHS.

18. The popularity and newsworthiness of hiring days is illustrated in the following sources: William Bailey Deposition, October 15, 1810, in Washington's Administrator v. Holleman, et al., 1814-088, Southampton County, VA, Chancery Papers, 1814, box 19, LVA; *American Beacon and Norfolk and Portsmouth Daily Advertiser,* January 2, 1839; Eggleston Family Papers, Mss 1Eg396b, sec. 1, VHS; *Petersburg Daily Courier,* December 23, 1814; *American Beacon and Norfolk and Portsmouth Daily Advertiser,* December 24, 25, 1839, January 2, 1840; Daniel William Cobb Diary, December 31, 1842; December 26, 1847; December 27, 31, 1849; December 28, 1857, VHS; B. H. Walker Diary (photocopy), January 1, 1858; January 1, 1859; January 2, 1860, LVA; Robert Henderson Allen Diary, January 1, 1858, Allen Family Papers, Mss 1AL546a, microfilm reel B1, VHS. The quotations are in W. V. Montague to T. C. Redman, February 6, 1862 (written from Princess Anne, VA), Lancaster County, VA, County Court Judgments, 1862, LVA; Robert Henderson Allen Diary, January 1, 1859; January 1, 2, 1861, VHS.

19. Britt et ux v. Hines' Executor et al., 1814-055, Southampton County, VA, Chancery Causes, Oversize box 2, LVA; Diary of Caroline Seabury, 1854–63, "New Year's Day/[18]56 'Hiring Out,'" at http://krypton.mankato.msus.edu/~susanna/diarycarolineseabury.html; Rhys Isaac, *The Transformation of Virginia, 1740–1790* (Chapel Hill: University of North Carolina Press, 1988), 317; Jack Larkin, *The Reshaping of Everyday Life, 1790–1840* (New York: Harper & Row, 1989), 284 (for the quotation on liquor); Donald L. Winters, *Tennessee Farming, Tennessee*

Farmers: Antebellum Agriculture in the Upper South (Knoxville: University of Tennessee Press, 1994), 133–34; E. Lee Shepard, "'This Being Court Day': Courthouses and Community Life in Rural Virginia," *Virginia Magazine of History and Biography* 103 (October 1995): 459–70.

20. Daniel William Cobb Diary, December 27, 31, 1849, VHS.

21. Shepard, "'This Being Court Day,'" 459–70; Ted Ownby, *Subduing Satan: Religion, Recreation, and Manhood in the Rural South, 1865–1920* (Chapel Hill: University of North Carolina Press, 1990), 2; chap. 2, passim; 49; Stephanie McCurry, *Masters of Small Worlds: Yeoman Households, Gender Relations, and the Political Culture of the Antebellum South Carolina Low Country* (New York: Oxford University Press, 1995), 91.

22. Walter Bowie, Jr. Journal, January 1, 14, 17, 7, 1861, Papers of Walter Bowie, Jr., box 1, acc. 8528, UVA; James F. Taliaferro to Miss J. M. Waller, 1850s, David Garland Waller Papers, 1842–61, DU. For southern white women's ladyhood and mastery, see Kirsten E. Wood, *Masterful Women: Slaveholding Widows from the American Revolution through the Civil War* (Chapel Hill: University of North Carolina Press, 2004).

23. Thomas Jefferson to John Minor, November 7, 1807, Thomas Jefferson Papers, 1780–1826, Mss 2J3595a11, VHS; Charles William Pollard Diary, March 13, 1852–December 9, 1854, Baylor Family Papers, 1779–1963, sec. 15, Mss 1B3445c46, VHS; Travel Journal, 5065-z, January–February 1847, February 3, 4, 5, 6, 1847, SHC.

24. GA, York County, VA, 1780–1823, 159, 179, 210, 216. White southern women's expected role in connection to slaves is treated in Marli F. Weiner, "Mistresses, Morality, and the Dilemmas of Slaveholding: The Ideology and Behavior of Elite Antebellum Women," in *Discovering the Women in Slavery*, ed. Patricia Morton (Athens: University of Georgia Press, 1996), 278–98.

25. William Braxton to W[illia]m R[oane] Aylett, 1859, Aylett Family Papers, 1776–1945, Mss 1Ay455a, VHS; John Marshall to Daniel Ward, May 27, [?] Keith Family Papers, 1709–1865, Mss 1K2694a149-160, sec. 19, VHS; John Augustine Washington to Louisa (Clemson) Washington, August 31, 1861, John Augustine Washington Letter, Mss 2W2774a1, VHS.

26. Charles W. Montague to Frances Thruston Hughes, November [?] 1845, Montague Family Papers, 1808–1939, Mss 1M7607a, sec. 5, microfilm reel B31, VHS.

27. Robert T. Taylor to Judith Willantina Frances (Robinson) Taylor, January 4, 1860, sec. 61 (folder 9 of 12); Taylor to Benjamin Temple, April 26, 1860, sec. 49; July 19, 1860, sec. 49; January 9, 1861, sec. 51; April 15, 1861, sec. 49; Elizabeth Skyren Temple to My dear Children, December 23, [?], sec. 51, Harrison Family Papers, Mss 1H2485a, VHS.

28. John Hill for Susanna Dabney to Thomas Chrystie, July 4, 1807, Thomas Chrystie Papers, 1784–1811, Mss 2C4695b, VHS.

29. Daniel and David Higginbotham Company (Amherst County, VA), Journals and Ledgers, 1818–43, Ledger F, Ledger H, cash accounts, February 10, 16, 1838; December 16, 1833, and passim, Local Government Records Collection, Amherst County Court Records, acc. 21597 and 21717, LVA.

30. The relationship between Page and Taylor was reconstructed from letters and accounts in Page Family Papers, Mss 1 P1465 c 11-58, sec. 2, VHS. Specific items cited in note 31.

31. W. H. Taylor to Elizabeth Page, April 15, December 17, 1845; May 2 [?], December 5, 12, 1848; June 14, 1849; April 12, 1850, Page Family Papers.

32. Cash Book of J. W. Twyman, ca. 1850–ca. 1870, January 2, 1857; January 1, 1858; March 9, 1859; June 15, 1860, and passim, Twyman Family Papers, acc. 7808, UVA; Beverly Hutchison to George Millam, March 28, 1858, Beverly Hutchison Papers, 3272-z, SHC.

33. Robert N. Trice to Miss Eliza B. Chowning, January 3, 1844, Harrison Family Papers, 1662–1915, Mss 1H2485a, sec. 32, VHS; Unidentified Compiler, Inventory, 1860, Mss 2Un3a24, VHS.

34. Robert Taylor Scott to Fanny Scott (Carter) Scott, January 3, 1861, Robert Taylor Scott Correspondence, Fanny Scott (Carter) Scott, folder 9 of 19, March 7, 1860–March 3, 1861, Keith Family Papers, Mss 1K2694cFA2, VHS; Free Schedule for Fauquier County, 1860; Freehling, *Road to Disunion*, 47–48.

35. These economic and occupational groups were derived from Free Schedule for Fauquier County, 1860, following identification of slave hirers in Slave Schedule for Fauquier County, 1860.

36. Edward Burke Account Book, 1840 and 1841 entries, Washington Family Papers, box 2, acc. 3683, UVA; GA, York County, VA, 1780–1823, 174, 187, 197, 225, 243, LDS.

37. Fauquier County, VA, Merchant's Journal, 1859–61, December 29, 1859 entry, wages paid Frank Lewis for 1859, Ms V Ame32u, WM; Free Schedule for Fauquier County, 1860, 80, 78, 123, 84, 151.

38. Free Schedule for Fauquier County, 1860, 78, 125, 137.

39. Joseph Lyler Deposition, October 28, 1871, in E. C. Fitzhugh, Trustee v. M. O'Brien, 1871, CFF 32h, FCCA.

40. John A. Selden Diary, January 6, 1843, Ms V D12, WM; Walker R. Carter and Larkin Stanard Agreement, August 25, 1809, and Bruce Chisholm Deposition, June 1, 1819, in Carter v. Stanard, 1818-02, Caroline County Chancery Causes, box 3, LVA; Mary Eliza Powell Dulany Diary, June 28, 1862, Mss 5:1 D8865:1, VHS.

41. Fred Arthur Bailey, *Class and Tennessee's Confederate Generation* (Chapel Hill: University of North Carolina Press, 1987); Freehling, *Road to Disunion*, 48–50 ("jealousy," 48); David M. Potter, *The Impending Crisis, 1848–1861*, completed and edited by Don E. Fehrenbacher (New York: Harper & Row, 1976), 398–400 ("African slave trade" quotations, 399). Quotations from petitions are from Digital Library on American Slavery, http://history.uncg.edu/slaverypetitions, under "poor Whites" in "Virginia."

42. Slave Schedule for Fauquier County, 1860; Bailey, *Class and Tennessee's Confederate Generation*, 64–65; Daniel W. Crofts, *Old Southampton: Politics and Society in a Virginia County, 1834–1869* (Charlottesville: University Press of Virginia, 1992), 133, 160, 180, 72.

43. Free Schedule for Fauquier County, 1860, 120, 84; Slave Schedule for Fauquier County, 1860, 42, 29.

44. Free Schedule for Fauquier County, 1860, 47; Slave Schedule for Fauquier County, 1860, 16.

45. Barton, "'Good Cooks and Washers,'" 436–60.

46. Free Schedule for Fauquier County, 1860, 6; Slave Schedule for Fauquier County, 1860, 2.

47. Free Schedule for Fauquier County, 1860, 46; Slave Schedule for Fauquier County, 1860, 16.

48. Free Schedule for Fauquier County, 118; Slave Schedule for Fauquier County, 40.

49. GA, York County, VA, 1780–1823, 182, 192, 193, 214, 215, 218, 219, 223, 224, LDS; James Galt Diary, December 27, 1841, Ms V D 10, WM; Edward Carter Turner Diary, December 31, 1839, Turner Family Papers, Mss 1T8596a, VHS; Anna C. Hoge to Susan C. Noland, December 24, 1849, Susan C. Noland Papers, 1847–62, DU; B. H. Walker Diary (photocopy), January 1, 1859. Whites' hiring of house servants is explored in Barton, "'Good Cooks and Washers.'"

50. Patrick Catlett to Elizabeth Catlett, January 4, 1847, Papers of John Catlett, acc. 9398-j, UVA.

51. John S. Miller to Jane Miller, September 17, 28, October 7, November 3, 1846, Letters of John S. Miller 1841–46, acc. 11702, UVA; Margaret Brooke to Robert Brooke, March 12, 1842, Brooke Family Papers, acc. 38–137, UVA.

52. Lorrinda McPherson to William Royston, April 10, 1838; April 18, July 15, 1842; January 26, 1847, William S. Royston Papers, 1823–98, DU.

53. Ibid., June 3, 1838; [?] 18, 1839, January 28, 1839; December 5, 1841; November 18, 1845.

54. The frequency of widows' hiring out of slaves is shown in Slave Schedule for Fauquier County, 1860, 3, 15, 16, 17, 18, 36, 46. Widows named are found in Free Schedule for Fauquier County, 1860, 9 (for Edmonds household), 72 (for Ogilvie household), 150 (for Sinclair household). Persons who hired slaves from Edmonds, Ogilvie, and Sinclair are found in Slave Schedule for Fauquier County, 1860, 44 (for Ferguson), 31 (for Fairfax County hirer), and Slave Schedule for Prince William County, 1860, 14 (for Meredith). Waller household is found in Free Schedule for Fauquier County, 1860, 115, and her hiring out of slaves is shown in Slave Schedule for Fauquier County, 1860, 54–55.

55. GA, Loudoun County, VA, 1838–52, LDS; Sarah Harriet Apphia Hunter Farming Materials, Lists of Slaves, Records of Slave Hire, Hunter Family Papers, 1766–1918, Essex County, VA, Mss 1H9196aFA2, box 28, VHS.

56. Perdue, Barden, and Phillips, *Weevils in the Wheat*, 39; Daniel William Cobb Diary, January 5, 1857; January 5, 9, 10, 1859; January 16, 1858, VHS. For reciprocity on the part of Cobb's neighbors, see November 23, 1858; January 5, 1859.

57. Walter Bowie Journal, June 18, 19, 20, 21, 22, 23, 25, 26, 27, 1860, in Stampp, *Records of Ante-Bellum Southern Plantations*, Series E: Selections from the University of Virginia Library.

58. Ibid.; Slave Schedule for Fauquier County, 1860, 26, 32, 34, 4?, 45, 46, 49, 57, 61; Free Schedule for Fauquier County, 1860, 74, 87, 90, 102, 107, 120, 147, 150.

59. John Walker Plantation Journal, September 11, November 5, 1832, in Stampp, *Records of Ante-Bellum Southern Plantations*, Series J: Selections from the Southern Historical Collection, Manuscripts Department, Library of the University of North Carolina at Chapel Hill; Jaqueline Plummer Taliaferro Diary, 1858–60, Mss 5:1T1434:1-3, January 4, September 2, 1859, VHS; Tho[ma]s Randolph to Joseph Watkins, January [?] 1796, in Papers of Joseph Watkins and the Shields Family, acc. 11433, UVA; Clinton M. King to Mollie King (incomplete), ca. March 1862, in Clinton M. King Papers, 1861–62, Mss 2 K5810b, VHS.

60. Accounts of Washington M. Carr, Orphan, in GA, Loudoun County, VA, 1838–52, LDS; William Faber Account Book, WM; receipt, Solemon Everhart to George Rust, June 16,

1854, "Memorandum of Negroes Hired For the year 1854," George Rust Papers, 1808–79, DU; William F. Martin (Mercer County, WV) Ledger, 1853–63, Local Government Records Collection, Giles County Court Records, LVA. Local neighborhood exchange is treated in John T. Schlotterbeck, "Plantation and Farm: Social and Economic Change in Orange and Greene Counties, Virginia, 1716 to 1860" (Ph.D. diss., Johns Hopkins University, 1980).

61. Daniel Anderson Account Book, 1844–53, September 22, 1848, Mss 5:3 An 234:2, VHS. The slave Nelson sent was sick, but the point is that the owner-hirer relationship was unaffected by hired slave Thornton's actions. Free and Slave Schedules for Fauquier and Loudoun counties, 1860.

62. On reciprocation, status, and respect, see Crofts, *Old Southampton*, 72. H. A. White & Co. Account Books, Mss 5:3 W5868:1–2, VHS.

63. H. A. White & Co. Account Books, Mss 5:3 W5868:2, VHS; Free Schedule for Fauquier County, 1860, 44; Slave Schedule for Fauquier County, 1860, 15.

CHAPTER 6. SLAVE HIRING, HIRED SLAVES, AND URBAN AND INDUSTRIAL SLAVERY

1. Lewis, *Coal, Iron, and Slaves*, 27–28; Takagi, "Slavery in Richmond," 21; Gerald W. Mullin, *Flight and Rebellion: Slave Resistance in Eighteenth-Century Virginia* (New York: Oxford University Press, 1972), 88.

2. Charles B. Dew, "David Ross and the Oxford Iron Works: A Study of Industrial Slavery in the Early Nineteenth-Century South," *William and Mary Quarterly* 21 (1974): 199–200; Ronald L. Lewis, "The Use and Extent of Slave Labor in the Chesapeake Iron Industry: The Colonial Era," *Labor History* 17 (Summer 1976): 403–4; Dew, *Bond of Iron*; Wilma A. Dunaway, *Slavery in the American Mountain South* (Cambridge: Cambridge University Press, 2003), 125–27; "Mining," in *Dictionary of Afro-American Slavery*, ed. Randall M. Miller and John David Smith (Westport, CT: Praeger, 1997), 472; John T. Schlotterbeck, "The Internal Economy of Slavery in Rural Piedmont Virginia," in *The Slaves' Economy: Independent Production by Slaves in the Americas*, ed. Ira Berlin and Philip D. Morgan (London: Frank Cass, 1991), 180n14.

3. Takagi, "Slavery in Richmond," 39, 41, 45.

4. Dunaway, *Slavery in the American Mountain South*, 123–25; Schlotterbeck, "Internal Economy," 180n14; R. S. Yeoman, *A Guide Book of United States Coins* (Atlanta: Whitman, 2007), 224–58.

5. Lewis, *Coal, Iron, and Slaves*, 64–65; Takagi, "Slavery in Richmond," 20–21; Lewis, *Coal, Iron, and Slaves*, 83–84, Heth quotation on 65; Miller and Smith, *Dictionary of Afro-American Slavery*, 472; *Richmond Enquirer*, December 28, 1858, 2.

6. John E. Stealey III, *The Antebellum Kanawha Salt Business and Western Markets* (Lexington: University Press of Kentucky, 1993), 133, 140, 141, 150, 151, 153, 155, 156, 157 (quotations on 156–57); Miller and Smith, *Dictionary of Afro-American Slavery*, 472; Dunaway, *Slavery in the American Mountain South*, 117–19.

7. Suzanne Gehring Schnittman, "Slavery in Virginia's Urban Tobacco Industry, 1840–1860" (Ph.D. diss., University of Rochester, 1987), 26–33, 112–14; Joseph Clarke Robert, *The*

Tobacco Kingdom: Plantation, Market, and Factory in Virginia and North Carolina, 1800–1860 (Durham, NC: Duke University Press, 1938), 197.

8. William H. Siener, "Charles Yates, the Grain Trade, and Economic Development in Fredericksburg, Virginia, 1750–1810," *Virginia Magazine of History and Biography* 93 (October 1985): 410; Takagi, "Slavery in Richmond," 19–20; *Alexandria Expositor and Columbian Advertiser*, December 29, 1802; Richard Blow Receipt Book, April 18, 1785; August 1, 1786, Business Records Collection, acc. 27744, LVA; Edwards, Clark, and McDaid, *Guide to Business Records*, 19.

9. Takagi, "Slavery in Richmond," 35; *Virginia Chronicle and Norfolk and Portsmouth General Advertiser*, December 15, 1792, 4; Wade, *Slavery in the Cities*, 330; Ira Berlin, "Evolution of Afro-American Society," 75–76; Evans v. Harrison's Administratrix, 1802-36, LCPSCV; GA, York County, VA, 1780–1823, 141, 162, LDS.

10. Orange County, VA, Legislative Petition, December 16, 1805, box 2, LVA, quoted in Schlotterbeck, "Plantation and Farm," 61.

11. Robert F. Hunter, "The Turnpike Movement in Virginia, 1816–1860" (Ph.D. diss., Columbia University, 1957), 134–36, 313; Nelson Conrad Depositions, September 3, 1836; March 29, 1837, in Graham v. Reid, CFF 78C, FCCA; Account Book (Journal), 1796–1820, Upper Appomattox Company Records, Mss 3UP65a, item a5, VHS.

12. Cornelia M. [Barksdale] Quarles to her brother, January 2, 1849, Peter Barksdale Papers, 1783–1895, Halifax County, VA, also Petersburg, VA, in Stampp, *Records of Ante-Bellum Southern Plantations*, Series F; Peter Way, *Common Labour: Workers and the Digging of North American Canals, 1780–1860* (Cambridge: Cambridge University Press, 1993), 49, 263, 125–29; James M. Harris to Iverson L. Twyman, January 4, 1859, folder 47, Letters to Iverson L. Twyman, 1859–60, Austin-Twyman Papers, 1765–1865, in Stampp, *Records of Ante-Bellum Southern Plantations*, Series L.

13. [Illegible] Burton to John Buford, November 10, 1854, John Buford Papers, 1804–98, in Stampp, *Records of Ante-Bellum Southern Plantations*, Series F; Kenneth W. Noe, *Southwest Virginia's Railroad: Modernization and the Sectional Crisis* (Urbana: University of Illinois Press, 1994), 29–30. In April 1851 Robert Mitchell informed Buford that he had secured thirty pairs of shoes and two hundred yards each of linen and cotton shirting for Buford's hired slaves, whom Mitchell thought numbered "about 30." R. C. Mitchell to John Buford, April 7, 1851, Correspondence 1850–59, Buford Family Papers, 1844–64, acc. 9782, microfilm reel no. M-2188, UVA; David H. Clark to John Buford, November 27, 1854, John Buford Papers; [illegible] Montgomery to Iverson L. Twyman, January 6, 1855, folder 45, Letters to Iverson L. Twyman, Austin-Twyman Papers, 1765–1865; see also entries for hired-slave labor in Buford and Mitchell's cash accounts in John Buford Papers; Noe, *Southwest Virginia's Railroad*, 82.

14. Hez[ekiah] Ford to James E. Cooke, January 20, 1852, Barker-Cooke Papers, 1809–89, folder 2, acc. 65 B24, WM; T. W. Leftwich to John Buford, May 13, 1854; R. M. Burk to John Buford, June 7, 1854, John Buford Papers; deposition of Isaac W. Davis, in Graham v. Reid, 1836, CFF 78C, FCCA.

15. Todd L. Savitt, *Medicine and Slavery: The Diseases and Health Care of Blacks in Antebellum Virginia* (Chicago: University of Illinois Press, 2002), 81–82.

16. James v. Keeling, Princess Anne County, VA, Circuit Court Judgments, 1856, box 3, folder 1, LVA; "Terms of Hiring" in Burwell Family Papers, Mss 1B9585b, sec. 15, VHS; slave-hiring bond, Benjamin S. Whitehurst and Pemmy Whitehurst to John Benthall, January 1, 1848, in Princess Anne County, VA, Circuit Superior Court Judgments, 1849, box 7, folder 2, LVA.

17. Stealey, *Antebellum Kanawha Salt Business*, 142–47; Jinnie Buford to Julius [Buford?], February 1, 1854, John Buford Papers.

18. Lewis, *Coal, Iron, and Slaves*, 90–94; R. [illegible] [Bailey?] to John Buford, October 28, 1854; C. T. Wells to Buford, February 25, 1854; Samuel Drewry to Buford, April 14, July 3, 1854; John [illegible] to Buford, February 17, 1855; Richmond Fire Association, "Slave Life Insurance Policy No. 244," a policy taken out by Southampton County slave owner Thomas Wrenn on "the Life of Charles a Slave labourer on [the] Va & Tenn R Road," John Buford Papers; Diaries of Robert W. Carter, 1818–59, folder 91, Carter Papers, in Stampp, *Records of Ante-Bellum Southern Plantations*, Series L.

19. Sam[ue]l Drewry to John Buford, December 13, 1853; February [9?], 1854, John Buford Papers.

20. Ronald L. Lewis, "'The Darkest Abode of Man': Black Miners in the First Southern Coal Fields, 1780–1865," *Virginia Magazine of History and Biography* 87 (1979): 196–202; Dew, "David Ross and the Oxford Iron Works," 204–5.

21. R. [illegible] [Bailey?] to John Buford, October 28, 1854, John Buford Papers.

22. Depositions of Isaac Davis and John Millan in Graham v. Reid, 1836, CFF 78C, FCCA.

23. Robert, *Tobacco Kingdom*, 204; Schnittman, "Slavery in Virginia's Urban Tobacco Industry," 143, 159, 172, 180–81, 185; Stealey, *Antebellum Kanawha Salt Business*, 142; Dew, *Bond of Iron*, 109; O. Nigel Bolland, "Proto-Proletarians? Slave Wages in the Americas between Slave Labour and Free Labour," in *From Chattel Slaves to Wage Slaves: The Dynamics of Labour Bargaining in the Americas*, ed. Mary Turner (Bloomington: Indiana University Press, 1995), 134; Schlotterbeck, "Internal Economy," 175.

24. Stealey, *Antebellum Kanawha Salt Business*, 135, 136, 156.

25. Dew, *Bond of Iron*, 67–70, 151, 161–62, 367.

26. Robert, *Tobacco Kingdom*, 203–4.

27. Wade, *Slavery in the Cities*, 62–67; Morgan, *Emancipation in Virginia's Tobacco Belt*, 65; Commonwealth v. Ezekiel, a Slave, Richmond City Hustings Court, Ended Causes, September 1854, box 195, LVA; Wade, *Slavery in the Cities*, quotation about Jack on 134; Robert, *Tobacco Kingdom*, 205; Commonwealth v. Ryland, a Slave, Richmond City Hustings Court, Ended Causes, October 1848, box 182, LVA.

28. Robert, *Tobacco Kingdom*, 203–5.

29. Commonwealth v. William Spurlock, a Slave, Richmond City Hustings Court, Ended Causes, October 1852, box 190, LVA.

30. Commonwealth v. Benjamin Jarvis, a Slave, Richmond City Hustings Court, Ended Causes, February 1848, box 180, LVA.

31. Commonwealth v. William, a Slave, Richmond City Hustings Court, Ended Causes, October 1847, box 179, LVA; McKenny v. Kello et ux, 1794-18, Southampton County, VA, Chancery Papers, box 7, LVA.

32. Commonwealth v. William, a Slave, Richmond City Hustings Court, Ended Causes, October 1847, box 179, LVA; Robert, *Tobacco Kingdom*, 205–7.

33. Wade, *Slavery in the Cities*, 239–86; Takagi, "Slavery in Richmond," 154.

34. Claudia Dale Goldin, "A Model to Explain the Relative Decline of Urban Slavery: Empirical Results," in *Race and Slavery in the Western Hemisphere: Quantitative Studies*, ed. Stanley L. Engerman and Eugene D. Genovese (Princeton, NJ: Princeton University Press, 1975), 433–35; Robert William Fogel, *Without Consent or Contract: The Rise and Fall of American Slavery* (New York: W. W. Norton, 1994), 108.

35. For employment of white workers at ironworks during the 1850s, see Dew, *Ironmaker to the Confederacy*, 28; and Gregg D. Kimball, *American City, Southern Place: A Cultural History of Antebellum Richmond* (Athens: University of Georgia Press, 2000), 173. Kimball outlines slavery's strength in Richmond and the white population's overall support for it (58, 59, 78, 93, 114, 134, quotations on 58 and 78). Richmond slave population figures are drawn from Wade, *Slavery in the Cities*, 330.

36. Takagi, "Slavery in Richmond," 156–57 (quotation), 263–67; David R. Goldfield, *Urban Growth in the Age of Sectionalism: Virginia, 1847–1861* (Baton Rouge: Louisiana State University Press, 1977), 130–37.

37. Goldin, "Relative Decline of Urban Slavery," 433–35. In 1860 Richmond slave men outnumbered slave women, but not by much: 6,636 men, 5,063 women. For population figures, see Wade, *Slavery in the Cities*, 330. In only two of Richmond's wards, a significant proportion of the city's female slave population worked as house servants. See Slave Schedule for Richmond City, First and Second Wards, 1860. For rising incomes, see Fogel, *Without Consent or Contract*, 108.

38. Goldfield, *Urban Growth in the Age of Sectionalism*, 132.

39. Noe, *Southwest Virginia's Railroad*, 34, 38, 70, 76–78, Olmsted quotation on 70.

40. Freehling, *Road to Disunion*, 162–66, 511–15; Noe, *Southwest Virginia's Railroad*, 84–86, 108, quotation on 86.

41. Henry T. Shanks, *The Secession Movement in Virginia, 1847–1861* (New York: AMS Press, 1971), 12.

42. Edward Carter Turner Diary, May 25, 1850; [Illegible] Burton to John Buford, November 10, 1854; Edward Carter Turner Diary, December 21, 1850, John Buford Papers, in Stampp, *Records of Ante-Bellum Southern Plantations*, Series F, Bureau of the Census, *Statistics of the United States (Including Mortality, Property, &c.,) in 1860; Compiled from the Original Returns and Being the Final Exhibit of the Eighth Census* (Washington, DC: Government Printing Office, 1866), 333.

43. Schlotterbeck, "Plantation and Farm," 301–7; Fields, "Agricultural Population of Virginia," 161; Daniel William Cobb Diary, January 1, August 31, December 18, 2[4?], 1857, VHS.

44. Edward Carter Turner Diary, January 3, 1850.

45. Bureau of the Census, *Statistics of the United States*, 333–36.

CHAPTER 7. SLAVE HIRING AND SLAVERY

1. John S. Miller to Jane Miller, September 17, 1846, Letters of John S. Miller, 1841–46, acc. 11702, UVA; Samuel Drewry to John Buford, February [7?], 1854, John Buford Papers, in

Stampp, *Records of Ante-Bellum Southern Plantations*, Series F; Fanny B. Ewing to her grandmother, July [?] 1862, Barbour Family Papers, VHS; Alex[ander] Findlay to W[illiam] Gray, September 15, 1850, William Gray Papers, VHS.

2. William Jerdone to George Pottie, January 18, 1845, Jerdone Family Papers, acc. 39.1 J47, box 9, folder 6, WM.

3. Alex[ander] Findlay to W[illiam] Gray, September 15, 1850, William Gray Papers, VHS; John A. Washington to his aunt [Louisa (Clemson) Washington?], August 31, 1861, John Augustine Washington Letter, Mss 2W2774a1, VHS.

4. Benjamin Brand to Martin Dawson, March 17, 1819, Benjamin Brand Papers, 1807–33, Mss 2 B7332b, VHS; Jane Watkins (Dupuy) Edmunds to William Thomas Scott, n.d., Edmunds Family Papers, 1826–1950, sec. 1, Mss 1 Ed596 a 1-27, VHS; John Whitehead to Floyd L. Whitehead, July 28, 1822, Papers of Floyd L. Whitehead, acc. 8712-d, UVA.

5. Unknown to William Gray, November 28, 1855, William Gray Papers, 1819–75, Mss 1 G7952 a FA2, VHS; Richard Blow to Samuel Proctor, January 21, 1806, Blow Family Papers, sec. 2, VHS; S[elina] Powell to "daughter" [Rebecca Powell], January 3, 1849, Powell Family Papers (1813–55), acc. 65 P875, box 1, folder 3, WM; William M. Cabaniss to Philip Howerton, August 11, 1833, Howerton Family Papers (359), series 1, folder 1, SHC.

6. Edward Carter Turner Diary, December 4, 5, 12, 16, 28, 30, 31, 1839; January 1, 2, 4, 1840, VHS.

7. Robert Mitchell to John Buford, December 11, 1851, John Buford Papers.

8. Samuel Drewry to John Buford, December 7, 1854, John Buford Papers.

9. Jonathan W. McCalley to William J. McCalley, January 7, 1849, Jonathan W. McCalley Letter, Mss 2M1245a1, VHS; Mark Anthony to William Ray, December 13, 1849, Mark Anthony Letters, December 13, 1849–January 8, 1852, acc. 38717, Personal Papers Collection, LVA; I[verson] L. Twyman to Frances A. Austin, December 31, 1852, Letters by Iverson L. Twyman, 1852–53, folder 27, Austin-Twyman Papers, in Stampp, *Records of Ante-Bellum Southern Plantations*, Series L; Samuel Drewry to John Buford, January 20, 1854; R. P. Clements to Buford, January 11, 1855; January 5, 1856; [illegible] to Buford, December 31, 1856; James Young to Buford, January 3, 1856; [illegible] to Buford, June [illegible], 1857, John Buford Papers; James F. Taliaferro to Miss J. M. Waller, 1850s, David Garland Waller Papers, 1842–61, DU.

10. Jonathan W. McCalley to William J. McCalley, January 7, 1849, Jonathan W. McCalley Letter; Wilson J. Cary to Virginia Cary, January 2, 1823, Carr-Cary Family Papers, acc. 1231, box 2, UVA; P. M. Tabb & Son to Robert W. Carter, November 18, 1846, Beverley Randolph Wellford Papers, 1773–1907, Mss 1W4597e92, sec. 90, VHS; Robert Baylor Lyne to Bro. Ware, December 12, 1859, Robert Baylor Lyne Letter, Ware Family Papers, Mss 1W2296a8–48, VHS; John B. Winfree to Christopher Winfree, May 27, 1859, Letters, 1843–59, Pertaining to Slavery and Slave Hiring, acc. 10969, UVA; "What would be my income in a certain contingency," George Rust Papers, 1808–79, DU; Travel Journal, 5065-z, January–February 1847, February 4, 5, 6, 1847, SHC.

11. A. Rives to Robert Rives, January 3, 18[?], Papers of Robert Rives Jr., folder 1832–82, acc. 4289, UVA; Henry Carrington Accounts, 1850–66, in Archibald Vaughan Account Book, 1835–66, Mss 5:3 V4654:1, VHS; M. M. Hastook to Elijah Fletcher, December 15, 1857, Indiana

(Fletcher) Williams Papers, 1804 (1846–92) 1900, DU; John R. Cary Memorandum Book, 1860, entry for January 21, 1860, John R. Cary Records, 1832–69, Local Government Records Collection, Gloucester County Court Records, LVA.

12. Benthall's Guardian v. Benthall, etc., 1857-01, Princess Anne County Circuit Court Chancery Papers, 1855–58, box 2, LVA.

13. Mrs. Roy Jones, "John Yeats and the Yeats Schools," Mrs. Roy Jones, Research Essay, typescript copy, Mss 7:1Y345:1, VHS.

14. Virginia County Guardians' Accounts, LDS; William J. Cary to Virginia Cary, February 3, 1823, Carr-Cary Family Papers, 1785–1839, acc. 1231, box 2, UVA; Ball Family Papers, Mss 1 B2105 b 1-32, 1829–1914, sec. 1, VHS; L. M.W[alton] to John T. Hargrave, February 10, 1837, The Reverend John T. Hargrave: Correspondence, 1820–52, Shepherdstown, WV, Papers, 1808–1945, acc. 11104, UVA.

15. William H. Carrick to William S. Royston, November 1, 1853; October 1, 1854; January 15, November 9, December 17, 1855; January 24, February 14, 1858; January 24, 1861, William S. Royston Papers, 1853–98, DU; Free Schedule for Norfolk City, 1860, 256.

16. "Petition of P.M. Tabb and Others to change the law concerning runaways," December 14, 1850, Richmond City, VA, Legislative Petitions, LVA.

17. Bickerton Lyle Winston Ledger, 1846–59, Mss 5:3W7334:1, VHS.

18. Letterbook of William McKean, 1809–18, James Dunlop Records, 1809–41, acc. 23873, Business Records Collection, LVA; Journal (Roslin, VA, w/inventory of property, inc. slaves), 1829–31, Business Records, 1821–1919, Papers of the McGill-Mahone Families, acc. 1627, UVA; Richard M. Cunningham Farm Diary, 1835–69 (item e), folder 2, Cunningham-Downman Family Papers, 1790–1875, acc. 28093, Personal Papers Collection, LVA; Seth Lunsford to Elizabeth Blackwell, January 13, 1845; John N. Grant to Blackwell, February 11, 1845, James D. Blackwell Papers, 1839–1929, Mss 39.1 B57, box 1, folder 1, WM; Slave Schedule for Fauquier County, 1860, 15; Daniel Anderson Account Book, 1844–53, Mss 5:3, An 234:2, VHS; Bureau of the Census, Seventh Census of the United States, 1850, Original Returns of the Assistant Marshals, microfilm, Schedule I, "An Enumeration of Free Inhabitants, Fauquier County, Virginia"; Folly Farm Papers, acc. 9380, UVA; David S. Baker Journal, 1860–69, 2, 21, 23, Local Government Records Collection, Fluvanna County Court Records, LVA; Slave Schedules for Loudoun and Fauquier counties, 1860.

19. Michael Tadman, *Speculators and Slaves: Masters, Traders, and Slaves in the Old South* (Madison: University of Wisconsin Press, 1996), 12; Ira Berlin, *Generations of Captivity: A History of African-American Slaves* (Cambridge, MA: Harvard University Press, 2003), 161; Slave Schedule for Fauquier County, 1860; Slave Schedule for Loudoun County, 1860; Brenda E. Stevenson, *Life in Black and White: Family and Community in the Slave South* (New York: Oxford University Press, 1996), 182; Morgan, *Emancipation in Virginia's Tobacco Belt*, 58; "Slave Hiring," tables 5.4, 5.9, 5.13, 5.16, in Wilma A. Dunaway, "Online Archives of Slavery and Emancipation in the Mountain South: Evidence, Sources, and Methods," http://scholar.lib.vt.edu/faculty_archives/mountain_slavery/trading.htm.

BIBLIOGRAPHY

PRIMARY SOURCES

ARCHIVAL COLLECTIONS

Albert and Shirley Small Special Collections Library, University of Virginia (UVA).
Church of Jesus Christ of Latter-Day Saints (microfilm) Church Records, Salt Lake City, UT (LDS).
Earl Gregg Swem Library, College of William and Mary in Virginia, Williamsburg, VA (WM).
Fairfax Circuit Court Archives, Fairfax County Judicial Center, Fairfax County, Fairfax, VA (FCCA).
Library of Virginia, Richmond, VA (LVA).
Loose Court Papers of Sussex County, Sussex Courthouse, Sussex, VA (LCPSCV).
Rare Book, Manuscript, and Special Collections Library, William Perkins Library, Duke University (DU).
Southern Historical Collection, Manuscripts Department, Wilson Library, University of North Carolina, Chapel Hill, NC (SHC).
Virginia Historical Society, Richmond, VA (VHS).

NEWSPAPERS

Alexandria Expositor and Columbian Advertiser.
American Beacon and Norfolk and Portsmouth Daily Advertiser.
Leesburg Democratic Mirror.
Petersburg Daily Courier.
Richmond Enquirer.
Virginia Chronicle and Norfolk and Portsmouth General Advertiser.

U.S. GOVERNMENT DOCUMENTS

Bureau of the Census. Eighth Census of the United States, 1860, Original Returns of the Assistant Marshalls (microfilm). Schedule I, "An Enumeration of Free Inhabitants" (Free Schedule for _____); Schedule II, "An Enumeration of Slave Population" (Slave Schedule for _____). National Archives.

———. Seventh Census of the United States, 1850, Original Returns of the Assistant Marshals (microfilm). Schedule I, "An Enumeration of Free Inhabitants, Fauquier County, Virginia." National Archives.

———. *Statistics of the United States, (Including Mortality, Property, &c.,) in 1860; Compiled from the Original Returns and Being the Final Exhibit of the Eighth Census.* Washington, DC: Government Printing Office, 1866.

EDITED WORKS

Miller, Randall M., and John David Smith, eds. *Dictionary of Afro-American Slavery.* Westport, CT: Praeger, 1997.

Perdue, Charles L., Jr., Thomas E. Barden, and Robert K. Phillips, comps. and eds. *Weevils in the Wheat: Interviews with Virginia Ex-Slaves.* Charlottesville: University Press of Virginia, 1976.

Rawick, George P., gen. ed. *The American Slave: A Composite Autobiography.* Westport, CT: Greenwood, 1972.

Stampp, Kenneth M., gen. ed. *Records of Ante-Bellum Southern Plantations from the Revolution through the Civil War.* Microfilm. Series E: Selections from the University of Virginia Library; Series F: Selections from the Manuscript Department, Duke University Library. Frederick, MD: University Publications of America, 1986.

———. *Records of Ante-Bellum Southern Plantations from the Revolution through the Civil War.* Microfilm. Series J: Selections from the Southern Historical Collection, Manuscripts Department, Library of the University of North Carolina at Chapel Hill. Bethesda, MD: University Publications of America, 1991.

———. *Records of Ante-Bellum Southern Plantations from the Revolution through the Civil War.* Microfilm. Series L: Selections from the Earl Gregg Swem Library, College of William and Mary in Virginia. Bethesda, MD: University Publications of America, 1994.

SECONDARY SOURCES

Appleby, Joyce. "Commercial Farming and the 'Agrarian Myth' in the Early Republic." *Journal of American History* 68 (March 1982): 833–49.

Bailey, Fred Arthur. *Class and Tennessee's Confederate Generation*. Chapel Hill: University of North Carolina Press, 1987.
Barton, Keith C. "'Good Cooks and Washers': Slave Hiring, Domestic Labor, and the Market in Bourbon County, Kentucky." *Journal of American History* 84 (September 1997): 436–60.
Berlin, Ira. *Generations of Captivity: A History of African-American Slaves*. Cambridge, MA: Harvard University Press, 2003.
———. "The Revolution in Black Life." In *The American Revolution: Explorations in the History of American Radicalism*, edited by Alfred F. Young, 349–82. DeKalb: Northern Illinois University Press, 1976.
———. "Time, Space, and the Evolution of Afro-American Society on British Mainland North America." *American Historical Review* 85 (1980): 44–78.
Boles, John B. *Black Southerners, 1619–1869*. Lexington: University Press of Kentucky, 1984.
Bolland, O. Nigel. "Proto-Proletarians? Slave Wages in the Americas between Slave Labour and Free Labour." In *From Chattel Slaves to Wage Slaves: The Dynamics of Labour Bargaining in the Americas*, edited by Mary Turner. Bloomington: Indiana University Press, 1995.
Breen, Timothy H. *Tobacco Culture: The Mentality of the Great Tidewater Planters on the Eve of the Revolution*. Princeton, NJ: Princeton University Press, 1985.
Breen, T. H., and Stephen Innes. *"Myne Owne Ground": Race and Freedom on Virginia's Eastern Shore, 1640–1676*. New York: Oxford University Press, 1980.
Bruchey, Stuart. *Enterprise: The Dynamic Economy of a Free People*. Cambridge, MA: Harvard University Press, 1990.
Byrne, William A. "The Hiring of Woodson, Slave Carpenter of Savannah." *Georgia Historical Quarterly* 77 (Summer 1993): 245–63.
Campbell, Randolph B. "Research Note: Slave Hiring in Texas." *American Historical Review* 92 (February 1988): 107–14.
Cowdrey, Albert E. *This Land, This South: An Environmental History*. Rev. ed. Lexington: University Press of Kentucky, 1996.
Crofts, Daniel W. *Old Southampton: Politics and Society in a Virginia County, 1834–1869*. Charlottesville: University Press of Virginia, 1992.
Daniels, Christine. "Gresham's Laws: Labor Management on an Early-Eighteenth-Century Chesapeake Plantation." *Journal of Southern History* 62 (May 1996): 205–38.
Dew, Charles B. "Black Ironworkers and the Slave Insurrection Panic of 1856." *Journal of Southern History* 41 (August 1975): 321–38.
———. *Bond of Iron: Master and Slave at Buffalo Forge*. New York: W. W. Norton, 1994.

———. "David Ross and the Oxford Iron Works: A Study of Industrial Slavery in the Early Nineteenth-Century South." *William and Mary Quarterly* 21 (1974): 189–224.

———. "Disciplining Slave Ironworkers in the Antebellum South: Coercion, Conciliation, and Accommodation." *American Historical Review* 79 (1974): 393–418.

———. *Ironmaker to the Confederacy: Joseph R. Anderson and the Tredegar Iron Works.* New Haven, CT: Yale University Press, 1966.

Dufour, Ronald P. *Colonial America.* St. Paul, MN: West, 1994.

Dunaway, Wilma A. *Slavery in the American Mountain South.* Cambridge: Cambridge University Press, 2003.

Eaton, Clement. *The Growth of Southern Civilization, 1790–1860.* New York: Harper & Row, 1963.

———. "Slave Hiring in the Upper South: A Step toward Freedom." *Mississippi Valley Historical Review* 46 (March 1960): 663–78.

Edwards, Conley L., III, Gwendolyn D. Clark, and Jennifer D. McDaid, comps. *A Guide to Business Records in the Virginia State Library and Archives.* Richmond: Virginia State Library and Archives, 1994.

Essah, Patience. *A House Divided: Slavery and Emancipation in Delaware, 1638–1865.* Charlottesville: University Press of Virginia, 1996.

Fields, Barbara Jeanne. *Slavery and Freedom on the Middle Ground: Maryland during the Nineteenth Century.* New Haven, CT: Yale University Press, 1985.

Fields, Emmett B. "The Agricultural Population of Virginia, 1850–1860." Ph.D. diss., Vanderbilt University, 1953.

Fogel, Robert William. *Without Consent or Contract: The Rise and Fall of American Slavery.* New York: W. W. Norton, 1994.

Freehling, William W. *The Road to Disunion: Secessionists at Bay, 1776–1854.* Vol. 1. New York: Oxford University Press, 1990.

Frey, Sylvia R. *Water from the Rock: Black Resistance in a Revolutionary Age.* Princeton, NJ: Princeton University Press, 1991.

Genovese, Eugene D. *Roll, Jordan, Roll: The World the Slaves Made.* New York: Vintage, 1974.

Goldfield, David R. *Urban Growth in the Age of Sectionalism: Virginia, 1847–1861.* Baton Rouge: Louisiana State University Press, 1977.

Goldin, Claudia Dale. "A Model to Explain the Relative Decline of Urban Slavery: Empirical Results." In *Race and Slavery in the Western Hemisphere: Quantitative Studies,* edited by Stanley L. Engerman and Eugene D. Genovese, 427–50. Princeton, NJ: Princeton University Press, 1975.

Gundersen, Joan Rezner. "The Double Bonds of Race and Sex: Black and White Women in a Colonial Virginia Parish." *Journal of Southern History* 52 (August 1986): 351–72.

Gutman, Herbert G. *The Black Family in Slavery and Freedom, 1750–1925.* New York: Vintage, 1976.
Hughes, Sarah Shaver. "Elizabeth City County, Virginia, 1782–1810: The Economic and Social Structure of a Tidewater County in the Early National Years." Ph.D. diss., College of William and Mary, 1975.
———. "Slaves for Hire: The Allocation of Black Labor in Elizabeth City County, Virginia, 1782 to 1810." *William and Mary Quarterly* 35 (April 1978): 260–86.
Hunter, Robert F. "The Turnpike Movement in Virginia, 1816–1860." Ph.D. diss., Columbia University, 1957.
Isaac, Rhys. *The Transformation of Virginia, 1740–1790.* Chapel Hill: University of North Carolina Press, 1988.
Jones, Jacqueline. "'My Mother Was Much of a Woman': Black Women, Work, and the Family under Slavery." In *Our American Sisters: Women in American Life and Thought,* edited by Jean E. Friedman, William G. Shade, and Mary Jane Capozzoli, 169–202. Lexington, MA: D. C. Heath, 1987.
Jordan, Winthrop D. *White Over Black: American Attitudes toward the Negro, 1550–1812.* New York: W. W. Norton, 1977.
Kimball, Gregg D. *American City, Southern Place: A Cultural History of Antebellum Richmond.* Athens: University of Georgia Press, 2000.
King, Wilma. *Stolen Childhood: Slave Youth in Nineteenth-Century America.* Bloomington: Indiana University Press, 1995.
Klingaman, David. "The Significance of Grain in the Development of the Tobacco Colonies." *Journal of Economic History* 29 (1969): 268–78.
Kolchin, Peter. *American Slavery, 1619–1877.* New York: Hill and Wang, 1993.
Kulikoff, Allan. "The Origins of Afro-American Society in Tidewater Maryland and Virginia, 1700 to 1790." *William and Mary Quarterly* 35 (1978): 226–59.
———. *Tobacco and Slaves: The Development of Southern Cultures in the Chesapeake, 1680–1800.* Chapel Hill: University of North Carolina Press, 1986.
Larkin, Jack. *The Reshaping of Everyday Life, 1790–1840.* New York: Harper & Row, 1989.
Lewis, Ronald L. *Coal, Iron, and Slaves: Industrial Slavery in Maryland and Virginia, 1715–1865.* Westport, CT: Greenwood Press, 1979.
———. "'The Darkest Abode of Man': Black Miners in the First Southern Coal Fields, 1780–1865." *Virginia Magazine of History and Biography* 87 (1979): 190–202.
———. "The Use and Extent of Slave Labor in the Chesapeake Iron Industry: The Colonial Era." *Labor History* 17 (Summer 1976): 388–405.
Link, William A. *Roots of Secession: Slavery and Politics in Antebellum Virginia.* Chapel Hill: University of North Carolina Press, 2003.
Martin, Jonathan D. *Divided Mastery: Slave Hiring in the American South.* Cambridge, MA: Harvard University Press, 2004.

McCurry, Stephanie. *Masters of Small Worlds: Yeoman Households, Gender Relations, and the Political Culture of the Antebellum South Carolina Low Country*. New York: Oxford University Press, 1995.

Morgan, Lynda J. *Emancipation in Virginia's Tobacco Belt, 1850–1870*. Athens: University of Georgia Press, 1992.

Mullin, Gerald W. *Flight and Rebellion: Slave Resistance in Eighteenth-Century Virginia*. New York: Oxford University Press, 1972.

Nettels, Curtis P. *The Emergence of a National Economy, 1775–1815*. New York: Harper & Row, 1969.

Noe, Kenneth W. *Southwest Virginia's Railroad: Modernization and the Sectional Crisis*. Urbana: University of Illinois Press, 1994.

Oast, Jennifer. "'The Worst Kind of Slavery:' Slave-Owning Presbyterian Churches in Prince Edward County, Virginia." *Journal of Southern History* 76 (November 2010): 867–900.

Ownby, Ted. *Subduing Satan: Religion, Recreation, and Manhood in the Rural South, 1865–1920*. Chapel Hill: University of North Carolina Press, 1990.

Potter, David M. *The Impending Crisis, 1848–1861*. Completed and edited by Don E. Fehrenbacher. New York: Harper & Row, 1976.

Ray, Suzanne Smith, Lyndon H. Hart, and J. Christian Kolbe. "Guardian." In *A Preliminary Guide to Pre-1904 County Records in the Virginia State Library and Archives*, xviii, compiled by Suzanne Smith Ray, Lyndon H. Hart, and J. Christian Kolbe. Richmond: Virginia State Library and Archives, 1994.

Robert, Joseph Clarke. *The Tobacco Kingdom: Plantation, Market, and Factory in Virginia and North Carolina, 1800–1860*. Durham, NC: Duke University Press, 1938.

Savitt, Todd L. *Medicine and Slavery: The Diseases and Health Care of Blacks in Antebellum Virginia*. Chicago: University of Illinois Press, 2002.

Schlotterbeck, John T. "The Internal Economy of Slavery in Rural Piedmont Virginia." In *The Slaves' Economy: Independent Production by Slaves in the Americas*, 170–81, edited by Ira Berlin and Philip D. Morgan. London: Frank Cass, 1991.

———. "Plantation and Farm: Social and Economic Change in Orange and Greene Counties, Virginia, 1716 to 1860." Ph.D. diss., Johns Hopkins University, 1980.

Schnittman, Suzanne Gehring. "Slavery in Virginia's Urban Tobacco Industry, 1840–1860." Ph.D. diss., University of Rochester, 1987.

Shanks, Henry T. *The Secession Movement in Virginia, 1847–1861*. New York: AMS Press, 1971.

Shepard, E. Lee. "'This Being Court Day': Courthouses and Community Life in Rural Virginia." *Virginia Magazine of History and Biography* 103 (October 1995): 459–70.

Siener, William H. "Charles Yates, the Grain Trade, and Economic Development in Fredericksburg, Virginia, 1750–1810." *Virginia Magazine of History and Biography* 93 (October 1985): 409–26.

Sorrells, Nancy. "Francis McFarland and the Black Community: A Case Study of the Hiring Practices within the Upper Shenandoah Valley." Paper, Carrier Library, James Madison University, Harrisonburg, VA.

Stampp, Kenneth M. *The Peculiar Institution: Slavery in the Ante-Bellum South.* New York: Vintage, 1956.

Starobin, Robert S. *Industrial Slavery in the Old South.* New York: Oxford University Press, 1970.

Stealey, John E., III. *The Antebellum Kanawha Salt Business and Western Markets.* Lexington: University Press of Kentucky, 1993.

Stevenson, Brenda E. "'All My Cherished Ones': Marriage and Family in Antebellum Virginia." Ph.D. diss., Yale University, 1990.

———. *Life in Black and White: Family and Community in the Slave South.* New York: Oxford University Press, 1996.

Tadman, Michael. *Speculators and Slaves: Masters, Traders, and Slaves in the Old South.* Madison: University of Wisconsin Press, 1996.

Takagi, Midori. *"Rearing Wolves to Our Own Destruction": Slavery in Richmond, Virginia, 1782–1865.* Charlottesville: University Press of Virginia, 1999.

———. "Slavery in Richmond, Virginia, 1782–1865." Ph.D. diss., Columbia University, 1994.

Wade, Richard C. *Slavery in the Cities: The South, 1820–1860.* New York: Oxford University Press, 1964.

Way, Peter. *Common Labour: Workers and the Digging of North American Canals, 1780–1860.* Cambridge: Cambridge University Press, 1993.

Weiner, Marli F. "Mistresses, Morality, and the Dilemmas of Slaveholding: The Ideology and Behavior of Elite Antebellum Women." In *Discovering the Women in Slavery,* edited by Patricia Morton, 278–98. Athens: University of Georgia Press, 1996.

White, Deborah Gray. *Ar'n't I a Woman? Female Slaves in the Plantation South.* New York: W. W. Norton, 1985.

Willis, John C. "From the Dictates of Pride to the Paths of Righteousness: Slave Honor and Christianity in Antebellum Virginia." In *The Edge of the South: Life in Nineteenth-Century Virginia,* edited by Edward L. Ayers and John C. Willis, 37–55. Charlottesville: University Press of Virginia, 1991.

Winters, Donald L. *Tennessee Farming, Tennessee Farmers: Antebellum Agriculture in the Upper South.* Knoxville: University of Tennessee Press, 1994.

Wood, Kirsten E. *Masterful Women: Slaveholding Widows from the American Revolution through the Civil War.* Chapel Hill: University of North Carolina Press, 2004.

Yeoman, R. S. *A Guide Book of United States Coins.* Atlanta: Whitman, 2007.

Zaborney, John J. "Slave Hiring and Slave Family and Friendship Ties in Rural Nineteenth-Century Virginia." In *Afro-Virginian History and Culture,* edited by John Saillant, 85–107. New York: Garland, 1999.

INDEX

Note: The plural ("slaves") is used in entries for slaves' names where there are several different persons with the same name.

Abington, Virginia, 143
Abolitionists, fear of, 92–93
Absalom (hired slaves), 126, 133
Accomack County, Virginia, 30, 35
Adams, John, 15
Agricultural diversification, and origins and pervasiveness of slave hiring, 3, 9–10. *See also* Hired slaves, demand and competition for; Labor requirements, wheat *vs.* tobacco; Livestock; Slaves, increasing population of; Slave hiring, as alternative to sale; Slave hiring, for harvest; Slave hiring, for hog butchering; Slave hiring, strengthens Virginia slavery; Slave surpluses
Albemarle County, Virginia, 9, 103, 153
Albert (hired slave), 21
Alexandria, Virginia, 37, 42, 110, 123, 125, 158
Allen, Robert Henderson, 21, 97
Alston, John, 36
Amanda (hired slaves), 12, 21, 78
Ambler, Thomas, 108
American Revolution, 10, 11, 12, 41, 42, 120–22
Amherst County, Virginia, 21, 97, 102, 156
Amy (hired slaves), 20, 34, 39, 40
Anacai (hired slave), 14

Anderson, Charles (hired slave), 49
Anderson, Daniel, 118, 161
Anderson, John, 42, 44
Anderson, Matthew, 124
Anderson (hired slave), 65
Ann (hired slaves), 21, 117
Anthony, Mark, 153
Appalachian (region), 121–22, 162
Appomattox River, 125
Armistead (hired slave), 96
Arrington, Edward, 55
Arson. *See* Hired slaves, and arson, committed against hirers; Hired slaves, resistance of
Ashby, Willis, 57
Augusta County, Virginia, 28, 47
Austin, Grace, 78
Austin (newborn of hired slave), 30
Austin, Zachariah, 93

B & O Railroad, 37. *See also* Hirers of slaves, railroad companies as
Baker, David, 161
Baley (hired slave), 24
Ball, G. W., 34
Baptist, T. C., 135
Barnett (hired slave), 115–16

INDEX

Barter economies, and slave hiring. *See* Slave hiring, in barter economies
Bartlet (hired slave), 116
Bath Iron Works, 121. *See also* Hirers of slaves, iron producers as
Beane, Leroy, 91
Beans, Aaron, 106
Beans, Edward, 106
Beans, Isaac, 106
Beans, Osker, 106
Beans, William, 106
Beavers, Margaret, 30
Beck (hired slave), 13
Beddingfield, John, 24
Bedford County, Virginia, 153
Belinda (hired slave), 23
Bell, John, 117
Bell, Samuel, 28
Ben (hired slaves), 17, 158, 161
Benford, James, 77
Benjamin (hired slave), 137
Benthall, John, 127
Benthall, Robert, 156
Berkley, Edmund, 30
Berlin, Ira, 162
Berry, Fannie (hired slave), 115
Berry, Sarah Ann, 115
Betsy (hired slave), 36
Betty (hired slaves), 28, 32
Beverly, Robert, 91
Beverly (hired slave), 15
Bill (hired slave), 49, 50
Billups, Robert, 39
Billups, Thomas, 96
Billy (hired slaves), 22, 24, 55
Black Heath Pits, 122, 130, 160. *See also* Hirers of slaves, coal mines as
Blow, Richard, 123–24, 151
Blunt, Henry, 95
Board money, 7, 134, 136–38, 140. *See also* Hired slaves, mobility of; Hirers of slaves, tobacco manufacturers as; Living out system

Bob (hired slaves), 14, 16, 40, 61, 81, 124
Bonds, slave hiring: manufactured and pre-printed, 26; as media of exchange, 25–26
Booker (hired slave), 93
Boone, William, 20
Botetourt County, Virginia, 121
Bowie, Ann, 109–10
Bowie, Arthur, 109
Bowie, Carlton, 109
Bowie, John J., 109–10
Bowie, Luther, 109
Bowie, Walter, Jr., 99, 115–16
Bowie, William, 109
Bowling Green, Virginia, 105
Brady, Daniel, 33
Brady, Emma, 33
Brady, Wilhelmina, 33
Branch & Company (mercantile firm), and slave hiring by, 26
Brand, Benjamin, 85, 150
Bransford, John, 44
Braxton, William, 100
Bray, Alpheus, 106
Bray, Mary, 106
Briery Presbyterian Church, and slave hiring by, 46, 48–49, 52–53, 55–56
Briery River, 48
Brister (hired slave), 51–52
Bristow, George, 40
Britania (hired slave), 30
Brooke, Margaret, 112
Brooke, Robert, 112
Brown, John, 152
Brown, Mandley, 106
Brunswick County, Virginia, 16
Bryan, Delaware, 29
Buckner, George, 105
Buckner, Richard, 71, 72
Buffalo Forge (iron works), 33, 121. *See also* Hirers of slaves, iron producers as
Buford, Jinnie, 128
Buford, John, 60, 126, 128–29

INDEX

Bumgardner, John, 96
Burke, Edward, 105
Burke, R. M., 126
Burrus, Lancelot, 33
Burt, Lewis, 15
Butler, N.B., 29
Byrd Plantation, 161

Cabaniss, William, 151
Cabell, William, 65
Cable, Alfred, 108–9
Cable, James, 106, 108
Cable, John, 106, 108
Cable, Mary, 108
Cain (hired slave), 16
Calvert, Thomas, 22
Campbell County, Virginia, 153
Carbon Hill Mines (coal mines), 122. *See also* Hirers of slaves, coal mines as
Cardwell, Wiltshire, Jr., 56
Caroline County, Virginia, 158
Caroline (hired slave), 30
Carpenter, Mahlon, 30
Carpenter, Marshal, 30
Carr, Dabney, 36
Carr, James, 36
Carrick, William, 158–59
Carrie, Sister (slave), 85–86
Carrington, Henry, 15, 67–69, 156
Carter, Elizabeth, 40
Carter, Joseph, 29
Carter, Robert, 79–80, 155
Carter, Walker, 22
Cary, Virginia, 154, 158
Cary, Wilson, 154, 158
Cary Street (Richmond), 135
Catey (hired slave), 32
Catherine (hired slave), 51
Catlett, John, 39
Catlett, Patrick, 36, 111
Cato (hired slave), 93
Chamblin, William, 59
Chapman, John, 38

Charles (hired slaves), 15, 55, 56, 89, 95
Charles (slave), 16
Charles City County, Virginia, 106, 150
Charlotte County, Virginia, 48, 67–68, 156
Charlottesville, Virginia, 36, 72–75, 156
Charlott (hired slave), 21
Charry (slave), 35
Chesapeake and Delaware Canal, 147
Chesapeake (region), 10
Chesterfield County, Virginia, 12, 44, 70, 122
Children, as hired slaves. *See* Hired slaves, children as. *See also* Hired slaves, as midwives; Hired slaves, pregnant and birthing; Hired slaves, and separations of family and friends; Hired slave women
Childs, William, 13
Chilton, Ralph, 90–91
China (hired slave), 36
Chloe (hired slaves), 14, 55
Chowning, Eliza, 104
Christmas, as slave-hiring season, 20–22, 24, 58–59, 61, 63, 65–66, 72, 89, 151. *See also* Hiring day (slave-hiring auctions); Slave hiring, season for
Chrystie, Thomas, 16, 81, 101–2
Civil War, 4, 6, 95, 105–6, 108, 114, 119, 122–23, 142, 146, 154, 157, 160, 162, 164–65
Clarissa (hired slave), 104
Clark, David, 126
Clark, William, 50
Clark County, Virginia, 107
Clarke, Mary Ann, 38
Clary (hired slave), 77
Clay, Turner, 21
Clayton, Sarah, 42
Clifton Forge, 121
Cloe (hired slave), 40
Clopton, William, 44
Clothing, of hired slaves. *See* Hired slaves, clothing of
Coal mines, 12. *See also* Hirers of slaves, coal mines as

Cobb, Daniel William, 18–19, 21, 23, 32, 35, 98, 115, 145–46
Colbert, Strother, 59
Cole, Robert, 20
Coleman, James, 81
Coleman, John, 93
Coleman, Samuel, 77
Colonel (hired slave), 128
Conn, Nancy, 41
Conn, William, 41
Cooke, G. B., 34, 42
Cooke, Harry S., 114
Cooke, James, 69–70, 76
Cooley, Ebenezer, 19–20
Coons, Robertson, 40
Cooper, Jane, 22
Cooper, Marmaduke, 43
Cooper, Samuel, 36
Cooper, Sarah Maria, 36
Corbin, Henry (hired slave), 15
Cotton gin, 11
Coughlin, William, 15
Cox, Eliasa, 137–38
Cox, Thomas, 50
Crafford, Carter, 22
Crenshaw, John, 128
Croxton, Philip, 16, 81
Crue, John, 58
Culley, John, 39
Culpeper County, Virginia, 17, 158
Culpeper Gold Mine, 127. *See also* Hirers of slaves, gold mines as
Cunningham, Richard, 71–72, 161
Curtis, Thomas, 63
Cyrus (hired slave), 71

Dabney, Susanna, 101
Dangerous work settings, hired slaves in. *See* Hired slaves, in dangerous work settings
Daniel and David Higginbotham Company (mercantile firm), and slave hiring by, 102
Daniel (hired slave), 16
Danville, Virginia, 123
Darne, R.B., 77
Darnes, Corbin, 131
Darnes, Gunnell, 131
Daugherty, Daniel, 106
David (hired slaves), 24, 78
Davis, Isaac, 130–31
Davy (hired slaves), 77, 89–90, 156
Day, William, 20
Dean, Gavis, 96
Death, of hired slaves. *See* Hired slaves, death of
Delaware, 7, 147–48
Delia (hired slave), 12
Delpha (hired slave), 94
Delphia (hired slave), 29
Deneale, James, 62
Deneale, Syble, 62
Deneale, William, 62
Dennis (hired slave), 89–90
Derest, Jim (hired slave), 133
Deshields, James, 94
Detter, John, 117
Dick (hired slaves), 23, 24, 90
Dickinson, Joseph, 50
Dickinson & Shrewsbury (salt manufacturing company), 122. *See also*, Hirers of slaves, salt mines as
Dido (hired slave), 40
Dinah (hired slave), 25, 40
Divided Mastery: Slave Hiring in the American South (Martin), 5–6
Doles, Rebecca, 35
Domestic slave trade, 11–12, 155, 162, 165. *See also* Lower South (region); Second Middle Passage; Slave hiring, as alternative to sale; Slave hiring, profitability of; Slave hiring, strengthens Virginia slavery; Slaves, increasing population of; Slave surpluses; Upper South (region)
Douglass, Pharoah, 31
Douglass, Richard, 56, 161
Drewry, Samuel, 88–89, 128, 149, 153

INDEX

Drewry, William, 20
Drewsville, Virginia (hiring-day site), 23, 98. *See also* Hiring day (slave-hiring auctions)
Duffie, Isaac, 49–51, 56
Dulany, Henry, 13
Dulany, Ida, 25
Dulany, Mary, 107
Dunaway, Robert, 89–90
Duncan, Maria, 110
Duncan, Murray, 110
Duncan, Thomas, 110
Duncan, William, 110
Dunlop, James, 12, 54–55
Dupuy, Asa, 36, 56
Dupuy, James, 56

Eastern Shore (region), 9
Easton, Betsy (slave), 133
Easton, Phill (slave), 133
Eaton, Clement, 1–2
Economic depression, 18–19, 146. *See also* Panic of 1819; Slave hiring, to alter labor-force size annually; Slave hiring, as solution to whites' problems
Economic diversification, and origins and pervasiveness of slave hiring. *See* Slave hiring, in diversified economy. *See also* Hired slaves, demand and competition for; Industrial slavery; Slave hiring, as alternative to sale; Slave hiring, strengthens Virginia slavery; Slave surpluses
Edmond (hired slave), 63
Edmonds, Cecelia, 114
Edmonds, Elias, 25
Edmund (hired slave), 77
Edmunds, Jane, 150
Elderly hired slaves. *See* Hired slaves, elderly
Elgin, Ignatius, 30
Elias (hired slave), 79
Elick (hired slave), 99

Ellick (hired slave), 70–71
Elizabeth City County, Virginia, 12–13, 22
Eliza (hired slave), 24, 28, 63
Eliza (slave), 146
Ellen (hired slave), 33
Embry, William, 59
Emily (hired slave), 54
Emmerson, C. M., 103
England, 10
Ephraim (hired slave), 15, 67–69
Essex County, Virginia, 14, 28, 37, 57, 93, 95, 97, 114
Eubank, Richard, 57
Europe, 10, 54, 121
Evans, Etheldread, 124
Everhart, Solemon, 117
Ewell, Ezekiel, 77
Ewing, Fanny, 149
Ezekiel (hired slave), 135

Faber, William, 117
Fairfax County, Virginia, 54, 62, 77, 81, 93, 97, 114, 125, 127, 130
Fairfax Courthouse, Virginia, 60
Family and friends. *See* Hired slaves, and separations from family and friends
Fanny (hired slaves), 12, 30, 40, 41, 43, 69, 70
Fauquier County, Virginia, 14, 18, 25, 29, 59, 71, 91–92, 100, 104–6, 108–11, 114, 116, 118, 144, 151–52, 161–62
Fauquier White Sulphur Springs Company, 100
Faulkner, Charles, 61
Ferguson, James, 114
Feutress, Elizabeth, 13
Fiduciaries, hire out slaves of others, 13. *See also* Guardians
Findlay, Alexander, 57, 149
Fishburn, 117
Fisher, Ellar Ann, 37–38
Fisher, John, 37–38
Fisher, Thomas, 37–38

INDEX

Fisher, William, 37–38
Fitzgerald, John, 13, 24, 78
Fitzhugh, Fenton, 106
Fleet, William, 11
Fleming, Beverly, 14, 57
Fletcher, Elijah, 156
Fletcher, Isaac, 13
Fletcher, John, 13, 25
Fletcher, Marion, 109
Fletcher, Mary, 109
Fletcher, Robert H., 109
Fletcher, William, 109
Flour, 10, 144. See also Agricultural diversification, and origins and pervasiveness of slave hiring
Flowers, William, 49–50
Fluvanna County, Virginia, 111, 161
Folly Farm Plantation, 96, 161
Ford, Hezekiah, 69–70, 126
Ford, Tom, 20
Fortune (hired slave), 24
Foster, B., 50
Foster, James, 52, 76
Foster, Patrick, 24
Foster, Thomas, 111, 152
France, 10
Frances (hired slaves), 21, 43
Frances (newborn of hired slave), 54
Frank (hired slaves), 49–52, 77, 127
Frank, Jr. (hired slave), 51
Franklin, James, 99
Franklin Street (Richmond), 135
Frederick County, Virginia, 62, 81, 107
Frederick (hired slave), 59
Fredericksburg, Virginia, 120, 124–25
Free blacks, population of, 11
Freeman, William, 135
Friend, Thomas, 132
Fuller (hired slave), 116

Galt, James, 111
Garland (hired slaves), 72–76, 160
Gault, John, 66

Gee, Thomas, 97
Gentry, James, 137
George, Wiley, 95
George (hired slaves), 1, 16, 22, 24, 40, 57, 77, 123, 154, 158
Gibson, William, 44–45
Gloucester, Virginia, 96, 102
Gloucester County, Virginia, 25, 39–40, 58, 97, 156
Gloucester Courthouse, Virginia, 67
Godfrey (hired slave), 124
Goldin, Claudia, 139, 141
Gold mines, 12, 121. See also Hirers of slaves, gold mines as
Gooch, Maria, 40
Goochland County, Virginia, 122
Gordon, Wellington, 59
Gordon, William, 34
Grain, 10, 123–24
Grant, John N., 118, 161
Grant, Sarah (hired slave), 61
Granville (hired slave), 14, 55
Gravatt, William, 95
Gray, William, 15, 20, 149
Green, A. G., 52
Green, Ann, 114
Green, Nathaniel, 16
Gregory, Mary, 84
Griffith, Ben, 116
Grigg, Richard, 28
Grinnan, Andrew, 59, 61
Guardians, 33; hire out slaves of orphans, 14, 37–39, 62, 96–97, 105, 114. See also Fiduciaries, hire out slaves of others
Guardians' accounts, 14, 105
Guardianship system 14
Gulick, D. F., 30
Gunnell, George, 77
Gurley, George, 97
Guthery, Jackson, 55

Hackerey, William, 36
Hager (hired slave), 32

INDEX

Haley, James, 50
Halifax County, North Carolina, 79, 125
Halifax County, Virginia, 13, 30
Halifax Courthouse, Virginia, 154
Hall, John, 124
Hall, Mary, 13–14, 55, 57
Halsey, Joseph, 59, 61–62
Hannah, Samuel, 37
Hannah (hired slaves), 29, 40, 90
Hanover County, Virginia, 33, 42, 44, 137, 160
Hardy, David, 42
Hargrave, John, 158
Harper's Ferry, Virginia, 37
Harrill, William, 106
Harris, James, 78, 125
Harrison, Alexander, 24
Harrison, Henry, 124
Harrison, James, 93
Harrison, John, 54
Hastook, M. M., 156
Hawkins, Ezra, 56
Hawkins, Hiram, 49–50
Hawkins, John, 51
Hawkins, William, 51
Healy, Alfred, 104
Henrico County, Virginia, 40, 122
Henrietta (hired slaves), 36, 111
Henry, John, 25
Henry (hired slaves), 20, 25, 70, 71, 93, 151
Hester (hired slave), 39
Heth, Henry, 111, 122
Hicks, Nelson, 94, 97
Hiden, Joseph, 94
Higs, Benjamin, 60
Hill, John, 101–2
Hill, Lewis, 15
Hired slaves: as apprentices, 124; and arson, committed against hirers, 43–45, 164; children as, 3–4, 28, 34–41, 45–47, 49–52, 54, 58, 61, 63, 77–78, 91, 96, 103, 106–7, 162; clothing of, 4, 14, 23–25, 28, 53, 66, 69, 76–77, 84, 88, 100, 102, 119, 126, 133–35; control over working conditions, 5, 83–85; conveyance, surveillance, and scrutiny of, 4, 6, 36–37, 43–45, 93–99, 105–7, 118, 131, 134, 151, 164; in dangerous work settings, 7, 16, 83, 122, 126–30, 160; death of, 34, 38, 41, 63, 77–78, 98, 127–31, 160; demand and competition for, 8, 75, 82–85, 87, 141–42, 146–48, 151–56, 160, 162, 165; discretions and advantages of, 5, 7, 132–38; elderly, 3, 63–64, 69–70, 162; experiences similar to those of non-hired slaves, 3, 5, 42, 65, 69, 71–72, 86, 91, 131, 136–39; as family units, 37–41, 45–46, 49–52, 58, 77, 91, 96, 103, 105, 108–10, 161; fear of, 92–93, 140–41; hired out for food and clothing, 29, 36, 39–40, 46, 49, 51, 58, 116–17, 150; hired out multiple times within year, 22; injuries of, 77, 95, 128–29, 131; life insurance on, 128–29, 154, 160; limited discretions and advantages of, 58–59, 67–69, 70–76, 79–80, 82, 87–97, 136–39, 148; limited mobility of, 29, 42, 104; medical care and expenses of, 4, 14–16, 31–32, 36–39, 49, 77, 79; as midwives, 32–34, 42, 164; mobility of, 1, 33, 42–43, 66–67, 136, 138–40; mortgage of, 16–17, 163; no special status or permanent experiences, 4–5, 42, 65, 67–76, 148; occupations of, 1–2, 4, 12, 16, 21–23, 28, 34–35, 41–44, 59–60, 62, 67, 70–76, 90, 102, 111–12, 116, 122–26, 128, 132–33, 135, 142, 161, 165; and poisoning, of hirers, 29; preferred over white labor, 120–22; pregnant and birthing, 3, 4, 29–32, 35, 38, 41, 49–51, 53–54, 62, 108, 163–64; removal from hirers' possession, 57; resistance of, 4, 29, 41, 43–45, 53, 59, 61–64, 71, 73–76, 78–85, 82, 87–88, 90–91, 93–95, 118, 122, 128–30, 136–38, 164; run away from hirers, 41, 59, 61–64, 71, 78–85, 87–88, 90–91, 93, 95, 118, 122, 128, 130, 137–38, 164; sale of, 29,

Hired slaves (*continued*)
41, 57, 63–64, 86, 90–91; select hirers, 5, 58, 66, 69–70, 82–85; self-esteem of, 7, 85, 134–38, sentenced to death, 43, 45; and separations from family and friends, 4, 5, 38, 42–44, 46–64, 164; shot, 79, 81; skilled, 2, 16, 22–23, 30, 42, 62, 66–67, 69–70, 80–81, 102, 106–7, 116, 121–24, 128, 156; taxes on, 14; unable to manipulate owners against hirers, 5, 43, 45, 87–89, 91, 93–97, 107, 118, 130, 165; in unhealthy living conditions, 7, 31, 53, 76–77, 84, 126–27, 130; whipped by hirers, 7, 16, 41, 44–45, 53, 78–79, 81–83, 86–87, 94–95, 131, 136–38, 164. *See also* Self-hired slaves

Hired slave women, 2–5, 13, 27, 28–45, 77; and hirers' expectations of, 34–35, 40–41, 45; and sexual relations with hirers, 41; and struggles with work and child care, 40–41, 164. *See also* Hired slaves, arson against hirers; Hired slaves, children as; Hired slaves, pregnant and birthing; House servants, hired

Hirers of slaves: blacksmiths as, 105, 124; builders as, 105; canal companies as, 125, 147, 165; carpenters as, 105; carriage makers as, 105; cattle drivers as, 105; clerks as, 164; coach makers as, 105; coal mines as, 12, 121–22, 127–30, 132, 151, 160; constables as, 105; couriers as, 105; elderly persons as, 105; fishing and water-transport businesses as, 127; gold mines as, 121, 127, 132; gunsmiths as, 105; hotel keepers as, 105; industrialists as, 3, 7, 12, 120–21, 131–32; 163; iron producers as, 120–21, 127, 130, 132–33, 153; journeymen as, 105, 109, 118, 164; laborers as, 105, 118, 164; lead mines as, 121; machinists as, 105, 118–19, 161; merchants as, 105, 112, 116, 164; milliners as, 105 ministers as, 105, 110; non-slave-owning whites as, 108–9, 116, 118; overseers as, 105; plasterers as, 105; poor whites as, 53, 58, 60, 108–9, 111, 113; railroad companies as, 16, 60–61, 84, 115, 125–26, 128–30, 142–45, 147, 149, 153, 165; railroad hands as, 105; river improvement companies as, 125; rope walks as, 121; salt mines as, 121–23, 127, 132; shoemakers as, 109–10, 124; slave owners' employees as, 117; tailors as, 105; tanners as, 105; teachers as, 105; tenants as, 77, 105, 108–10, 116–17; tobacco manufacturers as, 123, 132, 134–42; tollgate keepers as, 105; upholsterers as, 155; Virginia as, 42; urban whites as, 41–45, 123–24, 142; wheelwrights as, 105, 116; weavers as, 105; wood cutters as, 128, 154;

Hiring day (slave-hiring auctions), 6, 19, 23, 36, 39, 53, 58, 60, 97–99, 111, 119, 154, 163–64; as hub of white masculinity, 6, 97–99; and ladyhood, 6, 98–104; and white women excluded from, 6, 98–99. *See also* Ladyhood, preserved and enhanced by slave hiring; White men, roles of, in slave hiring; White women, roles of, in slave hiring

Hitt, Peter, 14
Hoge, Anna, 20
Hogg, John, 15
Holladay, 103
Holmes, Jack (hired slave), 133
Hopkins, John, 62, 81–82
Hord, Enos, 116
Hough, L. W. S., 34
House servants, hired, 28, 29, 34–36, 41–45, 60, 72, 111–12, 119, 141–42, 149, 155, 163, 165. *See also* Hired slaves, occupations of; Hired slave women; Ladyhood, preserved and enhanced by slave hiring
Howard, William, 20
Hudwall, William, 57
Hughes, Frances, 101
Hunley, Edwin, 14

INDEX

Hunter, Sarah Harriet Apphia (Sally), 15, 114–15
Hutcherson, Hill, 25
Hutchison, Beverly, 104

Industrial slavery, 119–48. *See also* Overwork payments; Task system; Urban slavery
Ingram, Charles, 29
Isaac (hired slaves), 23, 83

Jack (hired slave), 135
Jack (slave), 146
Jackson, Benjamin, 16, 61
James, William, 127
James City County, Virginia, 11
James (hired slaves), 21, 25, 103, 150
James River and Kanawha Canal, 125, 147. *See also* Hirers of slaves, canal companies as
Jefferson, Thomas, 9, 100
Jefferson County, Virginia, 37, 107
Jenkins, Creed, 51–52, 56
Jenny (hired slave), 40
Jenny Ann (hired slave), 20
Jerdone, William, 149–50
Jim (hired slaves), 99, 103, 106
Jincy (hired slave), 49–50
Joe (hired slave), 99
John (hired slaves), 49–51, 76, 81, 99, 152
Johnson, George, 81
Jones, Billy (hired slave), 25
Jordan, Stephen, 23
Jordan, William, 23
Joshua (hired slaves), 21, 151
Jourden, William, 21
Joyner, Thomas, 35
Judah (hired slaves), 40, 63
Judkins, Fanny, 24
Judy (hired slave), 32
Julia (hired slaves), 30, 97
Julia Ann (hired slave), 38
Julius (hired slave), 78–79

Kanawha County, Virginia, 122–23, 132. *See also* Hirers of slaves, salt mines as
Kanawha River, 128
Kanawha Valley (region), 122, 128. *See also* Hirers of slaves, salt mines as
Kane, Henry, 41
Keeling, Adam, 127
Keeling, Henry, 77
Kelly (hired slave), 58, 61
Kentucky, 61
Kerneysville, Virginia, 37
Keysville, Virginia, 48
King, Clinton, 116–17
King, Mollie, 116–17
King and Queen County, Virginia, 23, 60, 79, 111, 116
Kit (hired slave), 40
Knowles & Walford (insurance firm), 129. *See also*, Hired slaves, life insurance on

Labor requirements: seasonal, 22; wheat *vs.* tobacco, 11. *See also* Slaves, increasing population of; Slave surpluses; Wheat
Ladyhood, preserved and enhanced by slave hiring, 6–7, 98–100, 104, 109–14, 119, 165, 183 n. 22. *See also* Hiring day (slave-hiring auctions), and white women excluded from; House servants, hired; White women, roles of, in slave hiring, and desire for hired house servants
Lancaster County, Virginia, 25, 29, 31, 35, 40, 63, 89–90, 97, 161
Landon (hired slave), 99
Lattimore, Charles, 25
Laurence (hired slave), 93
Laurence (of Westmoreland County, Virginia), 116
Lavinia (hired slave), 31
Lawrence, James, 106
Lawrence, Lewis, 106
Lawrence, Thomas, 106
Laws, Edward, 22
Lawton, John, 25

Nead (hired slave), 94
Ned (hired slaves), 23, 78, 87
Nelly (hired slave), 40
Nelson, George (owner of Marcus), 67
Nelson, George (owner of Thornton), 118
Nelson, Nat, 55
Nelson County, Virginia, 117, 153
Nelson (hired slaves), 25, 115
Nelson (newborn of hired slave), 30
Newbill, Christopher, 14
New England (region), 19
Newsum, Isham, 97
Nick (self-hired slave), 66
Noland, Elizabeth, 92
Noland, Ella, 92
Noland, Susan, 20, 111
Norfolk, Virginia, 42, 58, 95, 102, 113, 124, 127, 158–59
Northampton County, North Carolina, 20
Northampton County, Virginia, 9
North Carolina, 79, 155
Northern Neck (region), 11
Northern Piedmont (region), 11
Northumberland County, Virginia, 57, 99
Northwestern Railroad, 144. *See also* Hirers of slaves, railroad companies as
Norton, George, 110
Norwich University (Vermont), 19, 22
Nottoway River, 78
Nutta (hired slave), 29

O'Brien, Matthew, 106
Occupations, of hired slaves. *See* Hired slaves, occupations of; House servants, hired; Industrial slavery
Ogilvie, Elizabeth, 114
Ohio, 84
Oliver (hired slave), 15
Olmsted, Frederick, 143
Orange, Virginia, 125
Orange County, Virginia, 22, 33, 47, 107, 121, 124, 127
Orrill, John, 96

Orphans, supported by slave hiring, 14, 37–39, 113–15. *See also* Fiduciaries, hire out slaves of others; Guardians
Osburn, A. F., 30
Oscar (hired slave), 61
Overwork payments, 1, 7, 85, 132–38. *See also* Board money; Hired slaves, mobility of; Hirers of slaves, coal mines as; Hirers of slaves, industrialists as; Hirers of slaves, iron producers as, Hirers of slaves, salt mines as; Hirers of slaves, tobacco manufacturers as; Living-out system; Slave hiring, and urban and industrial slavery; Task system
Owners and hirers of slaves: conflict between, 2–3, 5, 79–82; solidarity of, 2, 5–6, 87–89, 91–99, 161, 164–65. *See also* Hired slaves, unable to manipulate owners against hirers; White unity, behind slave hiring and control of hired slaves
Oxford Iron Works, 120. *See also* Hirers of slaves, iron producers as

Page, Elizabeth, 102–3
Page County, Virginia, 121
Pamelia (hired slave), 49–51
Panic of 1819, 18. *See also* Economic depression; Slave hiring, to alter labor-force size annually; Slave hiring, as solution to whites' problems
Parker, Elizabeth, 55
Parker, H., 99
Parker, Henry, 95
Parker, William, 23
Parks, Weldin, 97
Partin, Drewry, 23–24
Patience (hired slave), 35
Patrick (hired slave), 61
Patty (hired slave), 29
Paul, S. W., 42
Paxson, Charles, 60
Payne, Edward, 97
Payne, Rice, 59

Peay, James, 45
Penney, Joseph, 21
Perkins, Washington, 37
Perrin, John, 40, 58
Perrin, William, 33
Peter (hired slaves), 12, 22, 25, 62, 70, 71, 77, 78, 81, 87, 91, 155
Petersburg, Virginia, 66, 121, 123, 161
Philadelphia, 19
Philip (hired slave), 156
Phillips, James (hirer), 29
Phillips, James (owner), 22
Phillis (hired slave), 33
Phillus (hired slave), 28
Physicians, 15–16, 32, 79, 81, 111, 117, 130–31
Pierson, Joseph, 106
Pike, Moses, 135
Pippin, John, 96
Pittsylvania Courthouse, Virginia, 126
Plato (hired slave), 40
Pleasant (hired slave), 43
P. M. Tabb & Son (slave-trading firm), and slave hiring by, 155
Poisoning, of hirers. *See* Hired slaves, and poisoning, of hirers. *See also* Hired slaves, resistance of; House servants, hired
Pollard, Charles, 100
Porter, John, 22
Portsmouth, Virginia, 42, 123–24, 151
Portugal, 10
Powhatan County, Virginia, 25, 69
Pregnant women. *See* Hired slaves, pregnant and birthing. *See also* Hired slaves, children as; Hired slaves, as midwives; Hired slaves, separations from family and friends; Hired slave women
Preston (hired slave), 156
Price, Sam (hired slave), 56
Prince Edward County, Virginia, 46–48
Princess Anne County, Virginia, 13, 35, 77, 97, 127, 156
Prince William County, Virginia, 108, 114

Potts, Joseph, 1
Preddy, John, 50
Principal lessors of slave labor, 6, 116

Quarles, Cornelia, 125

Railroads, 1, 37, 145–47. *See also* Hirers of slaves, railroad companies as; Slave hiring, and prosperity of 1850s
Ralph (hired slave), 63
Randal (hired slave), 160
Randolph, Thomas, 116
Rawlings, Sarah, 114
Rawlings, Stephen, 114
Read, Thomas, 67–68
Reader, William, 30
Reason (hired slave), 55–56
Rebecca (newborn of hired slave), 54
Reid, John, 130
Repeat hirings, 20–21
Republican Party. *See* Slave hiring, and slave insurrection panic (1856)
Resistance, of hired slaves. *See* Hired slaves, resistance of
Rhody (hired slave), 161
Richard (hired slave), 61
Richardson, Hilery, 53, 56
Richmond (hired slave), 56
Richmond Academy (school), 72
Richmond and Danville Railroad, 61, 144. *See also* Hirers of slaves, railroad companies as
Richmond Fire Association (insurance firm), 128–29. *See also* Hired slaves, life insurance on
Richmond, Virginia, 2, 16, 26, 42–45, 66, 72–76, 105, 112, 121–24, 129, 132, 134–37, 140–42, 144, 155
Richmond, Virginia, Hustings Court, 138
Richmond and York River Railroad, 125. *See also* Hirers of slaves, railroad companies as
Riley, Westley, 30

Rives, Robert, 156
Roanoke, Virginia, 67
Robinson, Benjamin, 97
Robinson, Elenor, 43
Robert, Joseph, 136, 138
Robertson, Richard, 49
Rockbridge County, Virginia, 121
Rogers, James, 93
Rogers, Sanford, 92
Rose (hired slave), 35
Rosetta (hired slave), 31
Roslin Plantation, 12, 54–55, 93, 101
Ross, David, 120–21, 130. *See also* Hirers of slaves, iron producers as
Royston, William, 113, 158–59
Running away, of hired slaves. *See* Hired slaves, run away from hirers
Rust, George, 117, 155
Rutledge, Littleberry, 50
Rutter, John, 41
Ryland (hired slave), 135

Sadler, William, 95
Sale, Polly, 95
Sally (hired slaves), 39, 40
Salt mines. *See* Hirers of slaves, salt mines as
Sam (hired slaves), 13, 21, 26, 83
Sandridge's Store (hiring-day site), 99. *See also* Hiring day (slave-hiring auctions)
Sarah (hired slaves), 23, 28, 161
Saunders, Judy, 16
Saunders, Robert, 16
Savage, Teackle, 22
Schuse, Thomas, 93
Scott County, Virginia, 41
Scott, Edwin, 78
Scott, Fanny, 104
Scott, Robert Taylor, 104–5
Scott, Sam, 24, 78
Seaman, Emanuel, 43
Seavill, John, 96
Second Middle Passage, 162. *See also* Domestic slave trade; Lower South (region); Slave hiring, as alternative to sale; Slave hiring, profitability of; Slave hiring, strengthens Virginia slavery; Slaves, increasing population of; Slave surpluses; Upper South (region)
Seigert, Betty, 110
Seigert, Christine, 110
Seigert, Joseph, 110
Selby, John, 23–24
Self-esteem, of hired slaves. *See* Hired slaves, self-esteem of
Self-hired slaves, 65–67, 69–70, 73, 139. *See also* Hired slaves, discretions and advantages of
Seldon, John, 106
Sellers, Martha, 104
Sexton, James, 60
Shackelford, Robert, 40
Shaddock, James, 32
Shearwood, Thomas, 95
Shenandoah Valley, 96, 112, 144, 161
Shepherd, Sarah, 95
Shepherdstown, Virginia, 37
Shield, Samuel, 26
Sidney (hired slave), 61
Simon (hired slave), 150
Simpson, James, 30
Sinclair, Charity, 114
Singleton, John, 24
Skilled slaves. *See* Hired slaves, skilled
Skinker, Elizabeth, 29
Slaves: demand for, in Lower South, 11–12; freed by whites, 11; increasing population of, 7, 10–11, 28, 142–43; 149–50, 157, 162–63; legal importation of, banned, 11; outnumber whites, 11. *See also* Slave surpluses
Slave hiring: as alternative to purchase, 18, 146; as alternative to sale, 75–76, 143, 146, 148, 154–62, 165; to alter labor-force size annually, 19, 21, 146, 163; to assist white women, 109–13, 119; to avoid expense, 29–30, 35–40, 163; in

barter economies, 25–26, 163; bonds, 12–15, 23–24; definition of, 1; diminishes class resentments, 108; in diversified economy, 4, 148–49, 151, 160, 162–63, 165; as frequent topic of conversations, 20–23; as frequent topic of letters, 20–23, 163; for harvest, 21–22, 115–16; and hirers paid to hire slaves, 35–36, 38–39, 49–51, 105, 108, 117, 161; historiography of, 1–7, 65, 67, 69–70, 139, 141; for hog butchering, 21–22, 115–16; and increasing slave population, 3–4, 7–8; as integral facet of Virginia slavery, 3–4, 12, 27–28, 30, 36, 45, 71–72, 86, 96, 117–18, 149, 160–65; among neighbors, 21–22, 115–18, 156, 163; in newspaper advertisements, 28, 34, 42, 105, 121–24; origins and proliferation of, 1–28; in owners' wills, 16; and paternalism, 4, 39, 53; to pay debts, 16; pervasiveness of, 24–28, 148, 161–65; preference for, over slave owning, 125; private, 21, 23, 152, 163; and prosperity of 1850s, 146, 153; to purchase slaves, 16, 160; and quarterly payments, 101–2, 108; rate increases, 5, 8, 19, 34, 75, 82–85, 87, 97–98, 111, 122, 124, 146, 148, 153–60, 165; for regular income, 13–14, 19–20, 48–49, 113–15, 155–60, 163; among relatives, 22; to remove troublesome slaves, 76, 101, 150–51, and repeat hiring, 95–96, 111, 151; season for, 20–22, 24, 36, 88, 93, 97, 111, 118, 134, 152; short-term, 21–23; and slaves' family and friendship ties, 46–64; and slave insurrection panic (1856), 92–93; slaves' negative view of, 86; and slave surpluses, 3–4, 7–8; as solution to whites' problems, 4, 12, 16–19, 146, 149–51, 158–59; strengthens Virginia slavery, 2–3, 7–8, 119, 142–46, 148–49, 151, 154–65; to support heirs, 16, 19, 156–57; and transportation infrastructure, 3, 75, 124–31, 142–48, 153, 163; and urban and industrial development, 3, 12, 123, 148; and urban and industrial slavery, 119–48; and urban slavery's viability, 139–42; whites' familiarity with, 24–28; and white gender roles, 6–7; and white mastery, 5–6, 118; as whites' occupation, 26, 100, 104–5, 164; among whites' routine endeavors, 19–22, 26, 117–18, 160–65; and white society, 3, 5–7, 86–119; by white widows, 114–15

Slaves, self-hired. *See* Self-hired slaves

Slave schedules (census), 28, 96, 161

Slave surpluses, 3, 7, 11, 124–25, 142, 148–50, 162. *See also* Labor requirements, wheat *vs.* tobacco; Slave hiring, as alternative to sale; Slave hiring, profitability of; Slave hiring, as solution to whites' problems; Slaves, increasing population of

Smith, Coleman, 79–80

Smith, George, 13

Smith, John, 105

Smith, William (of Fauquier County, Virginia), 59

Smith, William (of Gloucester County, Virginia), 156

Sneed, James, 23

Sophia (hired slaves), 12, 40

Southampton County, Virginia, 18, 20, 23, 29, 35, 55, 60, 88, 97–98115, 128, 153–54

Southwestern Turnpike Company, 125. *See also* Hirers of slaves, turnpike companies as

Spain, 10

Spencer, Thomas, Jr., 56

Spencer (hired slaves), 25, 51–52

Spotsylvania County, Virginia, 124, 153–54

Stafford County, Virginia, 34, 39, 108

Stampp, Kenneth, 47

Stanard, Larkin, 22, 107

Staples, David, 37

Starke, Belfield, 16

Starke, Bolling, 16

Stephen (hired slaves), 61, 130–31
Stevensville, Virginia (hiring-day site), 23. *See also* Hiring day (slave-hiring auctions)
Strath, Henry, 110
Stuart, S. D., 51–52
Stubbs, T. S., 36
Sullivan, James, 29
Sussex, Virginia, 145–46
Sussex County, Virginia, 14, 16, 60, 77–79, 95, 97
Swift Run Gap Turnpike Company, 125. *See also* Hirers of slaves, turnpike companies as
Sydnor (hired slave), 57

Tabby (hired slave), 39
Tadman, Michael, 162
Takagi, Midori, 2
Taliaferro, James, 154
Taliaferro, James F., 99
Tarlton (slave), 44
Task system, 132–37. *See also* Hirers of slaves, coal mines as; Hirers of slaves, industrialists as; Hirers of slaves, iron producers as, Hirers of slaves, salt mines as; Hirers of slaves, tobacco manufacturers as; Slave hiring, and urban and industrial slavery; Overwork payments
Tavenner, Charles, 94
Taylor, Franklin, 93
Taylor, G. W., 97
Taylor, Jordan, 31
Taylor, Robert, 101
Taylor, S. F., 96
Taylor, Walter, 102–3
Taylor, William, 25
Tempe (hired slave), 29
Temple, Elizabeth, 101
Temple, James, 46
Tennessee, 58, 60–61, 107–8, 143
Thacker (hired slave), 40
Thackson, Roger, 50

Thomas, Henry, 97
Thomas, James, of Loudoun County, Virginia, 117
Thomas, James (hirer), 40
Thomas, James (owner), 33
Thomas (hired slave), 102
Thompson, Francis, 24
Thornton (hired slave), 118
Throckmorton, Eliza, 55
Tidewater (region), 11, 120
Timberlake, Mary, 61
Tobacco, 69, 142, 145; decline of, in eastern Virginia, 9, 10; export figures, 9; increased production of, in western Virginia, 142–43; and soil exhaustion, 10
Tobacco factories, slave hiring by. *See* Hirers of slaves, tobacco manufacturers as
Tom (hired slaves), 40, 102
Tom (slave), 62
Tomlin, John, 85
Toney (hired slave), 24
Towles, John, 31
Toy, Joseph, 34
Trail, Jake 117
Trice, Robert, 36, 104
Trice, William, 93
Tripletts, R., 30
Tune, John, 38
Turlington, John, 30
Turner, Edward Carter, 18, 91–92, 144–46, 151–53
Twyman, George, 95
Twyman, Iverson, 31, 65
Twyman, James, 12
Twyman, Joseph, 103–4
Tyler, Penelope, 54

Umphry (hired slave), 24–25
Unhealthy living conditions, hired slaves in. *See* Hired slaves, in unhealthy living conditions
University of Virginia, 74

INDEX 217

Upper Appomattox Company (river improvement company), 125. *See also* Hirers of slaves, river improvement companies as Upper South (region), 1, 107, 122, 147; sale of slaves from, 12. *See also* Domestic slave trade; Lower South (region); Second Middle Passage; Slave hiring, as alternative to sale; Slave hiring, profitability of; Slave hiring, strengthens Virginia slavery; Slaves, increasing population of; Slave surpluses

Urban slavery, 66; historiography of, 1–2, 66; and industrial slavery, 119–48. *See also* Board money; Hired slaves, mobility of; Hirers of slaves, tobacco manufacturers as; House servants, hired; Living-out system; Overwork payments; Self-hired slaves; Task system

U.S. Mint, 121

Valley of Virginia, 133. *See also* Hirers of slaves, iron producers as; Overwork payments; Task system; Weaver, William

Vermont, 19–20, 22

Vick, Josiah, 98

Vicksville, Virginia (hiring-day site), 23. *See also* Hiring day (slave-hiring auctions)

Vilet (hired slaves), 21, 51, 52

Vincent (hired slave), 89–90

Virginia and Tennessee Railroad, 126, 142–44, 147; and reduction of intrastate sectionalism, 143–44; strengthens Virginia slavery, 142–44. *See also* Hirers of slaves, railroad companies as; Slave hiring, strengthens Virginia slavery

Virginia Central Railroad, 142, 144. *See also* Hirers of slaves, railroad companies as

Waddey, George, 29
Waddill, William, 50
Wade, Joseph, 100
Wade, Richard, 1–2, 66, 139

Walker, Benjamin, 63
Walker, B. H., 23, 60, 111
Walker, John, 116
Waller, Elizabeth, 114
Waller, J. M., 99
Waller, Robert, 32
Waller, Sarah, 21
Wallis, Jesse, 24
Walter H. Taylor and Company (mercantile firm), slave hiring by, 102
Walton, Thomas, 23
Ward, Daniel, 100
Warner (hired slave), 61
War of the Austrian Succession, 10
Warrenton, Virginia, 109, 118–19, 152. *See also* Hiring day (slave-hiring auctions)
Washington, Charles, 34–35
Washington County, Virginia, 41
Washington, D.C., 125
Washington, George, 11
Washington, John, 100–101, 150
Washington, Sam, 96
Washington (hired slave), 128
Watkins, William, 49, 55
Watsey (hired slave), 161
Watson, Major (hired slave), 133
Watts, William, 69
Weaver, Horrace, 30
Weaver, Tilghman, 29
Weaver, William, 33, 83–85, 127, 133. *See also* Hirers of slaves, iron producers as
Webb, A., 51–52
Webb, Joel, 51
Webb, Martin, 87
Wesley (hired slave), 13
Westham Foundry (weapons manufacturing firm), 120. *See also* Hirers of slaves, industrialists as
West Indies, 10
Westmoreland County, Virginia, 99, 115
Wheat, 123, 144–45; demand for, 10; increased production of, 11; planters' shift toward, 10. *See also* Agricultural

SLOVER LIBRARY
Norfolk Public Library